BEAUTIFUL
BRUTALITY

www.transworldbooks.co.uk

BEAUTIFUL
BRUTALITY

Adam Smith

BANTAM PRESS

LONDON · TORONTO · SYDNEY · AUCKLAND · JOHANNESBURG

TRANSWORLD PUBLISHERS
61–63 Uxbridge Road, London W5 5SA
A Random House Group Company
www.transworldbooks.co.uk

First published in Great Britain
in 2012 by Bantam Press
an imprint of Transworld Publishers

A CIP catalogue record for this book
is available from the British Library.

ISBN 9780593067079

Addresses for Random House Group Ltd companies outside the UK
can be found at: www.randomhouse.co.uk
The Random House Group Ltd Reg. No. 954009

The Random House Group Limited supports the Forest Stewardship
Council (FSC®), the leading international forest-certification organization.
Our books carrying the FSC label are printed on FSC®-certified paper.
FSC is the only forest-certification scheme endorsed by the leading environmental
organizations, including Greenpeace. Our paper procurement policy can
be found at www.randomhouse.co.uk/environment.

Typeset in 12½/15pt Ehrhardt by
Kestrel Data, Exeter, Devon.
Printed and bound in Great Britain
CPI Group (UK) Ltd, Croydon, CR0 4YY.

2 4 6 8 10 9 7 5 3 1

To my fabulous wife, Jo, who is the most wonderful, supportive, sparkling and genuine family person. My rock.

To my three amazing children – Jessamy, Oscar and Tilly – who make each and every day a happier and better one.

To my family and lifelong friends, for always being there. Unconditionally.

To my childhood friend 'Dogger', and my boxing friend Diego Corrales, whom I miss lighting up my life.

Contents

Foreword

You need many components in order to become a world champion and reach the top in this, the hardest of all sports. Qualities such as dedication, desire, self-belief and an undying will to succeed. Plus the obvious requirements of talent, an exceptional trainer and manager, and a promoter who will match you carefully and always have your best interests at heart. The qualities you generally have to be born with, or have to work hard in order to get, or can be found in the gym. But one attribute I was fortunate to have, which can be equally as important but which some boxers are unfortunately not as lucky to have, is the support of a strong family.

You can have all those other components, but when they leave the gym some fighters don't have that family support, which can be the reason why sometimes even the most talented of boxers sadly don't reach the top. I wouldn't have got to the world title if I hadn't had a family behind me, to push me and put themselves out for me. To tell me when I was right or wrong, and even through the bad times, which we all have in life, staying in my corner and getting me back on track. My family means absolutely everything to me. They are why I work so hard. The older generation of my family set me up, did so much to help me when I was growing up and through the huge support they have given me in my boxing career. Everything I do now is to set my family up for the future. Fighters need families around them. It's a hard enough game, and you know they'll always love you, whatever happens.

My long-time friend Adam Smith, whom I met as a rookie professional at the age of eighteen when he worked with an array of world champions as one of the country's top pundits on Sky Sports, uses his wealth of boxing knowledge to explore this not-much-talked about area of the fight game, which readers will find fascinating. Boxing families, the support of a family, world champion brothers, fathers training sons – which surely can't be in the boxing manual – and mothers having to cope. The presence of families in this sport seems to be common, but is a part of boxing which, although it can only be seen as amazing, has never got the headlines – until now.

This is an exceptional read for boxing fans, lovers of sport in general and anyone who cares about family. Enjoy.

Richard Hatton MBE

Preface

Two things in life matter more than anything to me: people and sport. They are pure, simple, real passions. Almost obsessions, I guess.

I have always adored getting to know multicultural folk from all backgrounds, classes and cultures; equally I relish virtually every type of competitive regulated sport that exists, and which can excite us so much.

Let's narrow that down. I love my family above all else, and I crave boxing more than any other sport. I will do anything I can for my family; I will try anything possible to be ringside for a fight.

Family. Boxing. Boxing. Family. On the surface there might not seem to be too many parallels. After all, one is usually characterized by universal protection and comfort; the other is about defeating, even damaging, one's opponent in any way possible within the Marquess of Queensberry's rules.

Yet dig deeper and one finds, rather surprisingly, that these two fields can become fairly synonymous. Boxers need families. Families need fighters.

The essence of family is and always has been to support,

nurture, provide for, encourage and help. In ideal situations that is unequivocally 100 per cent of the time. Boxers must in turn give 100 per cent unconditional commitment to their cause, and often to their families, if they want to become a real success. They are also heavily influenced – in both positive and negative ways – by a whole range of weird, wonderful and truly ghastly family members.

When a promising athlete embarks on a professional, paid career in the pugilistic art, support is essential, for virtually all paths are riddled with dangerous roadblocks, and boxers don't have much time. They have short cycles and quick peaks, then sometimes fail to fully realize the decline of reflexes, punch resistance and optimum balance.

They also only get one serious shot at it. Losing a fight is not like losing any other sporting match. Lives can change for ever.

For every world champion there are hundreds, even thousands, of nearly men. Some scrape by on the barest of levels required to support human life. Yet titles, trophies and huge financial gain guarantee nothing. The fall from grace can be far swifter and more brutal. Snakes are more slippery than ladders. The number of sad stories in boxing concerning bankruptcy, illness, tragedy and death are often more associated with the famous stars than the journeymen triers.

The boxing ride is invariably a terrifying roller-coaster of ups and downs, highs and lows of real extremes. There are conflicting emotions, and decadent temptations set against the mundane boredom of clocking up miles and soaking gym sweat-suits – the austere regime of training that takes its toll. Questions arise over desire, ego, narcissism, triumph and failure. To earn a living in this harshest of ways obviously depends on that certain individual having an astonishing commitment as well as nerves of steel.

It's hard enough to become a fighter. It's far harder to make a global success of it.

Boxers have to operate in a sort of inner solitary confinement, and are often not well enough equipped to deal with the potential pitfalls alone. They must concentrate first and foremost on business inside the ring. Outside it can be a minefield, even for the sharpest of fighting folk. They need help, guidance and proper assistance.

Every boxer, whatever his standard, level or ambition, needs and relies upon the tightest of teams: his trainers, his manager, his promoter, his friends, and above all his family. They are all there to drive him on, push him that extra yard in training, pick up shattered pieces, comfort him, and love him.

Bumps along the way lead to disruption. Trainers can be blamed, and are usually the first to be fired. Managers and promoters may not be too far behind. Friends are sometimes seen as hangers-on, worse still parasites, and can, God forbid, end up as sworn enemies.

Families are the only constant. Yes, we all have our debates, disputes, arguments and troubles, but the love is usually unconditional. Blood is blood. Fighters shed blood for a living. They need blood brothers with them.

From time to time, people ask me what are the most important things in boxing. 'Levels and timing,' I reply. I've now realized that family must be added to the mix. For our brave, spirited and most admirable fighters, at the very heart of boxing lies the necessity and influence of family.

BEAUTIFUL
BRUTALITY

Prologue: The Boxing Family

Children of the same family, the same blood, with the same first associations and habits, have some means of enjoyment in their power, which no subsequent connections can supply.

Jane Austen

Fistic combat is so appealing, so scary, so physically and emotionally draining, that it harks back to a bygone age where this was plain to see: one wins and one loses. It's a simple, appetizing idea, but in modern society one that of course remains controversial, a fiery subject for a classic dinner-party debate.

Through the good, the bad and the plain ugly, there is constantly something happening in boxing. Events swing rapidly, and the basic gladiatorial battle brings out the primeval side in most of us.

Boxing is, quite simply, the most compelling of sports. The drama rivets us as the action twists and turns. Colourful and engaging personalities rise and fall, while the boundaries between life and death are brought frighteningly close.

Love or hate the sport, one simply cannot ignore the

fascinating, often mesmerizing, art that has evolved through the generations. It's the ultimate battle of machismo, pride, skills, wits and immense concentration. Mano-a-mano.

The lights, glamour and sadistic nature of boxing attract the wealthy, the poor, and the middle of the road. Everyone. Some loathe it, some desire it, but what is beyond any argument is the fact that virtually everyone has an opinion on one of the world's most ferocious and thrilling sports.

I am often amazed by how pre-fight predictions are dished up and dashed so rapidly. We, the 'experts', are sometimes made to look like fools as the toughest of men clash, and the predictable becomes the unpredictable – and often, ultimately, the down-right shocking. Strange events can materialize within seconds, and subsequently alter outcomes in weird but also dangerous ways. One just never knows.

We are consumed by this magnetic, marvellous world that is opportunistic, troublesome, gripping and addictive. Boxing draws you in, holds you there. You can never get out.

This is the only sport where the participants plan for months on how to dissect their opponents, yet the first thing they do when the final bell tolls is hug and embrace them. They may start as enemies, but often end as friends for ever. It is the theatre of life: one gets pulled from every angle possible as dreams are created, and also shattered.

I love other, more prominent sports too, like football, but I do find myself getting frustrated with some of the money-pampered players who only tend to say what their manager wants them to say in interviews, and so leave their public craving more.

Fighters are a breed of their own. They badly need the media. They know their next fight could be their last, and they are desperate for attention, appreciation and promotional building while they are developing their careers and chasing their fantasies. We get better access to their lives, and the lives of their families, than in any other sport.

There is something curious, something unique about boxers. Whether or not it is that they must have a small screw loose to venture into that lonely ring in the first place, I'm not sure. They certainly have bucket-loads of courage.

I will always admire each and every fighter, whether he or she becomes a world champion or just struggles to win a quick four-rounder. It takes a certain person, and a certain type of make-up, to become a boxer.

They are supremely dedicated, disciplined, rounded in-dividuals who know that they must be in phenomenal shape not only to cope with the predicaments presented within that strange squared circle, but also to handle the different pressures outside the ring. Boxing is the most alluring of professions; yet it can be horrible, brutal, even corrupt.

The promoters, managers, matchmakers, trainers, whips, doctors and journalists are merely the bystanders. The boxers are pure products as they enter the ring, and only they know why and how they can engage in the harshest, most competitive and riskiest game of all. These sportsmen are like no others. They are gentle, yet vicious; intelligent, but stupid; they are resound-ing characters who simply thrill and amaze us.

As a broadcaster, I have to remain totally unbiased, but it has been impossible not to become hugely emotionally involved. Having worked in television for more than twenty years – for the most part as a commentator, reporter and presenter, now as Head of Boxing at Sky Sports – I have been fortunate enough to spend vast quantities of time with most of the fighters of my generation.

Sky has been the home of British boxing for the last two decades, bringing viewers the best fights, the intense build-up, and so many tantalizing tales. I have been right in the epicentre.

From the finest talents to the toughest of scrappers, the headline hitters to the paid survivors, I have interviewed them countless times in different locations and in very varied situations around the world. Some questions have been hard, some chats have been light-hearted; some have been amusing, others deeply painful. Their stories can finish with glorious, even unbelievable, endings, but there are many sad outcomes too.

Boxing regularly dishes up quite blood-curdling conclusions that can have devastating effects on family. Recently we've seen the most fearless of warriors, Diego Corrales and Arturo Gatti, meet horrific ends; and the most humble of men in Darren Sutherland and Vernon Forrest also dying tragically young. So too one of the most spectacular types, in knockout king Edwin Valero. He was the Venezuelan who destroyed every one of his foes inside the distance but didn't make twenty-nine years of age himself. In a twenty-four-hour frenzy at Easter in 2010, Valero murdered his wife and was then found hanged in a cell. His family was ripped apart for ever, his own children cruelly orphaned. When Valero was found he had in his mouth a picture of his family.

Boxing is really like a circle of life, and that unfortunately includes, on rare occasions, an early death. This is, after all, 'Beautiful Brutality' – stunning and memorable, but at the same time so dreadfully risky, and way beyond the natural call of duty.

The family unit plays a more influential part in boxing than in virtually any other sport. Families are often ever-present for a fighter's full life cycle, and represent the very heart and essence of what can be the loneliest of sports.

In this book, I'll be delving deep into the way family inter-twines with boxing in traditional and non-traditional ways. For family allows one to be able to cope with the physical world. As far as possible, one is cocooned. A safe harbour exists to protect us from the strains of adversity. How crucial that is in the world of boxing.

Families, with all their love, disputes, break-ups and make-ups, go back to the very beginning of human nature, and encompass every kind of relationship and every type of emotion. A family's major function is of course to produce and reproduce. Parents then help to locate their children socially, and normally play a vital role in their development and education, thus influencing their subsequent place within society. Affinity, economics, culture and tradition all affect how families operate. Immigration, for instance, can change family life irreversibly.

Families have kept us gripped through the ages. My favourite playwrights, William Shakespeare and Oscar Wilde, wrote brilliantly about the full range of family ties, tear-ups, con-frontations and complications. The central theme in the Bard's works was family. His exploration of lust, lies, lost relations and loopy situations was profound. *Hamlet*, *The Winter's Tale*, *Twelfth Night*. How about *Romeo and Juliet*, where it takes the death of the two young lovers to unite their fiercely feuding families? Struggles between parents and children, and the reconnection of past circumstances, were Shakespearean traits. Wilde's wicked humour flitted around such subjects, but family mishaps were so often at the core. *The Importance of Being Earnest* remains a particular love of mine. Set in late Victorian England, the play's brilliance derives from characters maintaining fictitious identities to escape unwelcome social obligations. It satirizes not just the hypocrisy of the time, but the intricacies of family life too.

When I grew up things were little different really. There were the comings and goings of the Carry On family, while peculiar relationships were hysterically built around that family-oriented hotel Fawlty Towers.

Family breeds familiarity, and familiarity is what comforts us most. In modern society, whether one is part of a prestigious aristocratic family or just an average happy-go-lucky one with 2.4 children (and a suitable household pet), most of us are also keen to find out who we are and where we come from. Genealogy is a field that consumes increasing numbers of people. Family trees; the tracing of linear heritage and history; the tracking down of lost loved ones. This is why the British Red Cross, the Salvation Army and others spend huge amounts of time and resources to reunite families who are separated due to conflict, disaster or migration, and put them back in touch.

Think of the sight of thousands smiling and rushing to hug relatives with abandon at airports, or tearful and weeping farewells at bedsides and gravesides. Time together. Time lost. Emotions laced with huge relief or huge regret.

Families can be extremely close, or wide apart and disparate. Some children are raised as orphans, some are adopted, others have surrogate parents. The range is enormous, diverse and fascinating. Likewise, boxing families can be immensely tight – virtually unbreakable – or vindictive and at war, split and tragically absent.

I am passionate about family, from my own Smith clan to the tight-knit working group at Sky Sports.

My parents split when I was nine and my sister Anna was five. For our sakes they remained amicable, and were always hugely supportive. Tears at the time were soon wiped away. Anna and I have long had a very tight bond, and we chose to embrace new and interesting family members. As a unit we have all grown considerably over the years. My mum and dad were both from families of six children, so I ended up having twenty-plus first cousins!

My mother's family was largely made up of Jewish immigrants from Russia who settled in London. My dad's were descended from Black Country blacksmiths and nail-makers on his father's side, and from a massive Irish Catholic group on his mother's. His parents ended up in Leeds.

This mixture was made even richer by absorbing a contingent from the small town of Newbridge, nestled in the Welsh valleys. It was my step-mum who brought this lovely group to the party. Her dad had worked down the mines for forty years, and enjoyed his retirement by carving beautiful walking sticks out of rare wood found deep in the Welsh hill country.

I gained two half-brothers, John William and Edward, but we are so close that they are just my 'brothers'. I always refer to them as that. We are fourteen and seventeen years apart, but we offer each other a generational step that can often bridge the divide between parents and children. Both will, I'm sure, provide similar solace and support to my children.

Thus, amid the turmoil of a 'broken home', I was very fortunate. I grew up with a multicultural group of young and old characters, all of whom helped mould me. I have truly experienced the diversity of family life.

I have embraced my wife Jo's family in similar ways. My father-in-law, for instance, is descended on his mother's side from scores of Irish who ran farms in the stunning countryside of West Cork. We often travel to the tiny village of Drinagh to discover more. There are always amazing backgrounds to learn about, and many relationships to uncover and develop. Jo and I are determined to pass on to our three children the importance of their inheritance.

My Sky family is hugely important too. I started working at the 'Legoland' complex in west London way back in August 1994. Colleagues have come and gone, but there is a tight group who have knitted together over the years, and who provide real experience, camaraderie, authority and a 'togetherness' that is fairly unique within the media workplace.

With my eighteen seasons goes our reporter Ed Robinson's fourteen, while producers Declan Johnson and Charles Lawrence have done twenty-five or so years between them. Associate producer John Beloff – a distant cousin of mine – has been with us since university. Our directors Mike Allen and Sara Chenery have been with Sky virtually since it was launched; our PA Sarah Hornsby is another who's been with us for over a decade. We are surely the longest-standing unit in Sky Sports. There is often a warm, whole-hearted family feeling when we work.

We have also long been seen as the 'black sheep' of the company: boxing can be seen as an alternative sport that attracts at times, and repels at others. It's never simple in our world. Controversial, difficult, but always absorbing.

The 'talent' are very close too. Ian Darke, Glenn McCrory, Jim Watt, Johnny Nelson and I get on brilliantly, and we have grown together. We help each other, advise each other, and between us all work desperately hard to deliver the best boxing shows we can. Barry McGuigan has enjoyed much of his television career with us, so too Nicky Piper and Spencer Oliver, who have helped on a regular basis. Our latest inductee, Jamie Moore, gave us thrills and spills when he was fighting, and we have discovered how much the boxing community takes to him. Richie Woodhall and Carl Froch provide expert tactical analysis, Our long-time presenter Paul Dempsey went to Setanta after many years at Sky, but it seems like his replacement, Dave Clark, has always been with us.

From the managing director of Sky Sports – my boss, Barney Francis, a true boxing lover – to my editorial right-hand man and boxing historian Bob Mee, I work with the most professional team. They all play their part. To me, they're my other family.

They're not nearly as important as my 'blood' family though. Nothing could be.

*

So, having been brought up by a loving family, most of whom were steeped in retail, why on earth did I join the boxing fraternity in the first place?

My fellow prefect at St Paul's School in Barnes, London, was a certain George Osborne. Nowadays he's better known as the Chancellor of the Exchequer. One day, when we were around seventeen (and I had extraordinarily bad long hair), George and I had a little chat (he had just become 'George', having been known as Gideon throughout our schooldays). We talked about what might lie ahead when we were adults. Like you do.

'What will you become?' I asked the high-powered, super-bright, razor-sharp Osborne.

'I will be Prime Minister,' George replied. 'And you, Smith?'

I wasn't convinced he really cared what I would end up doing, but I told him anyway. 'I'm going to be a sports commentator, George,' I said.

'Great,' he said. 'Good luck.'

My mum was once a Conservative councillor. I remember it only too well. I had to drive around north London bellowing out 'Vote Veronica Soskin!' from a megaphone, and hide behind it when passing staunch left-wing neighbourhoods. It quickly became more like 'Vote Soskin – she's my mother. I bloody well have to!'

Mum met George recently. Apparently he was all set to tune into the latest big fight, and according to her was very proud of my journey in life. Well I am of his. Ruthless ambition and all that. The pair of us. Albeit in such contrasting ways.

George most definitely followed the conventional route of ascendancy to something major and serious. I went completely against the grain. Banking, accountancy, law, medicine and teaching just weren't for me.

But, amusingly, I beat him to it. He's not Prime Minister. Not yet, Mr Osborne. And I am that commentator I dreamt of becoming. Moreover in boxing, a sport that was practised at St Paul's back in the day, but long ago became extinct.

I'm sure that of the many captains of industry who have emerged from the school I remain the only captain of boxing television. Most Old Paulines are probably invited to high society dinners. I'm happy with fish and chips round at the Hattons'.

My love of boxing goes way back.

I grew up watching the superfights between that wonderful group Sugar Ray Leonard, Tommy Hearns, Marvin Hagler and Roberto Duran. Hearns was my favourite. The Hitman just epitomized everything gallant and gripping about the sport.

One particular night sticks in the memory: 15 April 1985, when the mesmerizing and brutal three rounds between Hearns and Hagler became etched in history. I was thirteen, and I cried and cried when Detroit's Hitman was knocked out. To this day I can recall how devastated I was.

During the build-up to the big Floyd Mayweather–Shane Mosley fight in Las Vegas in May 2010 I had the honour of interviewing two of those four greats, Hearns and Leonard. As we stood chatting before the camera rolled, I told Tommy about my adolescent adoration of him. He was hugely touched. Sugar Ray not so.

'What about me?' Leonard joked. 'Wasn't I good enough?'

'He liked the Hitman, Ray,' Hearns said. 'You have to understand that.'

'You're about to interview me,' Leonard continued, 'and you've just told me that Tommy Hearns is your hero? My God!'

'At least I'm honest,' I said.

Banter with two legends. It just doesn't happen every day. It continued even when the red light of the camera came on. Ray kept jibing in with reminders of who my hero was.

Inevitably there came the moment when Tommy talked about that devastating loss to 'Marvelous' Marvin.

'I was a young teenager watching in the early hours back in London,' I told the pair of them. 'I cried my eyes out when you were beaten, Tommy.'

'Well, guess what?' the Hitman said. 'I cried my eyes out too.'

'And you know something, I cried my eyes out too,' admitted Ray. 'We all cried, all three of us!'

There was laughter all round. Irreplaceable memories.

My other boxing hero was 'The Clones Cyclone'. Born Finbar Patrick, 'Barry' McGuigan was a national hero, of course. He attracted an enormous and loyal following in the mid-1980s, particularly at Belfast's King's Hall. A non-sectarian sporting ambassador, Barry would calm the violent feud between the Protestants and Catholics every time he fought during the Troubles. 'Leave the fighting to McGuigan,' it was often said. With his father Pat singing 'Danny Boy', there was huge emotion every time Barry fought.

Weeks after Hagler–Hearns had given me the boxing bug, I was still a small thirteen-year-old when on 8 June the great Panamanian Eusebio Pedroza turned up at Loftus Road to defend his world featherweight title for a record twentieth time against McGuigan. Pedroza had reigned for seven years, which was a division record. There were around twenty-seven thousand there that night on QPR's pitch, mainly decked out in green. I was one of the lucky ones, even though I was trapped right at the back. It wasn't even the 'nosebleed' section – just a long, flat, almost impossible view. But I was there.

I had just begun boarding at St Paul's, which was nestled on the south bank of the Thames by Hammersmith Bridge, little more than ten minutes away from Loftus Road. That Saturday night, I bought a ticket and sneaked in. I hadn't dared tell my mum, who was already appalled that I sugared my hair into a quiff and frequented psychobilly concerts at The Klub Foot in Hammersmith. Although my mum watches many of the fights these days, she certainly had no interest in boxing back then. She wouldn't have thought it was beautiful brutality, just brutally awful.

It was an incredible experience as Barry McGuigan became Ireland's first world champion in thirty-five years. Ironically, Barry's mum had stayed at home and her house was burnt down the same night. I will never forget the intensity of that evening. It felt like one big happy family. All together.

The following week I watched on the news as seventy-five thousand lined the streets of Belfast; two hundred thousand more went to Dublin's O'Connell Street to welcome McGuigan home. I couldn't believe it – and I had been part of this unforgettable sporting moment. Furthermore, it was all secret. No one knew I'd gone!

Imagine my shock years later, on one of my first days at Sky, when Barry McGuigan was due into the building. Moreover, he was joining our team. It didn't end there. Barry arrived, and we were introduced.

'Adam, you will be looking after Barry for the next season, taking him around the country to do features on different gyms and fighters,' my boss said.

I was simply gobsmacked. My idol, my hero. Working together.

I have now known Barry for over seventeen years. We have worked as colleagues and are firm friends. I have to admit, though, I still get a touch starry-eyed whenever I see him.

It was another event that secured my entry into Sky though – the event that catapulted me into boxing. At my first interview with Head of Sports Vic Wakeling, I was asked what had really drawn me to the sport. The answer I gave, about the time when I became utterly fascinated by it, was 'the night of the Fan Man'.

The unthinkable happened during the second encounter of that tremendous trilogy between Riddick Bowe and Evander Holyfield. Bowe had taken the world heavyweight title from Holyfield after an epic twelve-round war. The tenth, when Holyfield was seemingly out of it but came charging back, remains one of those three-minute sessions that defies logic and unites boxing fans in both adoration and disbelief.

On 6 November 1993, Holyfield was aiming to exact revenge. It wasn't going to be easy. Bowe was fresh, he was big, and he was good. As fine an inside fighter as you will see at heavy-weight.

I was doing an internship with CNN at the political bureau in Washington at the time and was transferred very briefly to their sporting department in Atlanta. While there, I spent time in Holyfield's training camp. I'm not sure I have met another individual like Evander. I like 'The Real Deal'; he's a family man, and a hugely inspiring fellow. From the first moment I saw him, as a wide-eyed CNN intern, Evander has always had a special place in my heart.

His guts were certainly never in question throughout his astonishing boxing career. I was, though, worried before he fought Mike Tyson in 1996. Critics were suggesting he would be carried home on a stretcher after a first-round knockout.

'Evander, everyone's writing you off,' I said. 'Everyone. Convince me to back you.'

'Do you believe in the Lord?' Evander replied.

'Not especially,' I said.

'I'll be just fine. I'm not scared of Tyson. Put your money on me to stop him.'

So for some reason I did. At ridiculous odds of around 33–1. He seemed doomed for the boxing scrap-heap. But I listened, I won, and Evander was just fine. He prayed, he believed, and he ultimately out-bullied the bully.

So you see I have always liked Evander Holyfield. He could surprise. The same could be said of one James Jarrett Miller, who three years before that Tyson fight dramatically entered the boxing world at Caesars Palace on the Vegas strip. I was sitting a few rows back from ringside, and what I saw – and heard – will live with me for ever.

In the middle of the seventh round of that Bowe–Holyfield rematch, this peculiar noise came from overhead, as the opportunist Miller descended towards the ring in some sort of paraglider. He crashed on to the top rope with his parachute tangled in the lights. Moments later he was pulled to the floor by fans and security and left unconscious in the enormous scuffle. The 'Fan Man' later joked, 'It was a heavyweight fight, and I was the only guy who was knocked out!'

The huge Bowe–Holyfield clash, which was in the balance, was held up for more than twenty minutes. I've always believed that the break helped Holyfield regain the biggest prize in boxing. The Atlanta warrior was naturally the fitter man. 'Big Daddy' Bowe, who promoter Frank Maloney tells me used to eat whole chicken after whole chicken, had a harder time. His muscles seized up down the final stretch, so I think the Fan Man's intervention crucially altered the outcome. Millions of dollars changed hands.

Only in boxing could this have happened. What a crazy world – befitting of a lunatic like Miller to enter. Was he mad? Was it a fix? What on earth had been going through his mind?

Whatever the truth, Miller became part of boxing folklore. A year later, he tried to land on the roof of Buckingham Palace. There were more madcap adventures until he was eventually found by hunters, long after he had hanged himself, in Alaska's remote Resurrection Pass Trail. A most grizzly end.

Describing the tale of the Fan Man opened the door to Sky for me.

'Expect the unexpected,' I told Vic Wakeling at my interview. 'You can never predict anything. Everyone in boxing must always be on their toes. It is a sport like no other. The range of emotions and outcomes, all the way from life to death, can be experienced.'

I am writing this chapter to a serene and stunning backdrop on Cape Cod, the arm-like peninsula that juts out of America's east coast around eighty miles from Boston. A light aircraft is buzzing around the sky. I think back to that night. It was an incredible, out-of-this-world experience that completely altered my view of sporting events, particularly boxing.

In our years at Sky, we have had outside broadcasts (in indoor centres!) abandoned due to flooding, had the lights go out mid-round, mid-fight, commentated under tarpaulin in torrential rain, been caught up in the turmoil of ring riots, witnessed fighters swimming in hurricanes and others fly in to battle on magic carpets. Many moments have come very close to equalling that bizarre experience at Caesars Palace. Nothing, though, has bettered it.

Nothing yet, that is.

From croquet on an English lawn with Oliver McCall to dominoes at Halloween with Hasim Rahman and chess duels in a honeymoon resort with Lennox Lewis, my job has often given me a unique and privileged insight into the make-up of the fabulous fighting folk.

Once we nearly sank a world heavyweight champion; and there was the time I collapsed in a heap after a ferocious altitude run with an Oscar De La Hoya at the peak of his powers. Then there was the moment when I really joined Team Barrera by diving into the snow to escape a runaway truck on Big Bear Mountain.

I have experienced truly inspirational days with miracle men like Michael Watson and Spencer Oliver, as well as fun nights out with Ricky Hatton and Joe Calzaghe. I've faced the frightening Mike Tyson entourage head on, and dealt with a fall-out with my long-time interviewee Naseem Hamed in the kitchens of an Atlantic City hotel as mountains of strawberry mousse were prepared around us.

Travelling throughout both the UK and the world as a broadcaster has enabled me to see and experience the human side of this often brutal sport. I've heard astonishing tales from the likes of Manny Pacquiao and his legions of fanatical Filipinos. I've witnessed Vernon Forrest's dedication to aiding the underprivileged with his 'Destiny's Child' programme. I cried buckets when my friend, former fighter Diego Corrales, was killed in a motorcycle accident. 'Chico' did some bad things, but you know what? He was rebuilding, he had learned, and deep down he had a heart of gold. Did you know that Diego Corrales personally helped deliver his final child? The man knew no fear. His family cherished him. So did I.

I've had the privilege of sitting six feet from ringside and 'calling' the fights, soaking up the cacophony of noise, the remarkable atmosphere, from the smallest and tightest of sports halls to the hugely hyped and starry Las Vegas nights. There is always a story.

So it is time now to tell some of those tales of the unexpected, as we delve deep into the training camps, families and lives of those who make boxing a beautiful but at the same time bloody brutality.

Family boxing businesses will be explored – the key relationships, from fathers and sons to brothers and mothers. There are absent, adopted and surrogate families, father figures, travellers, outsiders. There are the dynasties. There are the one-offs.

One of the great nights of the year is the Boxing Writers'

Dinner, when the scribes honour the fighters at a gala event in London. It is just like friends reuniting and recollecting, indulging in wonderful bonds. A big family gathering really. People said the same in the summer of 2010 when the WBC brought nearly a hundred champions together in Cardiff: it was like a family reunion.

Fighters come from vastly different backgrounds, but the respect and friendship they have for one another is second to none. They share their souls in the ring.

They also have a tendency to produce quite amazing vignettes, which help reveal the true sides of the Lords of the Ring, these bravest of men. In a sport perceived to be packed with lies, some of these stories may seem unbelievable, but they are true, believe me. We often have the footage to prove it.

So let's reveal a few of them, and admire the unbreakable bond boxers have with one another, and maybe more importantly the ones they desperately need to have with their families.

One

A FAMILY BUSINESS

1

A World of Fighters

August 2008. Bolton, Lancashire. A new town for me to visit. A new chapter in Sky's boxing history.

The big transfer news of the close-season was that Olympic boy wonder and unbeaten professional Amir Khan was moving from ITV to Sky. Opportunity was knocking for a new working relationship with an aspiring young star in the making. I couldn't wait to get to know Amir, and I was told that with Amir comes his whole family. The Khans are a unit. That this is, and always will be, very much a family business.

But who exactly were they? What would they be like to deal with? How many of them made up 'the family'?

Admittedly a little edgy, I arrived at their rather swish head-quarters on Bolton's Prince Street. It immediately made me think of my old interviewee/former partner in crime Prince Naseem Hamed and his offices for 'Prince Promotions'. So, this really is the way boxing is heading, I thought; there's a most noticeable shift in the way business is being conducted, particularly in the higher echelons of the sport. Fighters were taking control of their destinies; more and more big-name attractions were tending to employ members of their own family to help them.

The word 'loyalty' has for so long made one wince when mentioned in connection with boxing. The word 'trust' is a close second. Family is the nearest one can get to both loyalty and trust.

Based in these rather deluxe working premises at Bolton's Premier House were Premier Consultancy UK, the Khan family's company, and Gloves Community Gym. Amir met me at the front door. Talk about the main man. No entourage. No fuss. I liked him from the off. He showed me around this state-of-the art complex, which cost a million pounds to build.

'This was purely designed to help the youth of Bolton, especially in the rough parts,' Amir told me. 'It was my idea. I wanted to give something back to the community after all their support for me and my family. We've teamed up with the local college too, so that students can get an education in sports journalism for free. They come and share these computers, these desks, and any of the facilities. We charge a very small fee for the use of the gym – to encourage kids to get off the streets and do something positive.'

What he was too modest to tell me was that he put over £700,000 of his own money into the project.

I soon found out that Amir Khan was a very nice young man indeed, and quickly learned about his charity work as an ambassador for the NSPCC, plus his help for victims after the Indian Ocean tsunami and the Kashmir earthquake. Good parenting, I'd bet.

We went upstairs, and Amir introduced me to his father Shajaad, who was also instantly likeable. Then there was Amir's sister Tabinda and his Uncle Tahir. All of them had their own offices, each with their own role in this little empire.

Shajaad, or Shah as he is known, is involved practically 24/7. He has never missed one of Amir's fights, amateur or professional. Moreover, every important decision is run by him. Tahir, or Taz, appeared very sharp. He's university educated, and quit his job to help run the business side of Amir's career. Tabinda, or Tabs, is Amir's big sister. She makes sure the office runs smoothly and the numbers are checked. She even sometimes provides Amir's meals in camp.

Then I met two outsiders. Well, hardly big outsiders, but not true Khan blood anyway. Asif Vali is the business and commercial manager. 'I first met Amir at eight, when he came into the community club that I managed,' he said to me. 'I was told to watch out for him – even then he looked a champion. I owned a taxi firm in Bolton and helped sponsor some shows. I had no intention of being his manager but I became close to Shah, and I went full time after the Olympics.'

So Asif's almost part of the family, but can provide an independent voice if things become too close, too emotional, even if he hasn't been in boxing long. Likewise, Amir's best friend Saj has known him for years, and is treated as one of the clan. Saj organizes the fan mail and helps designing ring attire, logos, gift items and websites, as well as social media (if too vocally for some).

What a set-up, I thought, and all working for the most important commodity – the fighter himself.

We must have all got on well, because after we finished the tour of the business premises and the two excellently equipped boxing gyms my cameraman David Caine and I found ourselves invited back to Amir's house. Hospitable was not the word. We were treated like kings by the whole family, and there were lots more of them. There was Haroon, or Harry, Amir's funny younger brother and medal-winning amateur boxer, aiming for future Khan boxing glory. There was Mariyah, the younger sister who's never far from Amir's side. Shahid, or Uncle Terry, even made an appearance. He's the father of cricketer Saj Mahmood, a policeman and the pioneer of the family when he arrived from Pakistan.

The one person I really wanted to meet was Amir's mum. I am fascinated by boxers' mothers, and what they're like, as you'll find out later. Falak Khan was quietly cooking food, away from the hustle and bustle of her little nephews and nieces running everywhere. She was a lovely lady.

Again it was Amir who showed me around. This was his family home, next to which he still lives, amid all the noise, laughter and mayhem. It was one of the most communal, warm and inviting houses I've ever had the privilege of being welcomed into during my many years as a reporter.

'Every member of my family helps so much,' Amir told me. 'I wouldn't be here without them. When I get up in the morning, the only thing I have to worry about is training. Things are very different for a young Muslim growing up in England. It's not like being in other communities. The family mean more than anything in your life. That's why we all live together. You often find generations of the same family living under one roof, or very close to each other.

'My mum and dad have supported me from the beginning. My mum always tells me to be careful, and wants me to stop boxing. She prays for weeks before each fight. My Grandma Iqbal was very scared for me. She was my father's mother. I am so sad that she died before the Olympics; I wish she'd known I was safe and came out with my silver medal. Muslims have total respect for their fathers. They are everything, and I trust him more than anyone. We are so close as a family; [the business] is a family affair. I guess that's why so many Muslim families keep close together. Nothing is more important.'

Following in the tradition, in late 2011 Amir got engaged to young American, Faryal Makhdoom.

Back then it was a day to remember for me, and it was the start of life knowing the Khan family. I liked what I saw. This was different. This was modern.

Asif gave me his thoughts: 'All boxers should have their families involved. Mum, Dad, sister, brother, uncles, aunts, together with people trained in business. You have to have that trust. Without it, there's nothing. A great deal of boxers have declared themselves bankrupt in recent years – what does that tell you? Managers have ripped boxers off. They have not received sound advice. The taxman catches up with them. They just didn't know.'

Interesting words. Asif wasn't far off the mark. Mike Tyson: $300 million earned, declared bankrupt in 2003. Riddick Bowe: more than $75 million in the bank, declared bankrupt in 2005. Both were from the Brownsville slums in New York. Neither knew how to look after his fortune.

Over here, Chris Eubank could have won prizes for being the smartest dressed boxer of all time. The joke used to go that he used to throw his underwear away after one use. This came back to bite him in the bum. All his sartorial elegance coud not prevent Eubank being declared bankrupt in November 2005, owing £1.3 million in taxes.

Evander Holyfield made in excess of $100 million. I've visited his 109-room mansion on Evander Holyfield Highway in Atlanta. It boasts a baseball pitch, an Olympic-sized swimming pool in the shape of an IBF belt, a forest, a lake, a movie theatre and a garage filled with several luxury cars. Yet Holyfield recently defaulted on a $10 million loan that went towards the initial three-year building programme. It's so sad that he's still fighting given that he turns fifty in October 2012.

Boxing has always had these tragic tales of fighters squandering their money. The great Canadian Sam Langford was left blind and penniless; Joe Louis died indebted to the tune of $1.3 million. As I left Bolton that day in August 2008, I thought at least Amir Khan has his family right behind him: stable, solid, dependable and, most importantly, loyal. But as we would find out later, nothing is ever quite so simple.

Less than two weeks after the visit, we all watched in disbelief as Amir's perfect professional record of eighteen straight wins was blown apart in fifty-four nightmare seconds by unknown Colombian puncher Breidis Prescott.

Many critics wrote him off immediately. His family never did. And who better to pick up the broken pieces than your nearest and dearest? All of whom were ringside to watch one of the biggest upsets in a British ring in the modern era. Just ten months later Amir Khan was crowned world champion. It was one of the biggest and quickest boxing comebacks of recent times. The Khans were back in business.

Families have always been involved in the sport of boxing, from the bare-knuckle days right up to the Hattons, Khans and Mayweathers now. Some families have chosen to take on roles in the many different aspects of the boxing business. From the training to the promoting to the matchmaking, the careers of many successful boxers have become a family business. These family practitioners learn the skills necessary to liaise with everyone involved, from doctors to the matchmakers to the media.

From the eighteenth century some families used to make their money out of boxing booths, where fairground fighters would chin local hard men one after the other to earn their living. Coalminers and steelworkers took their chances, egged on by their mates. They would invariably lose in front of the baying crowds, because they were tackling skilled prizefighters. It was their business.

There were legendary figures like Tom Hickman, 'The Gaslight Man', who used to simply turn your lights out. James Figg pickled his knuckles in vinegar (I thought that was only done to harden conkers in preparation for duels in the school playground). Then there was Jem Mace, who I guess wasn't the ideal family man: he had fourteen children with five different women. Harry 'Kid' Furness was a 'boxing family' in himself. At various stages he was a fighter, a proprietor, a referee, a matchmaker and a promoter. He was a hugely important figure in the development of boxing. Many British boxing hopes emerged, like Jimmy Wilde, 'The Ghost with the Hammer in his Hand', and 'The Tonypandy Terror', Tommy Farr. Muhammad Ali once displayed his skills for charity at Ron Taylor's famous boxing emporium, in 1977.

Modern boxing was born out of these booths, which travelled with fairs, carnivals and circuses and were prosperous all over the English countryside for the best part of two hundred years. Step up and take your chance! Invariably a thoroughly good hiding followed. The money was collected, and the family business in boxing had well and truly begun.

One of Britain's most famous Romany bare-knuckle champions was a man called Absolom Beeny. At the age of ninety-five, Beeny saw his great-grandson head to the Beijing Olympics. Today, Billy Joe Saunders is a hot professional prospect. The Saunders clan are steeped in generational fighting history. All trying to make their way through the use of their fists.

While Absolom Beeny was rising to prominence in the fairgrounds, one Gershon Mendeloff was making his way into professional boxing, desperately attempting to earn some corn having been born in a gas-lit tenement in the East End. Mendeloff was the son of a cabinet maker and began at just fourteen, when he fought for sixpence and a cup of tea. He went on to box under the name of Ted 'Kid' Lewis and won around 230 of an incredible 300 bouts.

The Jews carried the torch for much of the late 1800s and early 1900s. Boxing was a favoured sport among the Jewish communities in London's East End; it was often seen as a route out of poverty for these huge families. Boxing was an escape, a way of making something of their lives, a means of erasing the inferiority complex of the immigrant. They were young, they were often penniless, and they chose to fight for pay.

Stateside, Jews in the urban ghettos were born fighting anti-semitism. From Abe Attell to Benny Leonard and Barney Ross, 'Slapsie' Maxie Rosenbloom to Jackie 'Kid' Berg, these boxers were seen as idols by children. Ironically, the Jewish press virtually ignored the sport, feeling it was thoroughly shameful. Fighters often had to hide their choice of career, fearful of family resentment. Some, like Mendeloff, made up new names. Benny Leonard was really Benjamin Leiner, and his mother had no idea that he fought. Such was the cloud of mystery. In reality, though, boxing was an excellent way of making money for families, and over time it became accepted.

Many of the Irish, too, were forced to become fighters, and some families benefited accordingly. The dreadful potato famine saw a period of death and disease that lasted from 1845 to 1852. This led to mass emigration, mostly to America, where men began working in canal building and construction works. Among these labourers hard men were formed, and it wasn't long before fighting became both a pastime and a profession. They had good strong genes for boxing success, and Irish communities began to grow, particularly in Boston, New York and Philadelphia. Enormous families and their circle of cousins headed to the east coast of the United States to find fame and fortune. They still do. Steve Collins, John Duddy and Andy Lee have all experienced the 'American dream' of late. Boston and New York are still favoured destinations.

Ireland has a rich boxing heritage. Native Irish and Irish-American boxers have always prided themselves on their inner strength and huge hearts. Countless legends are descended from the Irish, including 'The Greatest': Muhammad Ali's great-grandfather Abe Grady was born in the county town of Ennis. John L Sullivan was born in Massachusetts to Irish immigrant parents, Gene Tunney in New York to two Irish parents. Jack 'Nonpareil' Dempsey became the first recognized middleweight champion after knocking out George Fulljames in the twenty-second round. He was born in County Kildare, and his more famous namesake – 'The Manassa Mauler' – had an Irish father.

We had Mickey 'Toy Bulldog' Walker, who apparently laced his water bottle with gin during a middleweight title fight, and the 5ft 6in Jimmy 'Babyface' McLarnin. There was Billy 'The Pittsburgh Kid' Conn, 'Terrible' Terry McGovern, Packey McFarland and 'Sailor' Tom Sharkey. 'Irish' Micky Ward was one of my favourite modern fighters. His trilogy with the late, great Arturo Gatti will never be forgotten.

Ireland also boasted the super-flyweight great Rinty Monaghan, who was a terrific world champion from Belfast and became a cult hero in the post-war period. Monaghan was a part-time cabaret artist who worked with Vera Lynn and George Formby. Freddie Gilroy won the British, Commonwealth and European bantamweight titles, and challenged for world honours; Dave McAuley made five defences of the IBF flyweight title. 'The Pocket Rocket' Wayne McCullough struck silver at the 1992 Barcelona Olympics, and travelled to Japan to win the WBC bantamweight crown. Steve Collins was the steely WBO middle and super-middleweight champion who beat both Chris Eubank and Nigel Benn twice. More recently there have been Eamonn Loughran, Eamonn Magee, Damaen Kelly . . . the list is endless.

The Irish have been a poor nation for large periods of time. Boxing has long been seen as a way of bettering the lives of the many children these close families tend to have.

Then there were the Italian-Americans, of course, who also have an early and significant family link to the sport. Even today in New York's Little Italy, black and white pictures of boxing heroes, families and dynasties adorn the walls. Many more can be found at Jimmy's Bar in Times Square. Cult figures like Tony Canzoneri, Primo Carnera – 'The Ambling Alp' from the 1930s – and the starry Joey Giardello in the fifties and sixties. There were countless fighters who were so popular and colourful, like Rocky Graziano, Jake La Motta, Ray Mancini and Joey Maxim.

In modern times, Vinny Pazienza was the epitome of fighting spirit, proving medics and doctors wrong by boxing on after the most horrific of car crashes. I've even seen footage of Pazienza preparing for a fight with a metal neck brace on, a contraption that would have looked more in place as scaffolding on a sky-scraper.

One Guglielmo Papaleo, or Willy Pep, is a favourite of many people. Pep boxed almost two thousand rounds in over 240 fights during a twenty-six-year career. His reflexes and speed were quite dazzling. Perhaps the greatest of all, though, was Rocco Francis Marchegiano, more famously known as Rocky Marciano – the only heavyweight champion to retire undefeated: forty-nine fights, forty-nine wins, forty-three KOs.

However, along with the waves of Italian immigration to America, a family of a different kind began to rear their heads. Boxing was heavily influenced by the Mafia, or offshoots from the initial Sicilian Mafia. There were innumerable stories and instances of the Mob's racketeering, in which fights were fixed and boxers bribed, or in no uncertain terms told to take a fall. Fighters or their managers who did not play by the Mafia's rules were excluded from the world title contests that brought in the big paydays.

Criminals had always hung around the fringes of boxing in America. Some say it was the introduction of prohibition in the twenties that was the real driving force behind the rise of organized crime. With its brutality and potential financial gains, boxing was an obvious target for the mobsters. Even the biggest names in the ring, like Jake La Motta, could be bought. The Mafia were the tightest and toughest of families.

It was the 1950s when the Mob really took over, easing out more respectable figures like the Irish-Jewish promoter Mike Jacobs, who had run the legendary Madison Square Garden venue for twenty years and managed Joe Louis. Led by the sinister and ruthless Frankie Carbo, the underworld gained control. Carbo fixed so many fights that he became known as 'The Czar' of all boxing. He was also a gunman who was accused of countless murders, including possibly engineering the downfall of infamous American gangster Benjamin 'Bugsy' Siegel in 1947.

In this climate of fixing, results could be just a complete lottery. Symbolic of the Mob's sway was the rise of the heavyweight Sonny Liston, detested by many because of his savagery in the ring and perceived links to organized crime. Liston was a perfect tool. He'd been born in dreadful poverty in a cotton field in St Francis County in Arkansas, and was beaten regularly. Liston built up a long criminal record as a youth. He once admitted he didn't mind jail as it gave him three meals a day. At one stage he raped a maid but, using their judicial powers, the Mafia bosses made sure he escaped jail, and in doing so kept him permanently in their debt. Suspicion will forever remain over his losses against Cassius Clay/Muhammad Ali. Liston had revelled in his role of the 'world's baddest man', but he was also said to be charming, and worked hard for charities. Yet, as in some absent-family cases, Liston died in awful and strange circumstances in Las Vegas. There was no dream ending: he was buried under the flight path into McCarran airport with a headstone that simply read 'A Man'.

Another compelling story. Another sad waste.

With its air of malevolence and smell of blood, the Mafia gave boxing truly explosive years. The classic movie *On the Waterfront* came directly out of this. Marlon Brando's brilliant depiction of a former boxer denied the chance of competing for a title by the Mafia remains one of my favourites. 'I could have been a contender' has become an iconic line in cinematic history.

The influence of the Mafia eventually petered out, but some say the sport never quite regained its power as a serious cultural force. For all the qualities of that stream of Italian-American showmen, the darker side drawn in from those Sicilian roots did much damage to the integrity of our sport. It was one family business boxing didn't need.

2

Striking Out Alone

As the Khans showed me, families or boxing families have really evolved in modern times. They get ever nearer the heartbeat of the business.

While boxers hone their bodies into tip-top condition in training camp, they need their families to be the primary source of support. They can serve to alleviate the mundane regularity of the daily regime while also providing a set-up that makes the fighters feel good about themselves.

Yet there are still those boxers who choose to take on the world almost singlehandedly, without family really around them during the most important time of their careers. These fighters seem to want to handle their own business and take full responsibility for the consequences.

There are obsessive types, like former lightweight Wayne Rigby, who shut themselves in rooms with their opponent's name scrawled on the wall, or tear up pictures of their next foes.

I used to visit Steve Collins in his sparse hideaway in Jersey: biting winds, deserted beaches and rugged terrain. From these craggy rocks I went to the highest of mountains, where Nigel

Benn locked himself away on winding roads at twelve thousand feet on Tenerife's Mount Teide.

Two of the greatest middleweights of all time tended to take this approach to a different level. I was fortunate enough to get one-on-one with them.

The instructions were clinical, executed with precision by 'The Executioner'.

'Meet at South Beach. No later than five thirty a.m. A minute later and I'm gone. A minute. Do you understand that?' said the greatest middleweight of his generation.

It was spring 2004, and Bernard Hopkins was deep into training for a third fight with Robert Allen. At the time, the phenomenal Philadelphian just kept on turning back challenge after challenge for his world middleweight crown. The key to unlock the defence of this master was actually becoming tougher to find the older Hopkins was getting. Back then he was in his fortieth year; incredibly, he is still at the very top today. A victory in 2011 over Jean Pascal crowned B-Hop as the oldest fighter to win a world championship in history. A perfect, obsessive protection of his body has been vital to this longevity.

So there I was, waiting to run with this supreme fighter and awesome athlete. In one of the most vibrant cities in the world: Miami, Florida. At 5.29 a.m. he pitched up, and he was already in fairly full flow. It looked like he'd been running for a while.

'Come on,' Hopkins said. 'Time to work. Now.'

So off we went, pounding the long boardwalk stretch next to the white sand and the glorious ocean. The pace was sharp. We didn't even have a chance to film this magnificent insight. My excellent cameraman Cainey was, for once, left floundering, because we just couldn't get a vehicle in the right place. The experience, the dialogue, the moment was left just to Bernard and me – and the gentle early-morning waves.

'This just seems the perfect example of one man against the world,' I said to him.

'Yup,' he replied. 'There's no one else.'

It made me think of that eccentric middleweight from Watford, Ojay Abrahams, who always went by the phrase 'Me, Myself and I'. Boxing can be that lonely.

'Don't you need support? A family to surround you?'

'There are others,' Bernard replied. 'But if you had led the life I have, you'd realize you need to take care of number one. First and foremost. No one else will do that for you.'

I was really struggling to keep up with him. Yet I was desperately trying to, because you just don't often find yourself in such a unique or privileged position.

'I look after myself better than any other fighter,' he continued. 'That's why I'm where I am. I get up at five a.m. every morning in camp, without fail. By five ten I am warming up on the treadmill. I eat, sleep and breathe training. I don't drink, I don't smoke, I never ever abuse my body. I will not even have sauce on a pasta in a restaurant. Not if I don't know exactly what's in it. The lights go off at nine thirty p.m. eight weeks before a fight. Clockwork. After the life I've led, that's what I do. I was involved in gangs from childhood in the Raymond Rosen projects of north Philly. I mugged all sorts, and when I was in eleventh grade – yes, eleventh grade, at seventeen – I was sentenced to eighteen years in Graterford prison for armed robbery and around nine or ten felonies. Can you believe that?'

No, I couldn't. It was so far from where and how I had been brought up. Sheltered from all of this.

My time in boxing has given me such an eye-opener into life. I would never have had the chance to learn so much about the harshest of social and family situations if it wasn't for my work.

Even though he had committed all those terrible crimes, I still felt sympathy towards Bernard.

Plus, when Hopkins talks, he talks. It's fun to be part of the drum roll. Intelligent jargon, at freight train speed. It was magical stuff. It really was.

'The late seventies was just awful in my 'hood. Being anywhere near Diamond Street was a recipe for disaster. Locked me up, they did. Everyone in the prison thought that I would be back. Quickly. Not a chance. My inner spirit is strong. It took years, but I learned. Ever since I walked out of Graterford, I haven't so much as spat on the sidewalk.'

Bernard only goes back to Graterford to help motivate and educate today's prisoners. For the former jailbird now has a settled and happy home life and a prosperous future, and he is very much immersed in the Golden Boy promotional family.

After around fifteen minutes, my legs just couldn't keep up, and Hopkins tore off into the distance. I was left standing alone on South Beach, watching this fighting figure burn away.

Bernard Hopkins trains and fights alone, and that's what works for him. Family seems to play little or no part. He controls his business. It's a rare sight these days. But then there aren't many people as driven and as independent as Bernard Hopkins.

'Marvelous' Marvin Hagler was once the king of the middleweights in America. Ironically, he now lives in Italy. Hagler went the other way, to a country he adores, where he became a well-known actor in action films.

Hagler is settled now; but like the fighter who followed him in middleweight dominance, Bernard Hopkins, he was once a lone shark. When preparing for fights, this intense individual would isolate himself on Cape Cod in Massachusetts.

I have taken holidays on the Cape ever since childhood. Boasting beautiful beaches, scrummy seafood and an elegant but laid-back feel, it has a soothing air that entices visitors to relax and recharge. The quiet calm also offers an excellent arena for athletes to train without distraction, and I have frequented the spots where Hagler honed his body into supreme shape. It is amazing what you can find out by searching through the excellent public records service and old publications that the prestigious libraries on the Cape store.

Hagler used to lock himself away from virtually everybody at the very tip of Cape Cod, in Provincetown. Renowned today for its colourful, wild and gay scene, Provincetown attracts tourists with an array of entertaining transvestites, transgender and transsexual fairs and parades, especially during the summer. Autumn and winter are not such friendly seasons, due mainly to the damaging weather. The Pilgrims actually landed here, in November 1620, but were said to have turned back in horror, hauling up their anchors and moving across the bay to Plymouth. The winter winds make Provincetown one of the coldest places anywhere. Marvin Hagler would pound the beaches there in ice or snow. He could often be heard screaming in pain. Savage conditions, seagulls and solitude. The stunning Cape Cod seashore was Hagler's self-imposed prison.

'Sometimes as early as three a.m., seven days a week, I would run and sprint on Herring Cove beach and its surrounds,' Hagler told me when I chatted to him during a visit to the UK. 'I could do fifteen miles among the tough dunes, and I wore heavy combat boots. Running shoes, they were sissy shoes. I would run part of this backwards too as I always tried to replicate movements in the ring.'

Hagler holed himself up in remote, bare motels that were closed to the public. His team was sparse, just the Petronelli brothers – Guerino and Pat – and selected sparring partners, who according to sources still around today were 'brought in, beaten up and replaced regularly'. They were also never allowed to talk to Hagler on a social basis.

Between sessions, Hagler would stare intently at the ocean.

Lights were off even earlier than for Hopkins, at eight p.m. All to get into that zone. To prepare for that crucial moment in the ring.

It was the only way Hagler knew: fighting for himself – a trait stemming from yet another rocky boxing childhood. His family tenement was completely destroyed in the Newark riots during the summer of 1976. Twenty-six people were left dead after the multi-million-dollar disorder and devastation. Another tantalizing tale developed from deep-rooted domestic struggles.

Fighters are a strange breed. Many do what comes naturally to them. Complex and complicated family situations can drive them out on their own. They strive to reach the limits of their physical capabilities in order to mentally prepare for the wars that lie ahead.

So Hopkins and Hagler demonstrated that there were different strokes for different folks. Yet most prominent fighters, especially these days, tend to need people around them. Lennox Lewis was one of those.

When Oliver McCall shattered Lewis's perfect professional record at Wembley in 1994, lead trainer Pepe Correa was out and Emanuel Steward brought in. I spent loads of time with Lennox during his final fifteen training camps, all under Steward's tutelage. From Phoenix to Miami; Big Bear, California to the most well-used resort, Caesar's, up at three thousand feet, nestled among Pennsylvania's Pocono mountains. It was a spooky place. A honeymoon hideaway with round beds, mirrored walls, heart-shaped jacuzzis and ridiculously large plastic champagne flutes to bathe in. They used to freak me out those rooms, they really did.

Anyway, Lennox was always surrounded by exactly the same sizeable group of people, all of whom had an important role in the meticulous build-up to a world heavyweight title fight. This was Lennox Lewis's working family.

Alongside Manny Steward was the excellent assistant trainer Harold Knight, whom I rate highly, and who in his quiet, unassuming way was absolutely crucial to the rise of Lewis. Conditioner and oldest friend Courtney Shand ran the programme of training, dietary and media requirements. Patrick Drayton was the runner and pace-setter, while Egerton Marcus was the regular sparring partner, particularly good at imitating small fiery heavyweights like David Tua and Mike Tyson. Scott DeMercado and Ron Hepburn were Lennox's two great mates who were ever-present and helped on the conditioning and security side. Mum Violet was 'the mother of the whole group' – her cooking, support and love were essential. Lennox was of course guided for most of his career by the cheeky chirpy cockney Frank Maloney, who also spent weeks in camp, and always immersed himself in the family set-up. Adrian Ogun performed this role towards the end.

'I'm fortunate to have been surrounded by an amazing group of people, many of whom put their lives and the lives of their families on hold to help make me a better person and a better boxer through their loyalty, encouragement and support,' Lewis said on announcing his retirement in 2004. 'All members of Team Lewis were voices in my head that made me run a little further, bike a little faster, play chess a little better and punch a little harder.'

They were, indeed, a well-oiled professional outfit.

At the height of Lennox's powers, I used to be asked three things regularly by other fighters and by fans about this most cool, genial and laid-back of heavyweights.

Were some of these members of Team Lewis merely glorified hangers-on?

Were the camp members particularly camp?

And was our heavyweight champion of the world actually gay?

Rumours circulated for years. Speculation was always rife.

Lennox could be so chilled out that he appeared at times almost horizontal. He also seemed to surround himself with the same large group of guys, and some pointed to the fact he was particularly close to his mother. But so am I. What does that mean? Violet Lewis brought him up as a single mum. No wonder they have the closest of bonds.

Members of the media continued to speculate. The *Sun* ran a spread asking the big question: 'Is the World Heavyweight Champion gay?'

Lennox's personal life was always shrouded in mystery. Debate raged when Mike Tyson, following his farcical thirty-eight-second knockout of Lou Savarese at a sodden Hampden Park, felled referee John Coyle and then ranted extraordinary things at Lewis: 'Lennox, I'm coming for you . . . Lennox is no conqueror. I'm the best ever. I'm Sonny Liston, Jack Dempsey. I'm cut from their cloth. I want his heart, to eat his children.'

Not sure Mike had taken his happy pills that day.

Yet following this mad but fascinating diatribe, people were left saying 'Lennox doesn't have any children. In fact he doesn't seem to have a girlfriend.'

There was another unsavoury incident in the build-up to the rematch with Hasim Rahman, who had knocked Lewis cold in South Africa in 2001. Long before Lennox exacted revenge there was a punch-up in an ESPN television studio. It went back to a radio interview in which Rahman poured scorn on Lewis for suggesting he would take legal action against him, saying that sort of conduct was 'of a less than manly man'.

'Why did you say I was gay?' Lewis retorted. 'I am not gay.'

'I said you were acting gay, taking it to court,' Rahman replied.

'Listen, I'm a one hundred per cent women's man. If you're worried about that, bring your sister by.'

Rahman responded by smashing the table and saying, 'Do not say nothing about my family.'

It was sensitive stuff, but none of it really helped to quell the rumours about Lennox Lewis's sexuality.

Lewis once openly admitted to newspaper editor turned TV host Piers Morgan, 'When people started coming up to me and asking if I was gay, it really bugged me. It was so ridiculous and I couldn't do anything to stop the rumour.'

Lennox eventually married a college graduate, former beauty pageant winner and Miss Jamaica runner-up Violet Chang, on 15 July 2005. She is a delightful lady, and I recently enjoyed a casual supper with the two of them during which we talked about love, life and family. They now have four children – three daughters and a son, Landon. The Lewises also recently sent baby clothes to my wife Jo after the arrival of our third, Tilly. Lennox dotes on his family, and adores his growing clan. He told me he wants six children. 'It's the best thing that's happened to me,' he said. 'The time wasn't right before. I had my boxing family, now I have my real family. I want Landon to be involved in sport, but I have mixed thoughts about boxing. He can shadow box though!'

I married and had children in my mid- to late thirties. I too am close to my mum, my home life was on the unconventional side, and I put career before marriage for many years, until I found the right girl in my gorgeous wife Jo. So in many ways I can relate to Lennox.

Lennox is easy to chat to these days; there's now a contented, glowing feel to the former heavyweight king. Back in his fighting days, though, while always available for an interview, Lennox was tough to get close to.

I played countless games of chess through the night with him in camp, and while fiercely competitive, he rarely divulged anything. My Sky colleague Craig Slater and I also once took Lennox on a social boat trip in southern Florida. It was the cheapest vessel in the harbour, he brought his friend Scott along, and we nearly sank. It was a hard job getting much out of him though, bar the odd polite interjection.

He only once opened up to me. It was on the bridge from Miami to Key Biscayne in spring 1998. It was early, maybe seven a.m., and as the sun began to rise, we began to run.

The two people I never minded running with were Lennox and Naseem Hamed. Neither appeared to travel that fast. Not that I'd have told them that at the time. So I could keep up with Lennox. Just. The first time I ran with him was in ninety degrees of heat on a golf course littered with cacti in Arizona. I was in a pinstriped suit, and I was trying to conduct an interview. Troublesome conditions. This was a touch easier. I was better prepared, and little Frank Maloney was jogging at his own pace too.

I ran next to Lennox. He was deep into training for his fight with Shannon Briggs. We were both young, free, and very much single at the time. I have never really talked about that day until now. I feel this is an opportunity to set the record straight.

'Beautiful people in Miami,' I probed.

'The women are stunning,' he replied.

It was the first thing he said. His face lit up when he said it. I remember the conversation, crystal clear. There was a camera hovering around trying to film, but most of this was, like the Hopkins experience, rather secretive.

'You have to go out on South Beach,' he continued. 'Man, those girls are cute. Yo, really, really cute.'

Lennox then talked for some twenty minutes about women. Without a break. He spoke with passion and drive, and I felt, for the first and possibly only time ever, that Lennox had completely laid himself open. He suggested bars and clubs in Miami to go to, not just the predictable gay and expensive scene but the places to pitch up and pull the ladies.

Had it been a taped interview I would have been suspicious. But I never felt this was a planted 'chat' with a member of the media. I knew Lennox too well for that. I'd spent a lot of time with him. These were his real emotions. Laid bare.

I finished the run shattered, but at the same time utterly convinced that Lennox Lewis liked the ladies. I have since, of course, been proved right. Not that there would have been anything wrong if he had been gay – just hugely surprising given the bloody context of his chosen career.

'You put me in a room full of fighters, and I will be the last man standing,' Lennox used to tell me time and again.

So I learned that his close circle was indeed just that, designed to further his professional career and life. I'm sure Lennox and Violet, with their four kids, smile about the insinuations now.

The Lewis team was the first real 'boxing family' I had ever experienced, and boy were they tight-knit. They were also very, very successful. After that shock defeat to Hasim Rahman, when Lewis had been messing around on movie sets and believing in his own invincibility, he never lost another fight. Not to Mike Tyson. Not to Vitali Klitschko. Not to anyone.

3

At the Court of the Prince

The idea of boxing being a family business really hit home during the time I spent with 'Prince' Naseem Hamed.

For the second part of his career, Hamed shared the same coach with Lennox Lewis in Emanuel Steward. So they had to live together in camp at times. All of this had been brought about after the awful split between 'Naz' and his long-time trainer and mentor Brendan Ingle.

The tiny extroverted urchin from Sheffield and the old eccentric Irish chatterbox had been, to most observers, an unlikely but excellent match, even a match made in heaven. My close friend and colleague Johnny Nelson still can't quite believe what happened.

Hamed and Ingle had been together since Naz was seven. I remember an early interview with Hamed, shortly before he became a world champion, conducted at the back of Brendan's house, by the church opposite his St Thomas's Boys Club gym on that steep Wincobank hill. 'I will never ever leave Brendan. Dangle any carrot under my nose, any carrot. Nothing. I will not leave Brendan. For anything. Never.' That's what Hamed told me.

Talk is cheap, I guess. Or expensive if you listen to Naz. The problems were, as so often, largely financial. Brendan had expected to get both his trainer's and manager's cut, and as the Prince's purses began to rise into the millions, this became an issue. A fat piece of the pie and all that. With Naz's rise came an obsession with building the finest possible fleet of cars. I lost count of how many he had. Lamborghini, Ferrari, Aston Martin, Porsche, you name it. He said they were 'different cars for different moods'.

Brendan had given up much of his life to Naseem. He taught him how to box, he raved about his protégé. They went everywhere together.

In the late nineties I seemed to spend most of my time in the Steel City. Naz and I had a real rapport. I probably conducted about 150 official interviews with him over the years we worked together. I liked verbally sparring with Hamed. Cocky and controversial, he was probably the most enjoyable fighter to interview I have ever come across. Short in stature but hardly in attitude, Naz lit up rooms, and I have always been attracted to any person who does that.

At the time, Naz had two 'families'. Like Lennox Lewis, he was permanently surrounded by the same familiar boxing faces. His gym-mates were ever-present at his side. Johnny Nelson was one, the maverick heavyweight Clifton Mitchell another. The jokers were Kevin Adamson, a likeable light-middleweight, and a Robbie Fowler lookalike called Thomas Bradley, whom I always had time for. (Thomas was tragically killed in a motorbike crash in 2011 at just thirty-seven. I met up with Naz later that day. He was crestfallen.) Anas Oweida was another addition, a budding professional fighter who came from London. He became close to Naz through their Muslim faith. Naz's best friend was Ryan Rhodes. Inseparable buddies, they had been groomed side by side, and rose up the rankings together.

They were tremendously exciting times. I loved heading from London to the Steel City. I always yearned for that Sheffield train stop because I knew another fun roller-coaster ride lay ahead.

Naz's timekeeping was appalling. It still is, but I put up with it because I'm drawn to him. Once I waited eight hours for him to bother to come down from his suite at London's exclusive Grosvenor House Hotel, but I just didn't mind. Maybe I was young and keen. Maybe I just had a soft spot for him. Whatever it was, it seemed worth it in the end. There was always something golden at the end of the long, long rainbow.

That night in London ended at around 2.30 a.m. on the day – yes, the day – of Naz's vital unification bout with America's Tom 'Boom-Boom' Johnson. 'The boys', who all shared parts of whichever hotel suite they were in during the build-up to a fight, had been sent out for Naz's latest food request. It was usually Burger King or Kentucky Fried Chicken. Sometimes both.

Naz used to weigh-in on the eve of battle a shade under the featherweight limit of nine stone. Normally 8st 13½lb. Or thereabouts.

Once, when he was fighting Juan Cabrera, I saw Naz eat a chicken meal after the six p.m. Friday-night weigh-in. Then I heard he ordered a BK in the really early hours, and then KFC in the early hours. That family of boys apparently weighed him for fun at five a.m. on the day of the fight. Naz was said to have scaled in the region of 10st 4lb – a phenomenal statistic for one of the hardest-hitting featherweights who's ever lived.

These late finishes were hard for us, and that night the lobby of the Grosvenor House was turned into a no-holds-barred boxing ring as the entire team turned up with massive gloves. After my interview with the Prince, I was royally set upon by the whole lot of them. More weird and wonderful pictures for our Sky countdown programmes.

I've always had a close set of friends who go way back to when I was a small boy – some to nursery, when we were just three or four years old. Many of them are seen by my family as an extension of our family. So to see Naz with these unconditional supporters was refreshing for me. Once we even cut a *Friends* package that equated the Naz crew with the enormously popular TV series of the time.

We used to see the boys on the dodgems, at bowling alleys, racing their cars around, and playing umpteen practical jokes on one another. They would work hard and play hard. From tenacious boxing sessions to nightclub dancing of crazy proportions. 'I'll be there for you . . .' Isn't that the *Friends* theme tune?

So they were Naseem Hamed's boxing family. His real family were close-knit too, and became more and more involved in the development of his career as the relationship with Brendan Ingle and his sons John and Dominic began to break down. The Hameds went a step further than the Lennox set-up: they were an actual blood family who became heavily involved with the day-to-day running of their star asset's progress. Ultimately, Prince Promotions was born.

Sal Hamed's ancestors had been poor farmers in Yemen. He left his wife Caira in their homeland in order to seek work in the steel mills of Sheffield. He endured an arduous succession of boat rides to achieve his aim of pitching up in Britain, but family had always been key to Sal, and he was persistent. The family business began with a small corner-shop on Newman Road, less than five hundred yards up the hill from Brendan's sweatshop.

Sal was the patriarch of the family. Obedience and manners were important to him, and the media grew fond of him as the Hamed story began to gather steam. He was a pleasant and respected man who never seemed to get carried away with the fact that he had gone from being a newsagent to one of the best-treated men in all of Yemen. Sal used to rub shoulders with royalty from that Middle Eastern country. Sadly, he passed away recently. Naz, by then a father of three boys and a proud family man himself, was devastated. He has vowed to follow through with much of the charity work his father had been involved in.

The women in the family – there are four daughters – were hardly talked about in relation to business or work. The men – Sal and his five sons Riath, Nabeel, Naseem, Ali and Murad – were very much the providers. Some of the boys trained in the gym at times, but none was nearly as talented or as dedicated to becoming a sporting success as Naseem.

Ali tried, but it never quite worked out. He was the dark horse, or little black sheep, of the family. As polite and engaging as he was, I always felt sorry for him, because, at times, he seemed a lost soul. Yet I found him the kindest of them all. I liked him very much.

Riath, the eldest, was bright and had studied for a degree in political and social science; Nabeel always seemed keen to enter the business side too; little Murad, who looked most like Naz, tended to prefer the flash, partying lifestyle. Murad was forever coming up with extravagant and rather way-out entrepreneurial ideas.

They were an entertaining bunch – maybe not as witty as Naz's boxing boys, but interesting characters nonetheless. They were very close too, and were far more visible to the cameras as the fights became more and more important.

The tension between Brendan and the Hameds grew more obvious. The Ingles were beginning to feel that the family influence was becoming detrimental to Naz's training, and that Naz was starting to turn. I remember sitting with Brendan before he locked up the gym one summer's evening and asking whether he thought he would still be a part of the Hamed story at the end. When it was all said and done.

'That's a difficult question to answer, Adam,' he told me.

Brendan never had difficulties answering any question. He could fill up hours of tape at breakneck speed.

'I think that Naz is being badly advised by his family,' he told me. 'They don't have the faintest clue about the boxing business. Frank Warren is a brilliant promoter, and they're beginning to think they can do a better job. Very dangerous. The little fella's not training properly. His behaviour's arrogant and horrible. Money has become his god.'

Fiery stuff.

The problem stemmed from what Brendan's role was. Yes, he had trained Naz since the beginning, but he also claimed managerial rights because of the time spent nurturing him and therefore wanted 25 per cent for that too (the going rate for a manager, whereas a trainer is usually entitled to only 10 per cent. But then Brendan had been no ordinary trainer.)

Frank Warren promoted Naseem for the key part of his career, when the money rose from thousands to millions. This had a huge effect on the amount of money going out in percentage terms. Neither Warren nor Ingle could have been happy when Naz announced that Riath was to become his business manager. This was really the start of the family empire and Prince Promotions. Brendan was on their pay-roll, and his trainer's fees were subject to their negotiation.

It was something of a coup. The power base had changed dramatically, and the Ingles found themselves in a weak position. Warren was still the promoter – remember, he had made Hamed a great deal of money, and like many of us just had a soft spot for Naz. One birthday present was a special edition Aston Martin Vantage worth around £200,000.

The growing friction was glaringly apparent on my regular visits to Sheffield. I, like Brendan, didn't think it would be long before there were major changes.

The writing seemed well and truly on the wall with the publi-
cation of a book called *The Paddy and The Prince*. Nick Pitt's work
was a revealing and absorbing read. It seemed to me that Brendan
had used it to get his word across and to follow on from our
television interviews, speaking out via the ever-powerful written
word. It came over as a major criticism of Naseem Hamed, about
money, discipline and, most importantly, loyalty.

The wounds of this turbulent relationship were deepened by a
phone call I received from Naz late in September 1998.

'Adam, I want you to come up and interview me tomorrow.
I am going to give you an explosive exclusive. The truth about
Brendan. Bring the camera. I'll pick you up from the train station
myself.'

I booked my ticket instantly, spent the next twenty-four hours
preparing for this exciting journalistic opportunity, and hurried
north.

Naz was waiting for me in his Bentley. He was early. Naz was
never early.

He'd allowed me some privileged access to his life with fast
cars and other behind-the-scenes gems before. I'd even done a
documentary on his rise. But this felt different.

'Adam, we're going to my offices, and I want you to get my
story on film,' Naz said to me during the short ride in his extravagant open-top motor. 'You're going to hear things that will
shock you, and I'm giving this to you because I know you best.'

We arrived at Prince Promotions. The swanky office was
decked out with precious 'Prince' paraphernalia. We set up in
the huge boardroom. It felt like more of a place where important
company decisions were taken than an additional arm of his
growing boxing empire. Yet this is what Prince Promotions
had become. A business. A family one. The receptionist, Lynn,
wasn't a blood relative, but just about everyone else seemed to
be. There had long been a London-based PR girl on the scene

called Frankie Burstin, but it looked to me like the family was now calling the shots.

I have always tended to dislike the fact that the media are guided through endless streams of backroom public relations staff, or other such people who block you from the actual fighter. I can understand there is a job to do, and that sometimes there is a need to 'shield the product' – one more concern lifted from his shoulders – but I have always tried to build my own strong relationships with fighters. Especially the marquee names. I would always choose to approach them myself. Now Naz was approaching me.

He was, after all, the boss. The moneymaker. Even though it had become clear that biggest brother Riath was really starting to take control and run the ship as a commanding officer or chief executive. Meanwhile Nabeel was in charge of all the merchandise, ran the fan club and looked after that side of the shop. I remember thinking then that the real shift had happened. The Hameds were in control, rightly or wrongly. Was it a case of the blind leading the blind, or a sensible move within the sport, when a fighter becomes surrounded, protected and almost encompassed by the people he can trust most?

We set up the lights and camera, and then Naz and I were miked up. We sat either side of the wide, polished oak boardroom table. There was only one other person in the room: my cameraman from the 90s, Nick Bennett, who back then was a vital part of the set-up, and he knew Naz well. Riath wasn't present. There was an intense feeling of privacy. Rather like two fighters and a referee alone in that squared circle.

Naseem Hamed proceeded to give me the most amazing and revealing interview I have ever had the pleasure of taking back to our headquarters in west London. That hour will live with me for ever. It was Naz in full flow. Warts and warmth. Real Jekyll and Hyde stuff.

The first half was a savage verbal assault on Brendan Ingle. Arrows were flying as Naz used the opportunity to have his say. It was a planned assassination. Remember that Brendan was still his leading trainer, and they were building up to a clash in Atlantic City against Ireland's Wayne McCullough.

'Brendan is a Judas,' he hurled out. 'A total Judas. After all I've done for him. He's just a complete money-grabber. He never cared about me. I feel betrayed. Brendan Ingle has taught me absolutely nothing. Since I was seven years old. I taught myself. I never had one-to-one tuition. I have never had a proper trainer or a training camp. He has never been there. It was all about the money.'

For exactly thirty-three minutes Naz launched these fire-crackers. It was shocking, and it was mesmerizing. The family influence was clear.

'Riath is so clever. Blood is blood. I have got my family on the pay-roll. I make all the decisions in life, me and my family. I found out that after seventeen years, the only ones I can really trust down to the ground, in my heart, is my own blood.'

Then, suddenly, he took his microphone off and walked out of the room. Nick and I were left there gaping in disbelief at how much Naz had opened up. There was silence in the boardroom for three or four minutes, then Naz returned, holding his newborn son, Sami. He had never done anything like this before. Sami was adorable, a real smiler, and as I have always loved babies the connection between us intensified.

Naz's demeanour had changed. His body language, his tone of voice, everything. This was the soft, loveable side rarely seen on camera due to his propensity to brag and boast whenever the lights were on him.

'This is what all of this is about. My son. Nothing else matters as much as my family.'

A radiant glow exuded from him.

'I will do anything for my son. I cut the cord. It was the most amazing experience. This is where me and my family start making our decisions. Nothing is more important.'

It was Naseem Hamed as we had never seen him. Clucking and cooing, and more relaxed, and seemingly at ease, than ever. It was, quite simply, a compelling sixty-three minutes of material. The two sides. The two stories. The two videotapes I had to make sure made a safe transit back to Sky.

During the following week, the buzz and talk around Sky Sports was about little else. *What* did he say? Did he really bring his baby into the interview? When can we see it?

It was scheduled to air on our *Ringside* show that Thursday. We had a busy boxing week so we were only allowed to produce a twenty-minute piece out of the hour-long interview, which in terms of features in a sixty-minute programme is still a significant chunk.

Then I got a call. From Riath 'Big brother' was, at first, charming, and said that he'd heard the interview went wonderfully. Then came the twist. Riath wanted to travel down to our studios to make sure that it was 'edited correctly'.

What did that mean? Why did he want to try to wrest control of what was a Sky interview? Didn't he like what he had heard about it? Had Naz said the wrong things? Did they want to cut certain controversial issues out?

I told my boss. He rightly said that it was our material, and that we should cut it the way we thought was right for the most dramatic television. Provided we edited it fairly and gave Brendan the right to respond. We did. I asked Brendan outright if he was 'a Judas', and he of course denied this, blaming Naz's family for poisoning the relationship.

Given my close bond with Naz, I was nervous. I was young and less experienced back then; I was worried about the Hameds' reaction if we broadcast segments they would rather have cut.

Would Naz be angry? Was I putting my relationship with him in jeopardy? There is a danger of getting too close to one's subject, which in boxing is so easy to do.

My loyalty, though, is and always has been to Sky. I love my job, and I have worked very, very hard for the company. Furthermore, once a tape finishes rolling (which we call part of the 'rushes'), it is our property. No one else's. Remember, too, Naz had personally called me. He had driven this. Not me. Not Sky. It came from the man himself. If there was a lack of communication within the Hamed family, then that highlighted the problems of working in that way, as well as a failure to understand how the TV industry really works. I understood their concern, but they had approached us.

It was nonetheless our responsibility to mould the piece into a fair, balanced reflection of the material we had. Our press department went into overdrive. They did a super job. Many of the national broadsheets ran the story; most of the tabloids had back-page leads: 'Naz: "Brendan is a JUDAS"'.

The lighter side of the interview also made some of the front pages of the tabloids, the glistening shots of Naz and Sami, happiness personified, appealing to a different audience who could see a father's pride in his newborn son.

It was fabulous publicity for the build-up to the broadcast of *Ringside*, for which we more than quadrupled our regular viewing figures. I sat in the production gallery while the interview was played out. Our presenter at the time was Paul Dempsey, who, along with his guests, sat in total silence – in amazement really – as the interview went to air. You could not hear a pin drop in the packed gallery. It was unheard of. There's always the noise of the director, the PA, the tape machines. Not this time. Not until just thirty seconds was left of the play-out. It was extraordinary.

How Naz's statements ripped through the screens. Television adds phenomenal power. The body language, every detailed expression, and of course now those words were out there for all to witness.

Naseem Hamed had, however, made one thing clear: Brendan Ingle would not be fired as trainer. It was like a cat pawing a wounded mouse but not killing it off. Torture, but for Brendan at least it was paid torture.

It was a quite extraordinary atmosphere in which to be preparing for a vital high-profile world title clash. Thick dark clouds loomed overhead. They followed The Paddy and the Prince (both book and participants) to that rather murky gambling boardwalk in New Jersey.

We arrived a week before Hamed's match-up, set for Halloween night against McCullough. The Irish-American was in joyful spirits, so much so that he spent most of his week with his wife Cheryl, pushing the buggy containing their young daughter Wynona.

There was no sign of Naz and his large entourage. What followed was the most calamitous public relations week of Naseem Hamed's career. The first problem was a string of missed appointments to secure a visa for the States, due to the usual tardiness of the main man himself. The US Embassy was closed for the weekend, and the paperwork was delayed. Ironically a similar thing happened to Amir Khan before his battle against Paulie Malignaggi in May 2010. Khan was stuck in Canada for nearly two weeks, which severely disrupted his preparation. What fiascos these are. With the Naz issue, all parties pointed the finger at each other, Riath firmly blaming the promoters. That of course incensed Frank Warren, as well it might.

Naz turned up in Atlantic City just four days before the fight. Concorde might have helped alleviate some jet-lag, but it was a dreadful start.

I was nervous about Naz's reaction to the now infamous

interview, despite firmly believing, as I do to this day, that it put him in a glowing light. He had spoken honestly and openly about his grievance with Brendan, and I think the baby segment was some of the best publicity he'd ever done. Yet after Riath's attempted interference, I remained worried. Plus, this was just a few weeks later, so his words were particularly fresh in everyone's minds.

When Naz arrived, he was angry. Furious, in fact. I kept very much to the periphery. He conducted an open workout, training like a demon, before sitting down for an impromptu press conference. What followed did Hamed more damage than at any stage in the whole extraordinary sequence of events.

The American media had loved Prince Naseem when he lit up New York before, during and after the humdinger with Kevin Kelley. Now some were repulsed. He was in a filthy mood and turned on several people who had written unfavourably about him, especially boxing expert Colin Hart. Turning his chair around menacingly, Hamed launched a scathing attack on one of the most well-liked and respected men in the business.

'I don't like you, Colin. Colin Fart. Don't like you one bit. You're rubbish, and what you write is rubbish. You're useless.'

It was an awful moment, and a PR disaster. Others received a dishful of abuse, including the *Guardian*'s John Rawling.

'Enough! That's enough!' Sal Hamed shouted at his son.

There was silence. Naz and his team departed quickly. Safe to say the press were largely appalled by Hamed's behaviour.

I had earned a stay of execution. For now.

At the pre-fight press conference, Hamed still seemed fired up, telling all and sundry that McCullough would be knocked out early. Now 'The Prince' always tended to predict the round in which his foe would fall, and usually held out the corresponding number of fingers. For this one he changed his mind from two to three, and seemed altogether distracted.

There was needle with McCullough, and, as I was soon to find out, needle with me too. I gingerly approached Hamed for a live Sky interview after the presser was over. He took one look at me and said, 'I'm not talking to you. You've betrayed me. You're a Judas, Adam. After all we've been through.' Then he walked straight out of the room.

It hit me like one of his devastating corkscrew uppercuts, and I have to admit I was absolutely gutted. I thought we were inseparable. The 'Naz and Ads' team. We'd built something over the years. I just sat in this chair at Bally's Hotel on the boardwalk in tears. I've always been too sensitive, but at the time I felt my world had caved in.

I phoned my dad back home. 'The worst thing has happened to me,' I told him. 'Naz won't talk to me. We've fallen out.'

'Ads, the big fall-out might still lie ahead,' my dad replied. 'His brother is managing him. Who's in charge of the money? Plus, you're a journalist and a reporter. You have to remember that. You got too close to him. This is only the beginning of your career. There'll be many other fighters.'

Still, I thought to myself, Naz was special. He was my Muhammad Ali and Howard Cosell, my 'Arry and Frank.

Our commentary team for the big fight, Ian Darke and Glenn McCrory, were really annoyed at the treatment meted out to me. They had also previously faced Hamed's wrath. Glenn had been teased about his body-shot defeat to Jeff Lampkin, and both were verbally attacked after Ryan Rhodes's world title defeat to Otis Grant. Naz and I were forced to listen to that fight on phones set up in his New York suite before his American debut against Kevin Kelley, so only had the commentary to go on. Naz had refused to believe that his best mate had lost, and when Ian and Glenn arrived in Manhattan, they got it – with both barrels.

So Darkie and Glenn were never big fans. They admired Naz

as a fighter but had long thought that I had given him too many benefits of the doubt. They were enraged at this latest situation. Bob Mee had seen it all too, and he had had enough.

Bob took me to Riath and some of the other Hamed family members in an attempt to sort the situation out. As always, Bob kept his cool, but inside he was fuming. It was as if we were inching towards a battle-line. Like two sides gearing up for some sort of gunfight at the OK Corral.

Nabeel and Murad looked to me as if they were smirking, Riath seemed a little tentative to engage. Bob said that it was out of order for a main event fighter who was making millions not only from US television giants HBO but also from Sky Box Office to refuse an interview. Then he mentioned how much I had championed Naz's cause over the years, and how distressed I was. Which was fairly plain for all to see.

'Naz is angry,' replied Riath. 'He feels Sky and Adam let him down over the interview. But I'll talk to him.'

We waited a few minutes, then Naz appeared alongside his brother. 'You two,' Riath said to Naz and me, 'get through those doors and sort this out.'

We were almost thrown through these double doors like a couple of naughty school kids on detention. They swung open, and we found ourselves in a surreal scene. The location was the enormous kitchens of Bally's Hotel. A team of chefs were making strawberry mousse. There were in excess of five thousand people to cater for at Bally's, so you can imagine the quantities. For a moment I thought we'd been lobbed on to some sort of Carry On film set, and the two of us would end up covered in the bloody stuff. I detest strawberries too.

What we did do, away from everyone and away from any camera, was argue. Loudly. Nastily. Ferociously. Back and forth, like fighters.

'I trusted you, Adam Smith,' Naz shouted at me, 'and you

stabbed me in the back. You ran that interview when we told you we wanted to see the final cut before it went out.'

'Who do you think you guys are, demanding some sort of rights over what we show?' I retorted. 'What are you – producers?'

'You used all that stuff about Brendan being a Judas,' Naz bellowed back. 'Brendan is in my corner here. Why did you do that? You're the Judas, Adam.'

I took real exception to that. I pride myself on fierce loyalty. 'I have worked almost since I first met you on building your profile. I've helped make your family a fortune. And this is how I get treated.'

Naz said nothing.

'You called me up and asked me to interview you, Naz. It was *your* doing.'

It was fast becoming a monologue as he, perhaps, started to realize that he was being rather foolish.

'You used me to make your point,' I said, a little calmer now. 'You know exactly how television works.'

There lay the fundamental root of the problem. Did he really understand what happened when an interview was edited?

'When something is filmed by Sky, it becomes Sky property,' I explained. 'Not yours, ours. It is up to us what we show and how we show it. Obviously, if something is edited, we will use our experience to make sure that it is the best possible interpretation of events. When they edit a football match, do you think they leave out a goal? Of course not. So why were we going to leave out the crux of your premeditated thoughts? Remember, too, you instigated this. Riath never said anything to me about leaving out specific points, just that he wanted to see the cut version. Well, my boss decides what he wants, and we produce it. Don't shoot the messenger.'

Naz took it all in and replied, 'I didn't know the way it worked. I'm still not happy, but let's make up.'

We had always greeted each other with a warm embrace. This time a handshake sufficed. Something had changed, and it was going to take a great deal of rebuilding before that spark and connection between us returned.

Naseem Hamed was never himself that week in Atlantic City. Everything around him was crumbling. The Ingles were just peripheral figures. And just weeks after they had appeared to make another long-term deal, Frank Warren packed his suitcases to go home. On the Thursday morning. It took a massive plea from Sal Hamed to persuade Frank to stay, at least through the fight.

Recently, Frank Warren opened right up to me about it. 'That was one of the worst weeks of my life,' he said. 'The amount of abuse he gave people like you, Adam, was disgraceful. The money. The family's power and ego had gone to their heads. What did Riath ever know about boxing? He was a liaison officer for the Yemeni community in Sheffield. Riath screwed it all up. I was ready to go. Bags packed and everything. I only stayed for Sal. He was a good man, and the only man Naz seemed to respect. But the damage was done. I walked away when we got home. I just couldn't take it any more. I was actually relieved. I just couldn't deal with the brothers. But sad about Naz.'

The relationship with Brendan was obviously beyond the point of no return. During the lacklustre fight with McCullough, the old mentor was treated almost with contempt in the corner as Naz ignored his advice and at one stage pushed Brendan away. As if to make his point even clearer.

There was no two- or three-round knockout. It was a frustrating twelve-round affair in reality. A horrible fight to end a horrible night in the most horrible fight week I have ever experienced.

Hamed's eagerly anticipated ring-walk was in bad taste. The

Americans had set up this mock graveyard where Naz had to knock off skeleton heads on his way in. Halloween might be big in the States, but boxing is a sport where people can lose their lives. I thought it was totally inappropriate. An earlier world title fight between Marco Antonio Barrera and Richie Wenton had seen the Englishman forced to walk through this ghoulish set for his big chance. Wenton, who had experienced the nightmare of a previous opponent, Bradley Stone, dying after their British title fight.

In addition, there were scuffles between Hamed's fans and thousands of Irish, making it a rough atmosphere. Following his poor points victory, Naz then stormed out of his post-fight interview with Ian Darke with a dismissive 'Later, Curly'.

Oh dear. Oh dear.

Once the Atlantic City dust had settled, Darkie and I were told that Naz wanted to meet us for a coffee at London's prestigious Dorchester Hotel.

He arrived – late, surprise surprise – but looked a more mature young man. Naz had grown a goatee, his face had filled a little, and there was a completely different, relaxed feel about him. It was a good attempt at trying to start cleaning up the PR mess.

We kissed and made up and moved forward. Yet to this day I'm not sure Naseem Hamed ever totally recovered from what happened. Turning on the press who had built him was a catastrophic error in career terms. The pen is mightier than the sword and all that. From that moment, plenty wanted to see him fall.

Brendan and Frank no longer featured as the Hameds went their own way, on a sort of crusade against the world. Firstly Oscar Suarez, a likeable but little-known Puerto Rican, and then Emanuel Steward were brought in to train Hamed.

Barry Hearn was nominally the promoter for his British fights. The difference was that all non-family members were very much on the outside, paid specifically for their jobs. A way of saving money, maybe, but was it the right thing to do in the long run?

From October 1998 until the last time we saw Naseem Hamed in the ring, in May 2002, he only had six fights. The exciting Yorkshire derby with Paul Ingle. The wrestling mess with Cesar Soto. The obliteration of Vuyani Bungu. The terrific tear-up with Augie Sanchez. The only ever loss, to Marco Antonio Barrera. And the final twelve-round bore against Manuel Calvo.

Naz always generated magic and excitement for the fans. We did rebuild our relationship. We reminisce today. He's grown up, he's a loving family man, and I still like him very much. Yet some of those there for him on the way up, and who fell out, were not there to support him during his fall from grace. After Barrera and Calvo came a fifteen-month jail sentence for dangerous driving, and he was stripped of his MBE. Naseem Hamed has cut a bit of a lonely, reclusive figure at times.

On a positive note, Naz has started to get involved again and seems to have reconciled with Frank Warren. Time is a great healer.

'Frank Warren is the best promoter,' Naz told me over a cup of tea in a Chiswick café. 'Who knows how big I would have been if I hadn't left him?'

It seems like Mr Hamed now believes a family can't quite do everything in boxing for you.

We don't hear much about the rest of the Hameds today. Rumours are that Riath moved back to the Middle East. Naz's 'boxing family' also disbanded, which was a shame. Johnny Nelson fell out with him, for one. Sometimes you see Clifton and Kevin around the scene, but not with Naz. He does keep

AT THE COURT OF THE PRINCE

a close eye on Ryan Rhodes's continued success, though and is very proud of former stablemate Kell Brook's rise.

'Naz called me up a while ago,' Frank Warren told me. 'He was the size of a house, had no friends, and said he had not been fit for some of his later fights, particularly the Barrera one. He realized the mistake he made leaving me. In hindsight. I made him over fifteen million, gave him four exclusive cars, watches, even a diamond ring worth over £25,000. He sometimes got bonuses of £200,000 plus.

'Riath was dreadful for him. You have to know the way it works. After leaving me, he had Naz fighting only once a year. They didn't want to risk him getting beaten. What is the mentality in that? He should have been in the gym three times a day. Not just relying on his punch power, when he had one of the best boxing brains I have ever seen. It still makes me sad. He could and should have become a real legend. The best I've had.'

Frank blames the family set-up more than anything. 'Of course parents and family should be concerned about their son's career. I understand they want to be involved. In some cases, the brother, the father, would say, "Why pay him when we can do it?" Well, you'll find out why. We are the experts. This is what we do. I always use Theo Walcott as an example. Great young prospect, guided by Arsène Wenger. His family don't guide him on the pitch, do they? Leave it to those who know what they're doing. Take the Smiths in Liverpool. They have four successful boxers in the family. But they don't interfere. They let me do my job. I pick the right opponents at the right time. The problem, though, always ends up being about money. They think the grass is greener on the other side.'

At the height of his ring powers, Hamed would say that he could control his own destiny, and that he had been manipulated and exploited. The family took matters into their own hands, and Naz still went on to make a huge amount of money. He remains well up on Britain's rich list. The Hameds were out to set themselves all up for life, and every family strives to do that, whatever their profession. In that they succeeded. Naz will also go down in history as one of the most entertaining and hard-hitting little fighters of all time.

The Hameds produced a documentary themselves around the time of the fight with Barrera. Riath at last got his wish. You could see the brothers' influence: even with more riches promised, Naz was filmed messing around shortly before his acid test. People I spoke to in the trade couldn't believe that they had put their name to a documentary which basically made him look ridiculous. You want to give yourself every possible chance before your biggest fight. Imagine the money, the fame, if he had beaten Barrera.

Naz's family, Eleasha and his three boys, mean the world to him. Yet, was his boxing story largely unfulfilled because his siblings became too involved, with too little knowledge, too early? It remains one of those questions that will long be debated within boxing circles.

What is definitive about the Hamed family axis is that it was stronger than anything outside it. In many ways, they set the stall for family involvement which continues today. One look at the finances they conjured up has other families nurturing bright young talents dreaming of similar rewards. Families now play roles in almost all aspects of the fight business, from managing day-to-day needs to answering fan mail, running websites, dealing with media and charity requests, organizing competitions for the fans, designing clothes and dealing with medicals. Generally keeping the wheels in motion, allowing the boxer to concentrate on what he does best – box.

This is most noticeable among the sport's elite – the Klitschkos, Mayweathers, Hattons and Khans – where there is more to be involved in, and where the stakes are higher. At a lower level, family members tend to play supporting roles because the boxer can't afford to keep them on the pay-roll. It's usually just fathers involved.

Naseem Hamed's business manager was his brother, but Floyd Mayweather chose Leonard Ellerbe, an old friend, conditioner and now the CEO of Mayweather Promotions. He reminds me a little of the role Courtney Shand had with Lennox Lewis, but Ellerbe has more sway. He's a sharp power broker who knits Floyd beautifully together with his adviser and manager, the secretive but seriously impressive Al Haymon.

Ellerbe told me recently, 'The beauty is that Floyd is his own boss. He understands boxing. As his family does. Roger [Floyd's uncle] and Floyd senior know the game inside out. The difference is that Floyd junior has learned about business. He's become a very savvy and shrewd businessman. He's clever. We are looking way, way beyond the sport. We've co-promoted rock concerts, we have made commercials, we're doing a movie. A great team with great vision.'

With the world awaiting a decision as to whether Floyd would ever tackle Manny Pacquiao in one of the biggest fights of all time, Floyd posted this on his Twitter site in August 2010: 'A real boss moves when he is ready not when he is told. Follow to support, follow to hate. As long as you follow I appreciate.'

Cool, calm, and for the 'money' man fairly collected too. Floyd Mayweather has worked with Bob Arum and Golden Boy, and has been wined and dined by Don King. The difference is he seems to be calling the important shots, assisted by right-hand man Ellerbe.

Similarly, Vitali and Wladimir Klitschko have a long-standing friend called Bernd Bönte who is the managing director of the Klitschko Management Group. Like the brothers, Bönte is intelligent, worked in the media for years and has been a very useful adviser to the family for years. The team have used their brains far more than their brawn, and also brought on board one of the leading American boxing managers/advisers, Shelly Finkel, to help them overseas in selecting the right opponents and making the right moves.

Shelly is a deal-maker extraordinaire. He made his name in the music business promoting a few artists you might have heard of – Jimi Hendrix, The Rolling Stones, Paul McCartney, Billy Joel, Elton John. He's been in and around boxing for more than two decades, guiding the likes of Mike Tyson, Michael Moorer and Evander Holyfield. In the summer of 2010, Finkel decided that he wanted to return to his musical roots and was named the new chief executive of Empire Sports and Entertainment. Yet the wily New Yorker, whom I am fond of, has maintained his major marketing interest in boxing – advising the Klitschkos.

Of course the Klitschkos have brains themselves. Both have PhDs, speak numerous languages and are humanitarians: they enjoy leading roles in UNESCO (the United Nations Education, Scientific and Cultural Organization) and work with several charities, and Vitali has also dabbled in politics. One can see that this Eastern European family has worked the system. They know they are huge, talented athletes who are well-spoken and attract massive audiences in Europe. Sometimes the Klitschkos aren't the most exciting fighters. But they are admired, respected, and are excellent at their chosen trade. With Bönte and Finkel positioned alongside as 'outside' experts, their arsenal is very powerful indeed. Their joint family wealth is enormous.

My role as Head of Boxing at Sky has given me a new under-standing of, and a central role in, the process of making a big fight happen. Following the saga – say one between a Klitschko and our own heavyweight champion David Haye – largely rests on their close aides and advisers: Bönte and, for Haye, Adam Booth. While David's parents Deron and Jane played a major role in a close family upbringing, his professional career has not been steered by them, or indeed by a traditional promoter, but by Booth.

Adam lives and breathes boxing. A former amateur with the Lynn club, where he won forty of forty-eight bouts, Adam has been a mentor to David for over sixteen years. They have enjoyed good, bad and difficult times – your typical boxing roller-coaster really. He loves the sport, but hates the business. One gets the feeling that he will celebrate those moments when his champion Haye and protégé George Groves hang up the gloves more than any single win for either of them. Then Adam can sail into the sunset to enjoy his success. And go back to being a fight fan.

Adam has been belittled as an unheralded trainer, even scorned over his lack of know-how within the complicated world of boxing politics. Yet Adam's bright. He has proved to be an astute, intelligent trainer, tactically defusing champions like Nikolai Valuev and James DeGale, and as a manager has charted David's route through at times fairly treacherous waters.

They are survivors. They are winners. They have steered their way to the summit of two weight divisions by driving hard bargains, making carefully considered choices, and having total and true belief in themselves, despite that toe-curling night in Hamburg and the madness with Dereck Chisora in Munich in early 2012.

'It is a murky world,' Adam told me over breakfast one morning, 'but we have gone our own way, and I am proud of that. I sleep easily at night, knowing that everything we have achieved has been for the benefit of David. I am his trainer and manager, yes. But we are friends first and foremost. When this is all done, I just want people to know I did all I could.'

'Adam has been my right-hand man,' David continued. 'I owe so much to him. He's been like a brother. I trust him completely.'

Trust is something, of course, which when abused has damaged many boxing bonds over the years. Booth and Haye both have young families. They have neighbouring houses in Cyprus. They seem an odd boxing couple. Yet this unlikely combination and unusual partnership has worked quite wonderfully. They are brothers maybe, but not blood brothers. How important a difference is that?

In today's British market-place, the Hattons and the Khans are the prime examples of fighters relying largely on their families. Both sets of northern working-class families have taken control of their destiny. Ricky and Amir have put the trust in the ones they love most. But that is not to say they don't have advisers abroad like the Mayweathers and Klitschkos.

For the Khans, it is still very much a case of wait and see. All seems fairly comfortable with their alliance with Golden Boy Promotions, but there is still a long way to go in Amir's career. The megabucks might still be out there for our world light-welterweight star.

What did become apparent during the early months of 2011 though was that the Khan family, particularly father Shah, was calling the big shots. Amir was meant to tackle Irish southpaw Paul McCloskey on 16 April 2011 on Sky Box Office, but the card fell apart, and the family were offered the chance to put the fight on regular Sky Sports. They turned it down, taking the pay-per-view option of cable channel Primetime instead.

'They committed commercial suicide,' Matchroom's Eddie Hearn said. 'What a stupid, stupid decision. What on earth were they thinking of?'

After beating McCloskey, Amir's terrific performance against Zab Judah was still rather lost on a cable network, but, to my delight as Sky's Head of Boxing, he was desperate to return to our network, and a three-fight deal was agreed in the autumn of 2011 for Amir to fight on Sky Sports.

The first instalment was an important defence of his WBA and IBF belts against Lamont Peterson in the challenger's backyard of Washington DC. It was a fabulous fight, which thrilled the fans, but after Khan lost his titles, controversy reigned over the points deduction and then 'the man in the hat' stole all the headlines. Some criticized the Khan clan for their complaints, which overshadowed a fundamental omission in the contracts; while the IBF defence was mandatory, the WBA was voluntary, so a rematch clause should have existed but didn't. Who let that slip through the net?

Amir appeared, more mature, on *Ringside* early in 2012, having celebrated his recent engagement, and desperate for a return with Peterson. With the boxing powerhouse of Golden Boy behind them, the Khans finally agreed terms for a rematch on 19 May in the neutral Nevada desert.

4

The Hitman

While I know the Khans well, and felt the closest of bonds with Prince Naseem, the Hattons have seemed at times like family.

Ricky has always had his immediate family hugely involved. Dad Ray ran a pub, then a carpet business in Hyde, near Manchester, but still found time to take his eldest son all round the country as an amateur, and has been an ever-present during his professional career. Mum Carol helped out selling carpets at Glossop market, but has provided unflinching support, and brother Matthew even chose the same career path.

'We weren't happy that Richard and Matthew chose boxing,' Ray admitted to me. 'His mum was really not best pleased. We thought Richard would stick to football. They could have just joined the family business – I could sell a good carpet; mind you, Richard was a terrible, terrible fitter. Awful.'

The Hattons knew little about boxing at the beginning, so Ricky joined forces with Frank Warren, and the eccentric, likeable trainer honed in Moss Side's famous Champs Camp Gym, Billy Graham. A former police sergeant, Paul Speak, started as a friend, then became a driver, unofficial body-guard, agent and, as he always says to me, 'Ricky's general dogsbody'.

This team clicked, and Ricky Hatton had a phenomenal rise through the ranks. A star amateur, Hatton turned professional in Widnes in September 1997 and ripped through his early opponents. Gaining experience and exposure both at home and abroad, in prestigious venues like New York's Madison Square Garden and the Convention Center in Atlantic City, Ricky rocked and rolled, capturing the British light-welterweight title in his twenty-second fight, and the WBU bauble in his twenty-third. This propelled him into true international-class territory.

I had first seen Ricky when he was a chunky, blond, spiky-haired teenager, and few knew anything about this precocious talent outside Billy Graham's gym. I was up in Manchester filming their old favourites Steve Foster – with his Viking fans who brought replica longboats to his fights – and Ensley Bingham, who could put you to sleep if that sweet left hook of his landed. Billy took me straight over to this teenager who was whacking away on a grubby punch bag. But boy was he giving it some welly.

'This kid is the best young kid I've ever seen,' Billy told me. 'Honest to God. He's as pale as anything, but he hits like a mule. And he's got all the moves. He'd beat most current pros tomor-row. I'm telling you, Adam, this is the one to watch.'

Yes, yes, you always hear that. This time, though, it seemed Billy wasn't kidding about the young, wide-eyed hopeful. I've never forgotten that introduction to Ricky Hatton. What I liked straight away about him was that he was down-to-earth. No nonsense. No ego. But he was funny. He had personality. And he was one of the lads.

Ricky became my new Naz. Manchester the new Sheffield. I was sent everywhere to help build him up, and between Sky, Warren, Graham and the Hattons, I think we did a pretty good job.

I also loved his family. I was round his house in Hyde more than my own at times. Carol, Ray and Matthew were so hospitable. The tea was always brewing, the jokes flying out, the boxing videos rolling. The laughs, the camaraderie! They saw each other every single day and even holidayed together with loads of relatives. The Hatton cruise – once a year. I bet it's a total riot.

Ricky was, and has always been, incredibly grounded. Credit where credit's due – to his parents for the way they have brought him up. Carol was never afraid to keep her sons in line, still isn't. Incidentally, Ricky couldn't move out of the house for years because of the home-cooked meals and washing service. When he finally did, he moved a stone's throw away. And I mean a stone's throw.

From his love of *Only Fools and Horses* and driving around town in his 'Trotters' three-wheeler to his Elvis impressions and the fat suits he brought to shows later in his career for a little pop back at the critics who constantly went on about the wild yo-yoing of his weight, Ricky has never taken himself too seriously, if at all. He never lost touch with his mates from the Hattersley estate; we still see the greatest character among them, 'The Duck', to this day. Like Lennox and Naz, the popular 'Hitman' also had a 'boxing family' made up of a stream of fun, often crazy fighters from the north-west like Michael Gomez, Stephen Foster Jnr, Stevie Bell, Anthony Farnell, Paul Smith and of course Ricky's younger sibling, Matthew. Billy Graham added his tight-knit team of assistant Bobby Rimmer and conditioner Kerry Kayes to the working party. There is such a buzz about a gym when everything's on course and everybody's firing on all cylinders.

With his allegiance to his beloved Manchester City, and his love of a pint and a game of darts, the fans really began to latch on to the Ricky Hatton story. They then also became an extended family.

One night, Ricky drove me to a show at the small Wythen-shawe forum in south Manchester. It was early days in his professional career.

'What's Naseem Hamed like?' Ricky asked me. 'You've been working together for years. What's he really like?'

'Fascinating, fun, fiery, grips you, he really does, Ricky,' I replied. 'But he is always late for things, he turns up when he wants to, he's constantly surrounded by loads of people, and it can be tough. One on one, though, I love being with him.'

Ricky's gearbox made a crunching noise. He only had a banged-up old motor. It made me think.

'Naz has got every cool car out there,' I continued. 'Most you can't even see in the showroom. He has so many – one for each day of the week. People are jealous, and some dislike his attitude.'

'Has he changed over the years, Adam – become harder to deal with?' Ricky asked me.

'I guess,' I said. 'But he has become very famous. Plus, I find it a bit of a challenge, so I enjoy all of it really.'

'I just can't believe this,' Ricky replied. 'I'll tell you one thing, I will never ever change. My feet will remain firmly on the ground. I promise you that. I am desperate to get to the very top of this sport. I want to be world champion more than anything. But if I do that, you won't see me lording it all over the place. Not me. Not one little bit.'

Of course, everyone changes over the years, but I honestly cannot think of a fighter who has achieved so much since that rainy night-time drive in Hyde and who has remained more true to his word.

When the Hitman became a two-weight world champion years later, I remember him saying to me, 'I told you I'd never change. If I pranced around the street, and people were saying "There's Ricky know-it-all", it would kill me. I'd go home and throw my belts in the bin. Straight away. I'd hate people thinking of me like that. I'm just one of them. I really mean that.'

That's why the fans loved him. They were Ricky Hatton fans, not necessarily boxing fans. Everyone felt they knew him. He'd probably spoken to, signed autographs for or had a pint of Guinness with over half the crowd, even on his grandest nights at the MEN in Manchester.

That wonderful arena became Ricky Hatton's fortress, and after several thrilling dress rehearsals his dream came true in the early hours of 5 June 2005, amid an electric atmosphere of twenty-two thousand screaming supporters, when he upset and dethroned modern legend Kostya Tszyu. The Hitman had done it the hard way, walking through walls, to outgun and outlast one of the greatest fighters of his generation; he forced Tszyu to quit on his stool after eleven savage rounds. There was hardly a dry eye in the place. Not since Frank Bruno became world heavyweight champion at the fourth attempt, at Wembley Stadium in September 1995, could I remember such a triumphant night on home soil.

The first people Ricky ran over to hug were Ray and Carol. Matthew was next. They mattered more than anyone. All the team had played their part. The close family. The trainer. The promoter, who got the timing spot on.

The Guinness then flowed into the wee, wee hours, but even though we saw Ricky, I remember he could only drink sips of water – such was the exhaustion and the pain, even in ecstatic victory. And that was the best night of his life.

Beautiful Brutality.

*

The next time I saw Ricky Hatton was the following Saturday. I was standing at an altar in west London on the most important day in my life. The date of 11 June 2005 was lit up on my family's calendar – the day of my marriage to Jo. As I was waiting for my beautiful bride, I caught a glimpse of the Hitman. He gave me a little thumbs up from the back. Just part of the crowd. No fuss. But he was there. He had flown back from a celebratory few days in Tenerife, and he was there for us. Ricky understands the true value of family.

Despite the Tszyu triumph, Hatton's relationship with Warren had come to an end. Ray had more of an influence by now and the Hattons had their first real taste of running things. They stayed loyal to Sky, and brought on board a lawyer, Gareth Williams, and a new promoter in wealthy scrap metal dealer Dennis Hobson, who had guided Clinton Woods and had links to a US promoter called Art Pelullo. Basically, like the Hameds before them, the Hattons were playing the power game.

'This time it was the father's involvement,' Frank Warren told me. 'We handled Ricky well, and gave him the right fights at the right moments. Along with you at Sky, we also built him from scratch. Then they went to America on tiny shows. Why? Yes, the Mayweather and Pacquiao fights made them a lot of money, but he got badly hurt in both. Knocked out. Lasting damage. Why didn't his dad keep him off the booze? At least I kept him fighting regularly so he couldn't balloon too much in weight. When he left me, he didn't fight enough. Bit like Naz.'

The Hattons wanted to go their own way. Ricky only had eight fights in five years after leaving Warren, and the feeling is that no night was greater than that one against Tszyu, but his final bouts were lucrative. We were still treated to fantastic entertainment – the crushing of Carlos Maussa to unify the light-welterweight belts; the tough, tough American launch against Luis Collazo, in that rather odd location of Boston, when he survived to become a two-weight world champion; the twelve-rounder on a small show in Vegas against Juan Urango; and the fourth-round body-shot knockout of Jose Luis Castillo (incidentally the only Hatton fight that wasn't shown on Sky). Then there was the build-up to the clash between our unbeaten Ricky Hatton and America's unbeaten star Floyd Mayweather.

It was an amazing time to be involved. The transatlantic press tour gripped the boxing world – especially with Mayweather dancing in a Manchester United shirt in driving rain in front of thousands of baying Mancunians. By this time Oscar De La Hoya and his Golden Boy team had become involved as Ricky's American promoters, as Ray and Gareth took even more control of the growing boxing business. The Mayweather fight really captured the imagination and as many as thirty-five thousand British fans were said to have invaded Vegas. Yet it wasn't to be for Ricky. Outclassed, he lost in the tenth round – and for the first time in his life.

Ricky Hatton locked himself away and cried for days.

The Hitman vowed to be back – and he was, in an unprecedented homecoming in May 2008 against Juan Lazcano. This was the dream stage: the City of Manchester stadium. A crowd of fifty-five thousand was expected in the open air that spectacular night, but when all the numbers in the hospitality and private boxes were tallied up, fifty-eight thousand were said to have squeezed in.

Another promoter was brought in for this show with Frank Maloney on the payroll. So this family business was growing by the fight. They were pretty much in full control by now. Making all their own decisions.

I went round to Ricky's house to get a few shots on the morning of the fight. His lovely girlfriend Jennifer Dooley answered the door, but Cainey the cameraman and I were amazed to find a very subdued, edgy Ricky in his glasses, track-suit and slippers. It was the most nervous I had ever seen him. I hardly recognized the Hitman. It must have been the demons swirling around after the Mayweather disappointment. Did he still have it? Was he on the slide? Was the family business going to suffer? What if he lost again?

Fortunately, Hatton pulled himself together by fight time and, despite a couple of rather wobbly moments, managed to comfortably outbox the light-punching Tex-Mex Lazcano.

Yet another change followed. The fighter/trainer team that we had taken to our hearts was coming to an end. A storm had been brewing for quite some time at Billy Graham's Phoenix camp. I got the same sort of feeling I'd had for the last couple of years with Brendan and Naz. Growing divisions had developed in and around Team Hatton. Sides were being taken. Bobby Rimmer had been removed. Billy and Paul Speak seemed at loggerheads, and there was tension when Ray was in the gym too. Kerry Kayes, a good friend of Billy's, was trying to remain impartial. Billy used his office, a small smoky room that housed peculiar reptiles, more and more as a refuge from some of the others. He obviously thought he wasn't being allowed to do his job how he wanted to.

A debate raged over whether his way was still the right way. After the Lazcano fight, Billy Graham was dismissed amid stories of financial disputes and other claims, with several of Ricky's family and close aides believing that the Hitman hadn't been improving on Billy's body belt and with his other chosen training methods for a while. Billy had been struggling health-wise, but I was sad to see this end. I thought they'd see it out. Billy was devastated, and then became very angry, deciding to take legal proceedings against Hatton. They subsequently both appeared in court and settled, but never spoke directly. It was an unfortunate end to such a close and successful partnership.

The Hatton camp seemed to be in turmoil. The fighter himself was getting hit a bit too much by now, and the team decided to plump for a defensive strategist in rival Floyd Mayweather's dad, Floyd Snr. The critics just couldn't work this out. Ricky Hatton's main assets were his turbo-charged attacks and debilitating body shots. Why select a trainer who teaches shoulder rolls and defence? Maybe it was a way of tightening the Hitman up, but surely it was too late to adapt his style? It seemed a very strange choice.

On top of this, their characters were like chalk and cheese. Floyd dressed up in flamboyant suits and concocted weird rhetoric and made-up poetry; Ricky wore daft hats, cracked English jokes, laughed at himself, and wanted to fight.

They didn't have long together in Manchester and then Vegas before his next fight, with Paulie Malignaggi. I remember an early session when Ricky found it very difficult to get the rhythm on the pads right. He also found Floyd almost impossible to understand. It seemed far from the perfect match. Still, Hatton was way too strong and too good for Malignaggi, so at least he ended 2008 on a high.

Meanwhile Ricky's profile continued to grow with his after-dinner turns and comedy appearances; a new gym was being planned in Hyde, and a range of Hatton clothing and spin-offs began to push the commercial and marketing side. 'Hatton' as a name and brand started to make a great deal of money. Ray was winding up his carpet business because boxing had become a 24/7 job, and was now their livelihood. It was the most obvious example yet of a total family boxing business in Britain.

Ricky continued to manage himself, with his dad as his business adviser, looking after the money. More changes were rung on the boxing side, and assistant Lee Beard began to become more important inside the camp as worries mounted over Hatton's relationship with Mayweather Snr.

In May 2009, Ricky Hatton had his third blockbuster fight. He'd found the will to win as destiny called against Kostya Tszyu. He'd not been quite good enough for the supreme Floyd Mayweather Jnr, but there was an excuse: that fight was up at welterweight. Now he had the chance of redemption on the Vegas stage in his favoured class of ten stone, at which weight he had never lost. The problem was that he had to find a way of defusing the Filipino whirlwind Manny Pacquiao, who had sent Oscar De La Hoya into retirement.

The 'Hatton' brand was in full force. His initial company, Punch Promotions, where father Ray had cleverly squirrelled Ricky's money, was joined by Hatton Promotions, which was launched in the lead-up to the Pacquiao fight.

Ricky had initially taken out a cornerman's licence, and then a managerial one, so he could help brother Matthew; the latest addition to his qualifications was to become a licensed promoter. There was an announcement that a host of hot young prospects like Olympian Joe Murray and ABA champion Matty Askin would be under the Hatton banner. Gareth Williams was the external force, a shrewd lawyer who would have to get to know the boxing game fast.

As the family business began to expand, with Ricky at the epicentre, preparation for the Pacquiao fight was not going well. Manny drilled himself into prime condition in punishing sessions at Freddie Roach's Wild Card Gym in LA, but Ricky was struggling. A visit to the Vegas camp weeks before the fight was particularly worrying for me. When I first saw Ricky, he admitted he was homesick. He'd been out there a long time, undergoing hard runs on the mountains high above Vegas in heavy combat boots. It's a method that's a particular favourite of Floyd Mayweather Snr's, but one which some other trainers believe has a detrimental effect on the ankles.

The weight had come off quickly. Usually with Ricky it's a gradual process; he almost looked too fit for me at this stage. Top conditioner, nutritionist and expert at weight reduction Kerry Kayes was by now no longer part of the scene, mainly due to his loyalty to Billy Graham (although Kerry and Ricky do keep up on a social basis). Had Hatton peaked too soon? Had he overtrained?

The atmosphere had also changed. The buzz had gone. The camp was tiny. Just Mayweather, Beard, Speak, a bodyguard (Kugan), a couple of sparring partners and, for a while, brother Matthew. It was eerie.

Ricky had also become increasingly infuriated with the tardiness of his trainer. At times Mayweather seemed to me to be far more interested in the filming for HBO's excellent programme *24:7*, which provides exclusive behind-the-scenes access to the marquee boxers as they prepare for their mega-fights. The suits, the poems, the trash-talking in full flow; the training seemed secondary, even part-time to us. At one session, with our cameras present, Mayweather lolled in late, holding a fizzy drink, and set to work with the large cup still in his hands. How on earth could a trainer seriously be trying to teach moves on the pads while hampered by a plastic bucket?

The other thing that was glaringly apparent was that Ricky wasn't receiving the right tuition on the pads. Manny Pacquiao is a southpaw, therefore the sparring partners had to be south-paw, which they were (in the main), but Mayweather elected to train Ricky from the orthodox stance. I could not believe this from a trainer whom De La Hoya had dubbed 'the best ever, my secret weapon'. Horses for courses and all that, but despite the bravado and the predictions, did Floyd Mayweather Snr really believe Hatton would beat Pacquiao?

I was told that Mayweather couldn't do 'southpaw pads'. To me that's no excuse.

Ricky Hatton has always struggled against southpaws. Jürgen Brähmer, the troubled ex-WBO light-heavyweight champion, had knocked Hatton out in the amateurs; Eamonn Magee had floored him in their fight in Manchester; and Luis Collazo had given him real trouble. All southpaws. It is a well-known fact that Ricky had major trouble with them particularly because of the way he rushes in, all guns blazing.

Lee Beard, a close friend of Mayweather's and usually an advocate of what he teaches, was deeply concerned by what he saw. He even took me outside the gym, which was located in a remote suburb of Vegas, and asked me what I thought about Mayweather, and my impressions of Hatton's sparring.

I'd witnessed almost all of Ricky Hatton's training camps, and this one was worrying me more than any other. The best I had ever seen was before Tszyu. This was a far cry away. He was being hit too easily and he didn't seem – to me – to be receiving the right teaching.

Ray Hatton called me from England. 'Tell me honestly,' he said. 'You've seen Ricky all the way through. What do you think?'

I told him about my concerns, but also said that his son looked fitter than the proverbial butcher's dog.

The final thing Ricky said to us and the camera after our stint in Vegas was 'Put your house on me to win. Put everything you have. I am absolutely positive I am going to win this. Put it all on me.'

Hatton's camp for Pacquiao had, though, seemed a complete mess. My colleague Declan Johnson was with me to film both teams, and he immediately predicted a big win for the awesome Filipino. In hindsight, I should have too. I was never convinced that Hatton would beat Mayweather, but I did think he had a big chance here. I felt that if Hatton could survive the early rounds, he would prevail, because of his astonishing strength at ten stone.

On the basis of the camps, though, he was in deep trouble.

Things just seemed to get worse. I had chats with Ricky and Ray about ten days out, and they were agonizing. They had decided that Lee Beard had to get involved quickly. Mayweather was, to all intents and purposes, no longer the main man. Lee could do southpaw pads, and Ricky told me on the phone that they could turn this round. Yet was there enough time?

I spoke to the Hitman again on the eve of battle. 'It's all under control, Adam,' he assured me. 'This late change has got me right back on track.'

Hours later, Ricky Hatton's boxing career lay in limbo as the Hitman was iced cold by the Pac-man in two devastating rounds. It all went horribly wrong. On the night of the fight there was bad communication between Mayweather and Beard. Ricky looked extremely pensive as he came in. Then he charged out of the gates with all the naivety of an over-eager young pro. Where were the boxing skills, the tighter guard that Mayweather had tried to implement? The red mist had descended again, and Hatton walked right into Pacquiao's lair.

Down twice in a torrid first, Hatton was then laid out in the second by one of the most sensational left hands you'll ever see. It was horrific to watch, and the finish frightening to actually take in. There he was. Loveable Ricky. Stretched out on the canvas, and he didn't move a muscle. At first, those ringside thought he might even be dead.

Thankfully, Ricky was fine – pride shattered, but health in these situations is of course the primary and only real concern. Especially for the family.

*

It was the second devastating defeat for Ricky Hatton, and virtually everyone in the trade called for the Hitman to hang up the gloves.

Exciting career. People's champion. Achieved so much. No disgrace losing to the two best fighters of the modern generation in Mayweather and Pacquiao. No disgrace at all.

Ricky didn't make an immediate decision, which was sensible. He wanted time to reflect and recover. He was still only thirty. There were options.

I spoke to those closest to him. Carol, Jennifer and Paul said they wanted no more. Gareth, Ray and Matthew seemed open either way. I spoke at length to Jennifer. There had been some quite awful shots broadcast by the Americans of Jennifer's hysterical, raw reaction at ringside immediately after the crushing knockout. To many they seemed inappropriate, and back at Sky we had some extra shots of her which were never broadcast. The moment her fiancé went down, Jennifer let out a piercing scream. It was heartbreaking. I said to her that if Ricky ever decided to go back into the ring, he should watch that piece of footage first.

We have to remain totally unbiased as commentators when calling fights. At all times. Ricky had become a friend though, so this was a tough one. As a mate, I didn't want to see him in the ring again; and as a broadcaster I actually felt the same. Yes, it would generate excitement and interest, especially if there was a north-west blockbuster against Amir Khan. But why? What had he got left to prove? Absolutely nothing.

No one wanted to see him get badly hurt. Ricky had looked very shaky in recent performances, and the big question – which I know he thought long and hard about – was 'Had the punch resistance gone?' Probably, but no one can truly answer that.

More serious problems had also been revealed, as the Hitman

was hit hard by horror headlines about his social behaviour. Part of Ricky's charm and attraction is that he loves a night out. Yet it seemed that Hatton's depression after the awful Pacquiao loss had spiralled into chaos, with graphic pictures laid bare in the tabloids showing him snorting cocaine. A month in The Priory followed, and Ricky began another fightback. The British Boxing Board of Control also stripped him of his boxing, second's and managerial licences.

The trouble was, I knew Ricky. His pride hurt, the desire to fight on ran deep, because he felt he had let his beloved fans down with the Pacquiao performance. He had the angel on one shoulder, the devil on the other. Rumours of 'the comeback' continually circulated.

Fortunately, two years and two months after the Pacquiao debacle, Ricky Hatton announced his retirement. He chose to come to London for an interview with me, and I made sure it was conducted in the warm surroundings of my home. Calling it a day was most definitely the correct choice, but it hurt him right to the soles of his boxing boots.

'I know I have to go,' he told me. 'But it is the most agonizing decision of my life. I have to come to terms that it is over. Very, very, very hard, Adam.'

The decision over whether he fought again wasn't, as some believed it would be, a financial one, depending on the success of Hatton Promotions, and the linked businesses.

This isn't just a family business, it's really now his.

Ricky progressed well, has shed some weight, and is back training fighters in his gym. He dotes on his young son Campbell, girlfriend Jennifer and new daughter Millie, and he still has an enormous number of strings to his bow, from TV analysis to after-dinner speaking, coaching and promoting to clothing and whatever else he wants to do. Virtually everyone likes him.

Naseem Hamed made mistakes on the way up. Ricky Hatton has kept most people on side.

Ray told me, 'We've got Hatton TV, the website, Hatton products from gloves to T-shirts to hats and just about everything. We have a state-of-the-art gym, probably the best in the north of England – not just for boxing training, but for keep-fit classes, beauty treatment, you name it. For the local people in Cheshire. Richard is in charge of all of this. Yes, I've helped. I sold my businesses in August 2009. I've had a recent health scare, so I've slowed down from the crazy hours I used to work. I can advise Richard, but this is his future, and the family's, we're setting up. The gym cost £2.7 million. There's no loan on it. Ricky's new house is sorted. We've put a stash towards the promotional business; we know we might lose out initially, but we think it will be worth it in the long run.'

The gym is indeed sensational, the promotional idea fascinating, if risky. The family have made their money through having a talented and dynamic son. Was it the right choice to push on into unknown, even shark-infested waters rather than get out while the going was good?

Some point to greed, others to an obsession with the game. The truth is that fighters' careers tend to end in their thirties. That leaves a lifetime ahead. Even if financially they don't need to work, they'll want to do something that's going to keep them occupied. It's human nature.

The Hattons have pushed on even further than the Hameds. Will it work long-term? How long will the cash flow last?

Ricky told me recently, 'In ten years I want to be the number one promoter in the country. I am fiercely ambitious still, and I'll always be enthusiastic. I care about my fighters – deeply.'

Yet he has already experienced the difficulties of being 'on the other side'. Things that he didn't understand as a fighter. Shows fall through. Opponents pull out at the last minute. TV deals change. The British Board monitor so closely. There are failed medicals, injuries, staff wages. Constant headaches.

Then there's that word 'loyalty' that continually rears its ugly head. In his first year as a promoter, Ricky paid out a great deal of money to lure good fighters in. He threw out a six-figure sum to get his long-time friend Matthew Macklin a European title chance, which he won dramatically in the first round. Ricky thought he could steer Macklin towards a world title. No sooner had the celebrations begun, however, than their working relationship was over. His mate had gone off elsewhere. Ricky felt hugely let down.

Still, he put on as decent a set of bills as he could in his first year promoting, to show that he had serious intentions. Ideas like TV screens at venues and giving the crowds more value for money had not gone unnoticed. It was clear that he really wants to make a success of this and not be tempted to fight again.

Families have always run businesses. Many successfully, many not. It has been a tradition since time immemorial for family members to work side by side. The young learn from their parents, and gain the necessary experience to be able to deal with the volatile world. There is the familiarity of the family name, the assurances, the knowledge.

Against that there are obstacles to overcome. Feuding and arguments. An inability to separate one's personal and business lives (in family business it's always personal). There are strong emotions. There is the concern of nepotism too, and dealing with non-family members, jealousy and insecurity. Of course there are instances when things backfire. Families have fall-outs, separations, divorces and so on. Nothing is 100 per cent guaranteed.

Another worry is internal squabbling over who really is the boss. In boxing, it should be straightforward: the boxer is. Yet the business is always full of minefields because huge financial gains are often at stake, and so many people seem to want to try and grab a chunk of the gold. There have always been back-stabbers, liars, cheats, thieves and crooks – that's why all through history families have tried so hard to remain close. Yes, one has to have a star product, but generally the tighter they are, the more likely families are to make their business structure work.

As we have seen, while it is now trendy, and in many ways sensible in boxing, to have one's family in the trenches, or as near to the trenches as they can be, outside help is essential. Even if those people are just on the pay-roll, and have less power. There is definitely a place for business experts, top lawyers and nifty accountants. Boxers and their families need that help in this complex sport. There is, of course, always room for promoters and matchmakers. Those who know the game and the way it works, inside and out. They are the masters of the sneaky moves.

Frank Warren told me, 'I always hope that the mum and dad want the best for their kids. A good stable family is so important for a fighter. But if it's only money that motivates them, then that's where the problems start. Let us do what we do best. Don't interfere. We get results.'

Frank Maloney agrees. 'You need experts. Families provide important support and back-up, but if they don't know the business, don't interfere. It can cause real problems. I don't tell them how to do their jobs. Don't tell me how to do mine.'

Matchroom's maestro Barry Hearn is in no doubt either. 'Families can't run the boxing business. Nice that they want to support their kids, but come on – what do they know about the ruthless nature of the game? Amir once brought all his family to see me. There were loads of them. I asked each of them what their role was. Blank looks all round. None of them had any experience in boxing.'

Golden Boy's CEO Richard Schaefer, now Amir Khan's US promoter, picks up the theme: 'Family is important, but it's human nature that if there are problems in the family, they creep over into everyday life. No way can a family run a promotions business. Are they specialists in financial matters? Not many of them.'

Yet dipping your toes into this market seems to be more common for fighters and their families these days. Naseem Hamed with Prince Promotions, Lennox Lewis with Lion Promotions, and Oscar De La Hoya with Golden Boy Promotions led the way. Meanwhile Roy Jones has Square Ring, and Winky Wright and Juan Manuel Marquez have their own promotional companies. There are countless others. Here, we've seen mixed success with David Haye's Hayemaker – losing a TV deal with the collapse of Setanta, but still developing a world heavyweight champion – while Joe Calzaghe's Calzaghe Promotions has pretty much wound up already.

How many family boxing businesses will flourish? How many will fall by the wayside?

It is certainly a dangerous game. Being nice is no recipe for lasting success within the murky, money-obsessed boxing world. Especially in the current delicate financial climate. The pitfalls include legal wrangling, court cases and dealing with egomaniacs. Plus of course the issue that those closest to you can be over-protective (mind you, in a sport and business as savage as boxing, maybe that's not too bad a problem to have). Emotional disputes, private relationships that are opened up, and a lack of real know-how or necessary experience are further worries.

Yet nothing is more important than unconditional love. Families have this in abundance, and that is no bad thing when one's son or brother or nephew is putting his life on the line every time he enters that ring.

Two

FATHERS AND SONS

5

Blood in the Corner

Wembley Conference Centre, 11 August 2000. The one-sided carnage was over. America's latest bright hope, Omar Sheika, had been utterly outclassed. The Welsh contingent who had followed their hero to London erupted. Yet in a poignant and moving moment, two pivotal fight figures only had eyes for each other.

Enzo Calzaghe, as usual rather awkwardly, clambered through the ropes from his training corner. His fighting son Joe afforded himself a rare broad grin. The two then embraced, rolling over and over on the canvas.

It was a release, and the most pure emotional reaction. When nothing else matters in the world apart from a father's pride in his son's achievement, and a son's satisfaction that he has succeeded, not just for his father, but alongside him as part of the closest of professional teams.

'This one's for Dad,' Joe said, welling up in our post-fight interview. It's on nights like these that you know you're in one of the best jobs in the world. 'He puts up with me,' he continued, his voice thick with emotion. 'The moaning, the moods, the arguments, the freezing mornings in that tin-shack of a gym in

Newbridge. The time he's given to me is irreplaceable. It's down to Enzo.' And with that he planted a quick kiss on the glistening forehead of his old man.

I've followed Joe ever since he was a teenager, because my step-uncle lived doors down from the Calzaghe family in New-bridge. 'He's going all the way, Joe is,' I remember Uncle John telling me. Calzaghe must have been eighteen or nineteen and, incredibly, a three-weight amateur champion.

I have interviewed, reported and commentated on Joe since the mid-nineties, when the Pride of Wales won the British title. It's always a pleasure to catch up with him, like I did in the winter of 2009, as he relaxed in between his latest showbiz assignments. My wife and I had just been to see Joe 'perform' in *Strictly Come Dancing*. It was quite a night.

'Everyone used to laugh at us,' Joe told me. 'They thought we didn't have a clue. What we had was a special, amazing connection. Dad pushed the right buttons at the right time. I only lost nine of a hundred and twenty fights as an amateur, and won all forty-six as a pro. I never ever lost with Dad in my corner.'

Enzo was there, lively as ever, in his corner of the room, and piped up in his machine-gun-paced Italian-cockney-Welsh dialect, 'There was one loss as an amateur when I was in Joe's corner, just one, but that was when the referee was the opponent's father! Family is more important than anything. Who knows a son's character more than a father? I truly value Joe, and have always had his best wishes at heart. Love is strong. People don't realize that.'

'Any relationship's hard work,' Joe added, 'but we were great together. He not only taught me how to box, he taught me who I was in the first place. We shared everything, and above all, the love was always there.'

The problem in the tangling, complex male hereditary link

between fathers and sons is that love should indeed be unconditional but is often oddly absent.

The relationship between fathers and sons has long been a subject for psychological study. For examples of this you can take your pick from the annals of history and literature down the ages. From Virgil's classic first-century BC poem *The Aeneid*, in which Aeneas escapes Troy with his son Ascanius and father Anchises, to the parallel stories in Shakespeare's *Hamlet*, there have always been fascinating depictions of such relationships. The Mafia and many crime families were littered with strange bonds, like the Bonannos in late-fifties New York, while Ernest Hemingway's exploration of adolescence and identity-forming kept the theme alive well into modern times.

It's true to say that most men crave a son. For reasons of pride, arrogance and statesmanship, 'he' wants his family name to live on. This is especially evident in America, where the Christian name is regularly passed down too. Most families have Jnrs and Snrs. Some go even further: an old friend of mine was quite wonderfully named Webb Black Garrison the Third.

So having a son is in many ways a reward for us men. We have an heir to the throne. As fathers, we are there to guide, nurture and protect, but not in the same way as the mother. A father helps his son establish his manhood, and shapes his masculinity.

The majority of men also enjoy sports, and this is where the 'father and son' dynamic becomes most interesting. Many dads try to live out, even realize, their dreams through their sons. Unfortunately this can lead to careers breaking down, and more importantly to shattered relationships, some beyond repair.

Today, fathers want to be involved in their children's lives more than ever before. Standing on the touchlines at school football and rugby matches is a ritual observance. Determined and dedicated yet simultaneously angry and obnoxious, dads vent their frustration at anything that might not have put their 'special' son in the shiniest of lights. Are these men guilty of peering through rose-tinted glasses? Are they unconditionally supportive? Are they simply obsessed?

As their sons strive for perfection, fathers can be a huge embarrassment and burden, applying unwanted pressure rather than unflinching support. This can transfer quickly and often dangerously into professional sport. For there we enter the realms of a business: in professional sport one earns not just a living but sometimes vast quantities of money. There can be little room for emotions and sentiment.

Boxing is by no means the only sport to have grappled with such issues. On the surface, tennis is a beautiful, graceful game played by young, fit, committed athletes in wonderful arenas; but scratch the surface and this can be a lonely nomadic life for even the biggest of stars who endure quite horrific applications of pressure, particularly from fathers. Scores of youngsters have been burned out way too young; many subsequently turn against the fathers who tried to create 'the perfect player', having craved success almost at any cost. Richard Williams unashamedly admits that he pushed Venus and Serena too far. Jelena Dokic fired her father Damir amid claims of alleged abuse although in 2011, after he had been relased from prison, they did begin a period of reconciliation.

Maybe father–son ties exacerbate the adversity of a youngster following his path in life, which can in turn create the most awkward of scenarios. Things didn't always run smoothly between the supremely gifted John McEnroe and his father, John Snr. McEnroe might have been a genius, but his frequent mood swings led actor Tom Hulce to study him for his portrayal of Mozart in *Amadeus*. Meanwhile, McEnroe's rival Jimmy Connors was moulded into a sabre-toothed tiger of a player by his family. In this case, though, Jimmy's dad, 'Big Jim', a toll-bridge attendant, was rather overshadowed by Jimmy's mother, Gloria, who along with his grandmother moulded the aggressive tennis marvel.

Andre Agassi was another child prodigy. At the age of just two he had a racket taped to his hand and slept with a tennis ball above his bed. At nine, Andre beat an old NFL great called Jim Brown on the court. The prize he won for his dad, Mike, was $500 in a bet. Later, Agassi achieved his lifelong dream of winning Wimbledon. The first thing his father said to him afterwards was 'you had no business losing that fourth set'. Agassi grew to detest tennis because of his own dad.

In terms of family influence, not to mention one-on-one gladiatorial combat, tennis is probably the closest sport to boxing, a powerful mental and physical game of wits, explosive hitting and quick, classy skills. There is, though, an obvious and vital difference: the players in white on the lawns of SW19 do not get punched for a living.

The role of fathers and sons within the fighting game has always prompted fierce, lively debate. Leading American trainers Emanuel Steward and Teddy Atlas believe it rarely works to have fathers entwined in a fighter's career because emotion, sentiment and feelings become distorted. They argue that it is against natural law and order: fathers are there to protect and nurture their sons from birth, yet they then have to channel them into brutal confrontations.

And, as is obvious from the earliest traces of the sport – on a fresco on the Greek island of Santorini dating to 1600 BC – there's no more male or macho game than the one played out inside the squared circle. Many moons ago, in the old days of pugilism and prizefighting, boxing was rightly named the 'sport of kings'. It has won the acclaim of many a monarch and his dynasty. Fathers have long been seen as 'kings' of the family, 'head honchos'; they function as worker, provider, and the dominant and ruling force within the household. Many fathers are heavily involved in boxing. However, like those kings who have been sent into exile, or died suddenly, others are totally absent.

Mike Tyson's dad Jimmy Kirkpatrick abandoned his family in the squalor of Brooklyn's Bedford-Stuyvesant ghetto when Mike was two. Lennox Lewis's father Carlton Brooks was never involved in upbringing or parenting, and rarely gets mentioned, even today. That old great world heavyweight champion Jersey Joe Walcott (born Arnold Raymond Cream) lost his father when he was young and had to get a job in a soup factory to support his mother and eleven siblings. Jermain Taylor was deserted by his father when he was five; he cared for his mum and his three younger sisters, adopting the role of 'the man of the house'. When I visited Jermain in Little Rock, Arkansas, he told me, 'I was the father for my sisters, and the father for myself. We only ever watched soap operas on TV, never boxing. I grew up with girls. I have never known what it's like to have a father in my corner.'

Some dads tend to stay out of 'corners', choosing to remain on the periphery. One can regularly see them lurking in the background at fight venues. They seem to always offer a shoulder to lean on, but not obtrusively. Timothy Bradley's dad is a high-school security officer; Andy Morris's father is an inspector for our Central Area council; Michael Jennings's dad is often ringside, heading up the family's security firm. They all go about their own business while keeping a beady eye on the progress of their sons. These father–son relationships may benefit from the fact that the fathers have their own lives and careers, so are not reliant upon their sons. They choose to let them get on with it.

This is certainly the case behind the startling success of the Hatton family. Ray Hatton is one of those fathers who chose to be hugely involved, but mostly in terms of life guidance. His sons Ricky and Matthew stuck to the boxing; Ray looked after the managerial aspects, the finances, and in many ways their general well-being. His wife Carol is seen as the disciplinarian, keeping her boys humble and grounded, and Ray thinks this right: 'I never look at him as Ricky the superstar. He is Richard Hatton. If he's out of line, he'll get a kick up the backside from his mother. And me. Who does he think he is?

'All families have problems, and fall-outs,' he said to me when I started gathering views for this book. 'We've had right raging arguments. Rip-roaring barneys, we really have. But Adam, we can laugh them off. Parents should never be in awe of their children. I've seen that happen, and that breeds monsters. The real trouble between fathers and sons comes when there are egos involved.'

Despite never being happy that his sons chose boxing, Ray always gave them 'two hundred per cent support'. 'I used to take Richard a hundred miles a week to train,' he said. 'We used to travel the length and breadth of the country together in those amateur days. All things that could be done were done for my boys. I have had my concerns, primarily at the way Richard chooses to lead his life. But the beauty of our relationship is that I only ever comment on certain boxing things. "Listen, Cus D'Amato," Richard says to me, "you stick to the money, I'll stick to the boxing!"'

Ray laughs at the memory. 'You will never see me in the ring or jumping around. I never go backstage. It's not my place. I am not the trainer, I am their dad. I don't move from my seat at ringside. I don't go into the bars. It's horrible. I'm nervous, chewing my gum, everything's a blur, and it doesn't get any better. I can only enjoy boxing when Richard and Matthew are not fighting. I have to make sure they are financially secure. For every pound Richard's made, it's my job to make him another. Richard's set, he never has to worry, but he doesn't know what he's worth. He's on a salary. I understand about money from running my carpet business. I used to work sixteen to eighteen hours a day. I am so proud of my sons. I was proud the day they were born. As long as you're the best at what you endeavour to be. Stack the best shelves. Polish the best shoes. Whatever. That's my philosophy.'

His dad's homespun philosophy has kept Ricky's outlook on life simple too. Perhaps that was the key thing for his army of fans, who followed the fighter wherever he went – and in his final bouts, whether he won or lost. 'I have confidence in my dad,' Ricky says. 'Good parents give good advice.'

Amir Khan's father Shah has also been there through thick and thin for his eldest son. Shah's a kind and loving father with an infectious grin, and a real sense of family commitment. From ringside support in his Union Jack waistcoat at the Athens Olympics to embracing his son, in victory and defeat, Shah works doggedly hard – perhaps too hard – for Amir and the business. He always has. A grafter who used to fix cars in Bolton, Shah's always willing to help out.

Amir knows how important his father has been in shaping his life and career: 'Family is an enormous thing in Pakistan. Mine are a massive support. Without them I'd be nothing. Particularly my dad. He didn't miss one of my hundred and ten amateur bouts. He came all around the world, paying his own way. The time and effort he put into me was simply unbelievable. Whatever sport I would have chosen – and I was a good cross-country runner too – he would have helped and been proud of me. He also never applied any extra pressure. Even if I had sparred with guys who were better than me, he would mind his own business and not judge. Dad knew he wasn't my coach. Just my father, who's loved me from day one. I want my father to be my father, not my trainer. The coach sees you as a fighter, the father as a son. It's too risky; he wants to put a shell around you.'

I watched a crucial training day in Amir's rehabilitation, after his crushing knockout defeat to Breidis Prescott in 2008. His switch to Freddie Roach's notoriously tough Wild Card Gym in Hollywood brought him face to face with the king of the stable, Manny Pacquiao. Amir seemed relaxed and composed when Freddie told him that he would be sparring with the Filipino sensation. Not exactly for the faint-hearted after his boxing world had been left in tatters by Prescott in those fifty-four blistering and bewildering seconds.

It was one of those Roach masterstrokes. I witnessed the highly competitive session, which if anything Amir had the better of. Talk about a confidence booster. Then Amir told me that his dad would never have agreed to doing that. 'After I got knocked out by Prescott, my dad would have said no to sparring with Manny. That's the difference. He has deep inner feelings, and there's nothing you can do about those. It's far better to have a trainer who lives a different life and who is without those constant family worries.

'You have to understand my Muslim background too,' Amir continued. 'Fathers are there to protect. The respect sons have for their fathers within the Muslim community is like no other. My dad is my friend, but there is a huge line of respect, and that is key. I trust no one apart from my father. He does the accounts, and he will look out for me. I never have to worry with him there.'

James DeGale went one better than Amir in winning gold in Beijing, and as with the Khans, James's dad is the fulcrum of their family.

I was with the DeGale father-and-son team when James had his professional homecoming at Wembley. Leroy was ringside for James, as usual. 'My role is to be there unconditionally,' he told me. 'Always have been.'

James confirmed the arrangement: 'He's been there to look

out for me from day one. He leaves the training to Jimmy [McDonnell]; best way. Prevents arguments, and Dad knows that Jimmy's the boss with the boxing business.'

Father and son joke and nip at each other like Yorkshire terriers. It's fun to watch. I think young James should be just fine with his dad in that best supporting role.

So fathers can stand back in advisory, even managerial positions, much to the benefit of their sons: the sportsmen, the fighters. Fathers oversee the situation and offer their assistance and help when needed. In other words, they are best at just doing what dads do best.

That doesn't occur in every case. There's the tragic tale of Wilfred Benitez. The brilliant Puerto Rican was the youngest boxer to win a world title, at just seventeen in March 1976, when his high-school pals cheered him on to victory in San Juan over the WBA light-welterweight champion Antonio Cervantes. Yet, as is so often the way in this most perilous of sports, the fall was dramatic. His father, mentor, manager and idol Gregorio actually sold his contract on, allowing his son to dip into money that was meant to be placed into a trust and supposedly not to be touched until a year after he retired. Some at the time felt it was a father virtually pawning his son out for whatever cash he could get.

Unsurprisingly, there was no happy ending. Benitez suffers from an incurable degenerative brain condition and diabetes. Until his mother Clara died recently, Wilfred was living with her on a $200-a-month pension provided by the World Boxing Council. Many felt that Wilfred Benitez had been exploited by the person who should have protected him the most.

Situations like these are making the governing bodies of boxing increasingly suspicious of fathers getting too involved in their sport. At their annual convention in South Korea in 2009, the WBC called for fathers to be banned from working their sons' corners once and for all, after a study showed that it could prove fatal. President Jose Sulaiman led a group who believed that errors in paternal judgement needed to be eradicated for the safety of the fighters. Dr Paul Wallace, chairman of the WBC's medical board, stated, 'Our study shows that the most common factor which came from all the fatalities that have happened was having fathers in the corner. It's not a medical issue, but it's associated.'

Does the strong emotional link between a father and a son preclude the former from making rational, quick, impartial and sensible decisions in the ring? Is a father detached enough to make these often vital calls? Is he looking at what he loves rather than at what is actually unfolding? More dangerous still, is the father actually trying to be the fighter by proxy?

Throughout boxing history, fathers have become their sons' trainers, often from very early on. But, enter the working corner and you enter the line of fire.

I met Leavander Johnson and his father/trainer Bill on several occasions when reporting and commentating Stateside for Sky. They were a very pleasant team, and Leavander was a brave, gutsy, honest type of boxer who did ever so well to become the world lightweight champion.

It's typical of the fighter he was that Leavander complained and protested to referee Tony Weeks when he was stopped in the eleventh round of a world title defence against Jesus Chavez in Las Vegas in September 2005. Yet Johnson had been on the end of waves of savage attacks – he was outpunched 409–148 on the statistics – was badly hurt, and five days later, the thirty-five-year-old father of four tragically passed away.

Bill Johnson was naturally heartbroken. He'd worked his corner, he'd kept on sending Leavander out round after round, father and son obviously convinced that they could somehow prevail.

'He was fighting for a world title, then a few minutes later he was fighting for his life,' Bill relayed at the time through Leavander's promoter Lou DiBella. 'He fought like a warrior,' a tearful DiBella added. 'There will be all these people who will come out and say this is the brutality of our sport. But Leavander didn't want to be a drug dealer, he didn't want to hustle on the streets. He wanted to become a world champion, and that's what he became. You can't blame anyone.'

Yet it is a fact of human nature that people point fingers. We are constantly thrilled by boxing's action, yet we are sickened when a tragedy occurs. Most spectators at ringside that night in Vegas were aghast during the one-sided beating, but Leavander's lead corner man – his father – might not have actually quite grasped what was going on in front of him. It was initially reported that Bill Johnson warned his son that he was going to stop the fight.

But at the start of the eleventh round, Jim Lampley, HBO's lead broadcaster, said this: 'In the recent history of the sport, when you look at fights where one fighter has been badly, maybe permanently damaged, two constants seem to be part of the formula. Number one, the opponent who is doing the damage is a harder hitter, but not a big enough hitter to put the opponent away. Second, the guy who is getting worked over has his father in the corner constantly sending him back to take more punishment.' Lampley's colleagues Larry Merchant, Emanuel Steward and Harold Lederman all felt the corner should have stopped the fight a few rounds earlier. Bill has since admitted that Leavander just wasn't himself from as early as the third round.

Now, nobody with any heart or decency should blame Bill Johnson. I am sure he plays the fight over in his mind on a regular basis and wishes, beyond anything, that he could turn back the clock. Leavander's brother Craig certainly hasn't blamed his dad, feeling that there was always better security with his father in Leavander's corner. Knowing that Bill would have helped him most.

The family had not been concerned in the ring afterwards either, as Leavander congratulated Jesus, or even back in the dressing-room – until he collapsed. For the Johnsons had seen Leavander in previous fights taking what they felt was more of a beating. Ironically – again, as is often the case in these rare but tragic circumstances – the systematic lighter punches of Jesus Chavez had in fact done far more lasting damage than if Johnson had been wiped out with one shot.

A statue of Leavander Johnson was unveiled in Atlantic City in 2011, and Jesus Chavez has kept in touch with the family; the boxer left standing typically acts in this decent manner. The Johnson family attach no blame to a fighter who was just doing his job. Chavez, like Barry McGuigan, Richie Wenton and others who have seen an opponent lose their life, has to live with it too. Always. So too Bill Johnson, who, rightly or wrongly, didn't pull his son, his boy, his love, out of the fray.

But as I said, it would be too cruel to blame Leavander's father for what happened. Still, it must be asked: if there had been someone not as tied to the fighter in the corner, would they have made a different, more practical, less emotional call?

One could delve deeper and look at the referees in these situations. Does it alter their approach knowing that a father is in the corner? Maybe they should be more aware when the action is becoming one-sided; at least go and have a word in between rounds. If Dad is not the most objective judge when in the corner, should referees be more vigilant and step in earlier, or is that simply not their concern?

Safety must be paramount of course, and with every tragedy,

lessons need to be learned from all sides. I remember the interview we did with Leavander before the fight. I watched it back in the weeks after his death, and he hadn't quite seemed himself. Maybe he was weight-drained. Maybe he just wasn't right. There could have been many reasons before or during the fight why this unfortunately happened to Leavander Johnson.

It was, of course, never meant to end this way. Bill Johnson obviously helped his son strive for a better life. Leavander left behind a wife, four children, and a daddy with a shattered heart.

As the cliché goes, there's no room to hide in the ring. As a result, these up close and personal scenarios can haunt fathers, and their families, for ever.

Undefeated welterweight Billy Collins took a severe beating from Luis Resto at Madison Square Garden in June 1983. After the fight, Collins's father and trainer Billy Snr went to shake Resto's hands, and felt them through his gloves. The New York commission subsequently discovered that Resto's trainer Panama Lewis had removed an ounce of padding from each glove. Lewis was effectively banned for life, although I continue to see him around the current boxing scene. Resto never fought again. Both men were jailed for two and a half years.

Collins had suffered a torn iris and permanently blurred vision which prevented him from continuing his boxing career. This broke him both physically and mentally, and the following year he crashed his car into a tree. Billy Collins was dead at just twenty-two. His father has never recovered.

Billy Collins Snr still lives in the same house in Nashville, and he still asks the same question: 'Why didn't I know? We instilled it in Billy never to quit, but I should have done something when he told me during the fight that it felt as though his opponent had a rock in his glove.'

Billy has taken down all boxing pictures and trophies of the son he trained, managed and adored. They mean nothing now. Boxing may as well not exist for the Collins family.

That's probably exactly how the Rushtons view the sport in their Yorkshire home. John Rushton has always been known as the 'Mr Doncaster' of the domestic game, a jovial character whose son Jason was a fighter. Another rare but unfortunate incident saw twenty-six-year-old Jason collapse after losing a tough Central Area light-middleweight title fight against Brian Rose in October 2009.

I was backstage in Bolton when Rushton slumped to the floor right in front of me, and having been present at the three most tragic events in British boxing in the last fifteen years, I felt straight away it was extremely serious. And extremely frightening. Jason's father John was also his corner man and found it virtually impossible to deal with the drama.

Jason was rushed to hospital and was placed in an induced coma after suffering a tear of the brain tissue. It was touch and go for a while, but Jason is now making a slow recovery. He says, 'It was nobody's fault, nobody's to blame – it's just one of those things.'

It's refreshing to hear that he hasn't criticized his father in any way for not pulling him out, but some insiders felt that Jason was beginning to be matched too hard for the talent he possessed. One went further, complaining that 'as a responsible dad, you should know how tough your son is'.

I'm sure that the father-and-son team from Yorkshire were just trying to make the best possible living, even though Jason had quite clearly slipped from a promising prospect to a decent journeyman doing the rounds. John Rushton said he'd quit the game after what happened to his son. Jason is hoping his dad changes his mind. His aim is to manage and train fighters himself, and he wants his father alongside. We wish them well. Even if mistakes were made, the bonds between father and son are astonishing; so too the draw and power of this most addictive of sports.

6

No Love Like That

The great boxing trainers tend to be just that – great trainers. They can motivate, they can plan strategies, they can work psychology and they can remain cool, impartial, even aloof while maintaining close, important and professional working relationships. A stranger can take the emotion out of the situation.

Ray Arcel guided eighteen fighters, from Ezzard Charles to Roberto Duran, to world titles; Whitey Bimstein looked after legendary names like Benny Leonard and Rocky Marciano; Al Silvani trained twenty world champions, Henry Armstrong and Jake La Motta among them. The astute Eddie Futch was behind Joe Frazier, Ken Norton and Riddick Bowe. Freddie Roach benefited from late Futch wisdom and is currently one of the hottest trainers in boxing, his stable of stars headed by pound-for-pound great Manny Pacquiao, along with our own Amir Khan.

As the finishing touches were being made to this book in early February 2012, the boxing world lost one of the most iconic trainers of them all, Angelo Dundee, who was steadfastly loyal to Muhammad Ali and led him to glory in the ring (he always said of Ali that the boxer had the reflexes, Dundee simply directed them). Over six decades in the sport he trained fifteen world champions, among them another all-time great, Sugar Ray Leonard. The famous American broadcaster Howard Cosell once said that Dundee was 'the only man in boxing to whom I would entrust my own son'. Personally, it always meant a great deal to me that I shared a birthday with the great man – 30 August. In 2011, Angelo Dundee turned ninety on the day I turned forty.

Many of the boxers I've mentioned saw their trainers as 'father figures', but they weren't their actual blood fathers. Big difference.

Take the case of Gil Clancy, the excellent coach who was indelibly linked to Emile Griffith, but who also trained George Foreman. Clancy then moved to help Gerry Cooney try to dismantle big George. Imagine a father having to move camps to plot his son's downfall. Or the Kronk's Emanuel Steward who, having steered Tommy Hearns to multi-title triumphs, was used as 'a hired gun' in the nineties. Steward trained Oliver McCall to knock out Lennox Lewis, then switched allegiances to rebuild Lennox, who ultimately exacted revenge on 'The Atomic Bull'. I remember Manny Pacquiao once telling me that you have to pick your loyalty and your decisions in boxing most carefully.

Young boys are loyal and idolize their fathers early on, but can rebel or discard parental advice in their teens. That's when boxing development is very important. So many fighters are led into battle by their 'old men'. Yet blood ties make it very tough to make impartial decisions; it's almost impossible not to be compassionate if you are a father, and there's normally overwhelming emotion whether it works or fails.

I've known Joe and Enzo Calzaghe for over twenty years. In my eyes, they have been *the* father-and-son team of my career so far, arguably of all time. Together, Team Calzaghe won everything. Joe notched up three ABA titles at different weights, and after a fabulous fifteen-year career enjoyed the rare honour of retiring undefeated, while Enzo still stands as one of the most decorated trainers of all time.

So what were the secrets of succeeding in the very role that has caused so many families so many problems over the years, and what happens if and when it all starts to fall apart?

'Firstly, you never lose the love of your child for boxing or anything,' Enzo said. 'Secondly, it is about respect. I am from a very tough Italian background, where my father was in total command. He was the hardest man in Sassori. He was on the go 24/7, and my mother worked in the morgues. We got smacked, yes, but there was plenty of love. Here in Britain, the children become the boss, but the father must have the power. That went for my daughters Sonia and Mel as well as Joe. With Joe, we just had flow. I'm his father and his friend. My companion on equal terms. But when I said no, it meant no.'

'Love and respect were the key,' Joe agreed. 'Dad taught me the boxing basics. Yet I admit that there were times when I was thinking about another coach.'

Enzo explained what happened. 'Mickey Duff didn't think I was good enough. Then later Frank Warren felt Joe needed to move on. It was 1999, and he felt I had taken Joe as far as I could. Cruel to be kind and all that. I said to Joe, whatever decision you make will be fine with me. When a father tries to tighten the grip, that's when there's a fall-out. I let Joe and only Joe make the call. He tried some other trainers, looked for the holy grail, but the bird always came back to roost. Joe said he valued me, and loved my style of training. That I was a positive influence on him.'

Joe, for obvious reasons, does not regret the decision to stick with family. 'We clicked, and Dad was the one person who could really motivate me. To give me that kick up the arse I needed. We had our rows but they would always be forgotten quickly. Never any grudges.'

'Never hold grudges,' Enzo echoed. 'We rowed but an hour later we would hug. In the gym, he looked at me as a trainer. For that time. I had the ability to make him move. Then we'd finish, and he'd see me as his father again.'

Of course Enzo never really saw Joe in serious trouble in the ring, never had to make that crunch decision on whether to withdraw his son from battle. However, he did have to cope with Joe being decked more often during the latter stages of his career. 'When he went down against Byron Mitchell, that was the first time in his life,' Enzo told me. 'I was as cool as a cucumber. My soul was prepared. Remember, I was born hard, pushed into the army. Travelled alone. A steely character.'

But what of the emotions involved? I asked him.

'There's no time to worry,' he replied. 'You just worry about the next shot. It's a job.'

'He was the calm for me in the corner,' said Joe. 'I'm normally a chilled, relaxed guy. If I was in trouble, I didn't want to hear anything. Just feel it. The passion. Keep myself together.'

'It just made him more comfortable seeing me in the corner,' added Enzo. 'Joe's my only son. Whether he'd been a dustman, worked the sewers, or been a cook, he's my flesh and blood. I guess it worked better than others because of our trust.'

'I can't judge other father-and-son teams,' said Joe. 'We came from a different world. There was never any ego, no entourage. Just us.'

'What we achieved will never be done again,' Enzo concluded. 'Not just the accolades, but the fact we stayed together through thick and thin.'

'Ironically,' added Joe, 'I now have a son who's keen on boxing. Joe junior. He's a bit of a target because of his name. I would never push him into it, and keep telling him how much hard work it takes. But maybe I'll just let him get it out of his system!'

*

Left: An early publicity shot at Sky Sports. I've aged a bit in my nearly two decades there!

Below: Johnny Nelson has become my perfect partner in crime on our *Ringside* show.

Bottom: The Sky Sports boxing team is like another family to me: (*left to right*) Glenn McCrory, Andy Scott, Nick Halling, Jim Watt, Johnny Nelson, me, Ed Robinson, Dave Clark.

Right: This is my commentary sheet from one of my favourite ever fights, when Diego Corrales rose twice in the tenth round to stop Jose Luis Castillo. I miss Diego terribly.

Middle and bottom: Commentating at ringside with Jim Watt, Ian Darke and Glenn McCrory. Jim and Glenn's expertise are invaluable and Darkie has been the voice of so many great fights.

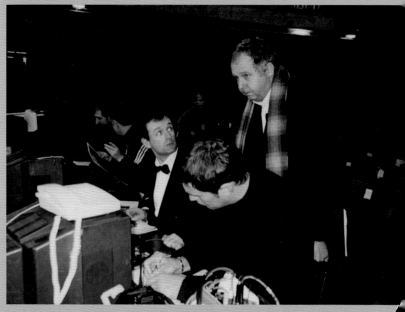

Left: I'm lucky enough to have travelled across the States filming for Sky. This was with my producer Declan Johnson at Southfork Ranch, home of Dallas, when filming Texan Paulie Ayala before he tackled Erik Morales in 2002.

Left: In Phoenix, Arizona, while seeing Lennox Lewis for his training camp ahead of his rematch against Oliver McCall.

Below left: Overlooking Brooklyn Bridge in New York. We filmed Danny Williams there before his sensational win against Mike Tyson.

Bottom left: Doing live links in Las Vegas during Ike Quartey's challenge to Oscar De La Hoya back in February 1999.

Bottom right: On location in Colorado with cameraman David Caine and producer Charles Lawrence, filming Robbie Allen before he tackled Bernard Hopkins for the third time. Cainey has been everywhere with me and producers like Charles and Dec are also good friends as well as valued colleagues.

Right: Talking to Russell Crowe in Manchester for the epic Ricky Hatton – Kostya Tszyu clash put the gloss on that fabulous night – a real highlight of my career.

Middle: In the Vegas desert with the 'Pocket Rocket' Wayne McCullough. My producer Dec (*left*) and my cameraman Cainey (*right*) were again on board for that one.

Bottom: The Klitschko brothers are always welcome guests on *Ringside*. Here is Wladimir with (*left to right*) producer Charles Lawrence, reporter Andy Scott, the show's PA Sarah Hornsby, Johnny Nelson and assistant producer James Tynan.

Left: The Sky boxing team gets to let their hair down every now and then. This was a few years ago with (*left to right*) Cainey, reporter Ed Robinson, former assistant producer Ben Compton, assistant producer Jon Beloff and Dcc.

Middle: Along with my family, friends are so important to me. The Green Boys livened up Princeton University on tour in the nineties! (*Top row, from left*) Jamie 'Pussy Dollar' Szpiro, Oli 'Of Ulay' Glasgow, Simon 'Shelvis' Levitt, Charlie 'Chops' Curtis, me (Adam 'Sledge' Smith) and (*bottom row, from left*) Sophie 'Flooders' Ludgate, Rob 'Favero' Baruch, Dan 'Tiggler' Somers, Toby 'Warf Man' Szpiro and Ben 'Digits' Rickard.

Bottom: This was on my stag weekend when we went on a boat round Boston then down to Cape Cod. (*Left to right*) Toby Szpiro, 'Sir' Geordie Corsiglia, my best mate Levitt, Jamie Szpiro, Will 'Chips' Davies, Chops, Hodges, Lewers, me and Dec.

Top left: My family: (*from left*) my brothers JW and Edward, my stepmum Joan, and my dad Alan (with my son Oscar in his arms). I'm holding my daughter Jessamy and my wife Jo is on the far right.

Top right: Liverpool FC is another love of my life. Here I am at Anfield with my sister Anna (*left*) and my mum Veronica (*right*).

Middle and bottom right: Anna and I have long had a tight bond, and my brothers JW and Edward come from the Welsh side of the family. My grandma Joyce Peregrine lives near the Calzaghe family in Newbridge.

Bottom left: My in-laws Chris and Jenny Brown (here with Jo and my kids Jessamy, Tilly and Oscar) make us a tight-knit group.

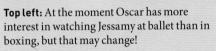

Top left: At the moment Oscar has more interest in watching Jessamy at ballet than in boxing, but that may change!

Top right: At home in the snow in west London.

Above left: The Three Amigos!

Right: My wife Jo is my rock.

Right: My youngest Tilly shows her support for my line of work and for 'The Greatest'.

Middle: Ricky Hatton and I have shared some wonderful moments over the years.

Bottom: Boxing may have a tough image, but as Oscar De La Hoya shows, it's all about family.

It could be said that the Calzaghes are proof that the father-and-son system works, and we've seen some other success stories in Britain. Peter Harrison steered Scott to a terrific tenure as the world featherweight champion and is still standing behind his son despite all his problems out of the ring, while Paul Cook led his boy Nicky to the world super-featherweight crown. After Nicky lost his title to Roman Martinez, he attributed no blame to his father, saying, 'Me and my dad will always be together. After I was beaten, he asked whether I wanted to move on, and he said it wouldn't be a problem if I chose to do so. But we have a partnership, and I wouldn't just give that up.'

England also has the quality father-and-son training team of Jimmy and Mark Tibbs. Both were decent former pros, and they now work side by side training good young fighters like Kevin Mitchell and Billy Joe Saunders. Going well too are the Calzaghes' neighbours, the Cleverlys. Father Vince and son Nathan, who lived up to his name by getting a mathematics degree while learning the fight game, boast an unbeaten slate, and are motoring up the world rankings side by side.

Yet there's always the flip side, and there are many pitfalls. I will never forget being ringside at the MEN Arena in Manchester on 28 September 2002. Ricky Hatton had what looked like a comfortable night's work in front of him against Stephen Smith, a talented but light-punching part-time model. Smith was trained by his father Darkie, who had himself won nine of forty-two fights. A torrid first round saw Smith hit the canvas, and look to his dad in the corner for help; the second saw Smith suffer a nasty cut to his right eye (on account of an accidental Hatton elbow), and what followed was one of the most bizarre ring incidents in the modern fight game.

The fan man's Vegas flight was seriously wacky, but this was almost as odd. At the MEN, Darkie Smith ended the bout by jumping through the ropes during the action and attacking referee Mickey Vann. His anger stemmed from his belief that Vann had ignored infringements by Hatton, thus failing to protect Stephen. Smith was disqualified and his father's boxing licence subsequently revoked.

It was a disgraceful scene, but to me, it was tinged with sadness. Stephen and Darkie split, and the damage was done. They didn't speak for months. Darkie had just seemed to want his son out of the ring; maybe he realized he was out of his depth, getting a beating, and felt he did the right thing. Fathers want to protect their sons. Yet a fighter wants to protect himself; he certainly doesn't want his daddy pitching in to fight his battles. That is the cruel truth of being a boxer.

'If my dad had done that to me,' Ricky Hatton told me later, 'I wouldn't have talked to him for a long, long time. Corners are no place for a father. I really mean that. One hundred per cent. I would never ever have fought with my dad training me. No way. It's just insane. Enzo and Joe are a one-off. Trust me, it doesn't work.'

If a father and son can't put their personal feelings to one side for their chosen profession, maybe Ricky's right, and they shouldn't be in it together. Not when lives are on the line.

The problem is that fathers send their kids into dangerous situations and when they get hurt they either send them back to prove a point, worry and want them out, or do what Scottish trainer Stevie Maguire did: Stevie Snr simply stormed out of his son's corner, mid-fight, and gave up! He was that annoyed and upset with young Stevie's performance. There's passion, and commitment, but there can be blind panic, or overwhelming frustration.

In January 2012 at the York Hall, I saw another instance of this. A few seconds after the bell to start the ninth round of an electric English light-middleweight title clash between Erick 'The Eagle' Ochieng and Nick Quigley, Nick's dad Tony waved the white towel to pull his son out of the war, to the loud protests of his boy. Quigley had set a red-hot pace from the off, was tired and was losing the fight, but it seemed a strange stoppage so soon after a minute's rest in the corner. I was sitting ringside with former world super-middleweight champion Richie Woodhall, who immediately said, 'That was the father in him coming out. Protecting his son. There lies the issue with fathers training their boys.'

Richie should know of course. His own dad Len guided him all the way.

'My dad nearly pulled me out a couple of times,' Richie continued. 'After the eighth round of my European middleweight title fight with Silvio Branco, he said enough, and almost stopped it. I was at home in front of my Telford crowd. I pleaded, and I'm glad I did. I knocked Branco out in the next round. Adam, I could see that same thing with the Quigleys. I saw it straight away in Tony's eyes.'

Tony Quigley has three fighting sons in Tony Jnr, Nick and John. He is an accomplished trainer, but he is also a protective dad. Such a very hard balance to deal with, especially in the heat of battle.

Boxing history is packed with father-and-son training combinations that often end in blood, sweat and tears; the occasional feel-good tales usually come when there are no axes to grind. The Byrds are one such partnership. Father Joe Byrd, a 5ft 6in heavyweight who fought the dynamite-punching Earnie Shavers, only had a record of 13–20–1, but he trained and managed his son Chris to the world heavyweight title. They had a really strong relationship, because there was never any jealousy. Joe was totally self-sufficient and settled. He just wanted his son's best effort.

So too did Yoel Judah, who managed to guide his talented, if wayward, son Zab to the undisputed world welterweight title.

This has largely been a positive relationship, but people have questioned the partnership because for all of Zab's flashy early dominance of a fight, he tends to run out of ideas. Is that a problem with the fighter, or the fact that he remained for so long with his father?

Judah recently decided to change his corner, choosing the legendary Pernell 'Sweet Pea' Whitaker to guide him into his major match with Amir Khan in July 2011. It wasn't Judah's finest hour. Outclassed from the very first bell, the temperamental talent made a meal out of a borderline body blow in the fifth round, and tried to get Khan disqualified. Virtually every critic saw this as an easy way out; whatever the truth, Judah had decided upon this action in a split second of heated battle. Personally, I don't think it would have mattered if Yoel or Pernell had been in the corner. Sometimes the fighter himself dictates a swift course of action from within, not after close or even cosy instruction.

The truth is that most father-trainers are successful only when their fighting son is exceptionally gifted.

'It's far easier polishing a gem,' Vince Cleverly told me. 'Father–son teams can work, but it's all down to the natural qualities of the fighter. My son Nathan always wanted to box; even if he was a journeyman, I would have stood by him. But he would have been much, much harder to train. I really think it's largely down to the skill-set of the individual boxer. For us fathers who choose this profession, that's what you have to be – a professional. It's a job. But it's easier when good genes pass down the line.'

Nathan's quality is even more impressive given the huge difficulties he endured before and during Vince's divorce from his mother Jackie. The young fighter coped with the animosity around him and is now active in supporting children's charities.

What has come out of it is a strong bond between father and

son, a deep love; their relationship has come to define them. Professionally, like Joe and Enzo Calzaghe before them, they can leave any argument in the gym. And they can be extremely tempestuous. Vince also has to take his fair share of punishment, all to see his son succeed.

Ironically, Nathan – who remains very close to Joe – was also trained by Enzo Calzaghe. Boxing politics put a halt to that, and Nathan was straight back into his father's arms. It would be fascinating if we could know how Nathan Cleverly's career unfolded first under Enzo and then under Vince. Would Enzo have guided Nathan to more successful fights than his father? Or would it turn out that the fighter did just as well, or as poorly, with either of them training him?

So far so good for the Cleverlys. Nathan is, after all, the WBO light-heavyweight champion, and whatever happens on his boxing journey in future years it seems obvious that father and son are entwined on the same path for ever, even if Vince doesn't remain the lead trainer. 'If Nathan and I feel that I have taken him as far as I can, and he needs someone with more expertise to take him to the very summit, then so be it,' Vince said. 'I have no problem if he wanted Freddie Roach to fine-tune him. I would learn so much too, just being a part of it. As long as it's the best for Nathan, that's all I care about.'

Says it all, really, about the powerful connection between father and son.

Felix Trinidad won five national amateur titles, forty-two out of forty-five professional fights, was a three-weight world champion, and one of the greatest boxers ever to emerge from that Caribbean jewel of Puerto Rico. He too was trained by his father, Don Felix, from the moment he first donned the gloves at twelve. This father-and-son team became multi-millionaires while, most importantly, staying close.

There were wranglings, of course. Felix Snr, a former Puerto

Rican national champion, had his differences with the Puerto Rican authorities who wanted to take his son to the Olympics. And, like many, he also had his ups and downs with promoter Don King.

Perhaps most famously, Trinidad was pulled out of his mega-match with Bernard Hopkins by his father who, having seen his son take too much, climbed into the ring in the twelfth to save him. It was an important moment. Not many boxers are rescued in the final round. If this had been a pride issue, Trinidad's dad may well have let him go the full course; alternatively, if Don Felix had simply wanted 'to get his fighter out of there' he would have stopped the bout sooner. This was no Stephen/Darkie Smith situation. Felix Trinidad had bundles of talent, but his father knew when to say enough. That may just have been an instinct, but once again it shows that these relationships can work.

The Trinidads retired together, came back together, and retired again together. 'Felix was a special talent,' the elder Trinidad, often affectionately called 'Papa', said. 'I never pushed him into the ring. First of all, we have respect for each other. We're friends. He will always have my support.'

Like Trinidad, Shane Mosley is one of the finest fighters of the modern era. The smiling Californian was a brilliant lightweight, and – again like Trinidad – went on to win world titles in three weight classes. Through most of his career, Shane was guided by his gentle and softly spoken father Jack, who was voted Trainer of the Year after their superb victory over Oscar De La Hoya in 2000.

'You have to separate the two different sides,' Shane told me. 'I have always been able to separate my father from my trainer. He'll always be my father, even if he's not my trainer.'

Jack might always be fighting Shane's corner, but he's not in the thick of it now. In fact the father was removed by the son on a couple of occasions. When Mosley was floored twice and faced his first real moment of crisis against Vernon Forrest in 2002, Jack seemed shell-shocked. Critics blamed Shane's father for an inability to adapt tactics during the difficult situation.

Shane hired the excellent Joe Goossen for the rematch with Forrest, and although he lost again, it was much closer. More recently, Naazim Richardson has taken the lead corner role. This lends weight to the argument that fighters might – at times, at least – be better off without their fathers.

Interestingly, Shane has a son, Shane Jnr, who is training to be a fighter, and follow in his father's footsteps. How will Daddy treat the next generation? Will grandfather Jack be involved? We wait with interest.

Egos can bump. Egos can collide. Egos can ruin, especially if the sons are better boxers, and become more famous than their fathers. Some modern greats, like Roy Jones and Floyd Mayweather, have also fired their dads.

Jones was taught to box by his father Roy Snr from the age of five. Yet even in those early years their relationship was often turbulent. Jones became annoyed with his father one time after his dad shot and killed his favourite dog. There was also a meeting involving Emanuel Steward and the Jones family, when Roy Jnr apparently ordered that his father's position be lessened. Steward felt particularly uncomfortable as he didn't want to steal a son from his father. As Roy's career really took off, his father was out of the picture.

After a twelve-year split and a great deal of animosity, Jones re-hired his father as part of the team. It was crunch time in Roy Jnr's dwindling career as he reached back to the man who had once provided security for him.

During a third fight with Antonio Tarver, there were arguments in the corner between Roy Snr and the long-time trainer Alton Merkerson. At one point they were trying to shove each other off the ring apron. Astonishingly, Jones claims that he made a conscious decision to lose that fight against Tarver, because he didn't want his dad to get any credit if he won! 'He would have got the glory,' said Roy. 'The critics would have said it was because of him. But where was he the last twelve years? I couldn't win that fight.'

Punishing stuff, and if it's true that he virtually threw a fight out of spite for his father, what warped relations they must have had, presumably stemming from something deep in the past. Jones claims that he was abused.

Floyd Mayweather Jnr talks of being knocked about at the hands of his father too. 'My dad used to beat me,' he said. 'It just gave me the motivation to take it out on my opponents. Life was hard. I used to share a room with seven family members. My mother [Deborah Sinclair] was a crack addict and used to steal Christmas presents for us. My father was just a hustler. I was the man of the house.'

Lil' Floyd is of course the son of Big Floyd and the nephew of Roger and Jeff. They have all been good fighters, but there is no question that Floyd Jnr's the best. In my opinion he's the finest fighter to have laced on the gloves since Sugar Ray Leonard. Floyd Snr couldn't get past Leonard when they met, and he ended with a record of 29–6–1. 'Jazzy' Jeff chalked up a 32–10–5 slate. The 'Black Mamba' Roger was the most success-ful of the three brothers, winning world titles in two weight divisions and finishing with a 59–13 record. Yet the brilliance of the son/nephew in winning world titles in five weight categories and continually increasing his undefeated tally puts Floyd Jnr in a league of his own. Has this led to competition, jealousy, anger, even wrath among a family who have all trodden similar paths? Wouldn't pride be a more common and natural feeling?

Family Mayweather seem dysfunctional at best. Nothing has ever been simple, and none of them is a saint. The two Floyds have had a rocky relationship, virtually since the day when the boy was just one and his daddy used him as a human shield when an uncle from his mother's side pulled a gun on him. Floyd Snr was subsequently shot in the leg. It's possible that subconsciously Floyd Snr somehow harbours a grudge against his son for that unsavoury incident. What is beyond question is that Floyd Snr taught Floyd Jnr much of his classy style of reflexes, shoulder rolls and speed.

Yet when Floyd Snr was jailed for drug trafficking in the early to mid-nineties, Uncle Roger assumed pretty much complete control of Lil' Floyd's corner. Floyd Snr was back at the helm briefly after his release, but a bust-up, during which Floyd Snr was basically kicked out of the house, meant that firstly Jeff and then Roger took over. The rifts between the two elder brothers then really began to rage. Floyd Jnr added fuel to the fire by saying that his 'Uncle Rog' was a more superior trainer than his dad.

As for father and son, it has been one long, sorry soap opera. I have been around the Mayweathers for the last fifteen years, and it really is one of the most complex yet idiotic situations. 'They're snakes, especially Roger,' Floyd Snr tells me on regular occasions. 'I really have no time for him. Everyone's aware that I taught Lil' Floyd everything he knows. I'm the innovator, motivator, creator.'

In a quiet moment of thought a while back, I remember Floyd Jnr telling me that his father 'always thinks he's bigger than the fighter'. That, he felt, was the real issue – one of self-importance. Floyd Snr's enormous ego certainly drives him on, and I've found he plays up to the camera almost obscenely at times. Despite the flashy suits, he seems so desperately insecure, so hopeful of instant recognition, more in love with himself and the idea of fame than with anyone or anything else.

One spring day in Vegas in 2009, after Ricky Hatton had trained in the lead-up to his match with Manny Pacquiao, I spent a couple of hours around Floyd Snr, and actually came out of it having warmed to him. He cuts quite a sorry figure these days, even when he's banging on constantly about the dollars he feels he missed out on. He coughs badly now too, because of his long-suffering fight with the lung disease sarcoidosis, and just seems at odds with most things. 'My son has got all the money,' he told me. 'Doesn't care about me. I gave him the gift. I am dying. I don't know if my son needs me. I don't need him. Got my eight grandchildren. I gotta do what I've gotta do. It's not about money, but look at him, and look at me. I'm his father.'

The Mayweather muddle can ramble on and on, and everyone has an opinion on them. For Ricky Hatton, 'this is a prime example that there are too many egos in boxing; they think they are all stars'. Joe Calzaghe believes that 'this obviously stems from real bitterness from when Floyd was a kid at home. Maybe he was just more talented, and his father couldn't handle that.' Joe's father Enzo goes further: 'Regarding the Mayweathers – it's total vanity. The father's trying to outshine his son. You must be humble. He's the polar opposite. Pathetic.'

Roger's no angel. He was sentenced to six months for smashing two of his son's grandmother's teeth. Then he was banned for a year from his nephew's corner, and fined $200,000 for causing mayhem in the ring at the end of the fight with Zab Judah. Roger has also been arrested on battery and strangulation charges against one of his female boxers.

Meanwhile, Floyd Jnr's brushes with the law have led to a ninety-day sentence, throwing away further months of his boxing career. Floyd Jnr's got his haters too; he's been criticized for being arrogant, irritable and obnoxious – particularly for the manner in which he tosses hundred-dollar bills into crowds, calls himself 'Money' and has a record company called 'Philthy Rich'. Maybe not the ideal humble image in our recession-hit world.

Surely the most outrageous Mayweather offering was that Floyd Snr was prepared to train Oscar De La Hoya to beat his son. That is just totally incomprehensible to most of us. 'How could he prosper financially for preparing someone to hurt his son? How distorted is that scenario?' asks Mayweather's former promoter Bob Arum.

Incidentally, I remember one diabolical instance in middle America where a father and son actually fought each other in the ring. Why oh why was that ever allowed? It just tears up every-thing about such a precious and special relationship. The least said about this obscure, appalling incident the better.

At the time when Floyd Snr was debating the possibility of plotting against his own son in the ring, he said, 'I'm going to train that old man [De La Hoya] to go and kick his [Floyd Jnr's] ass.' Nice. Fortunately, the Golden Boy showed sense. 'I just didn't feel comfortable with him training me against his son,' said De La Hoya. 'You just hate to see a father and son apart for so many years. Hopefully it will help bring the Mayweathers together.'

Recently, it does indeed seem like they have found some peace, or at least common ground. Maturity, especially on Floyd Jnr's side, has led to a thawing of the icy tension. For now. The quiet and often forgotten young Uncle Jeff told me, 'It was really nice when the four of us got round a table for dinner. That was a long time coming.'

'Time is a great healer,' added Floyd Jnr, who welcomed his father back into the camp following his short retirement.

Uncle Roger remains in charge of the team, and maybe that is the sensible and right outcome – leaving Floyd Snr to try to become a proper daddy. Roger and Floyd Snr are still a long way from being bosom buddies, but at least there's more tranquillity in the Mayweather household. Or so it seems.

Hiring uncles is a possible compromise in these training scenarios. I very much fill the 'uncle' role with my two brothers. They see me as a mentor, or supplemental figure – someone especially useful to help advise them on problems that maybe they don't feel as comfortable talking to our parents about. I am their inter-generational buffer.

'Uncles can work in boxing,' long-time British corner man Frank Hopkins told me. 'Even though I'm Tony Oakey's uncle, he's always been like a son. Dads can tell you off, and give you the right hump. Uncles can step in and say just calm it down as you don't want to upset your dad. Nicer job. That's why it works with Roger and Floyd. In boxing, fathers are almost always too hard or too soft.'

Some children can resent or even fear their father. An uncle doesn't expect as much, but values his nephew, and can give alternative advice and direction. For a while, this was the case with Miguel Cotto, another of the fighting idols from Puerto Rico. Some years ago, when Miguel was a young prospect, I visited his home in Caguas. We ran around the dusty roads of his city together at five a.m., and I remember Miguel telling me, 'Nothing is as important as the relationship between a father and son. For me, it's with my dad, Miguel Snr, and my son, Miguel Jnr.' Both ways. 'My dad has been the biggest influence on me,' Miguel continued, 'but in boxing terms, an uncle is good. It's a different relationship.'

For the early part of his career, Cotto was trained by his Uncle Evangelista. It was a solid and successful partnership, but cracks began to appear due to Evangelista's increased work with other fighters. A major disagreement followed, and Miguel admitted that the nephew-and-uncle relationship had been effectively over years before.

Cotto eventually replaced Evangelista with a non-family member in Joe Santiago (who ironically should have pulled Cotto out of his beating from Pacquiao in November 2009). The strain then turned to Cotto's own father. Miguel Snr was forced to choose between his brother and his son.

Miguel Snr stayed loyal to Miguel Jnr, and became very much part of Cotto's camp. He reiterated the words that the fighter had told me: 'There is no love like that of a father and son.'

Miguel Snr hoped that one day the family rift would be healed. Unfortunately he died suddenly in January 2010, at the age of fifty-seven. It would be good to see the Cotto family bonding fully again, if only for the memory of Miguel Snr.

Meanwhile, Miguel Cotto fought on, under the tutelage of Emanuel Steward, neither his father nor his uncle. Just a highly experienced trainer.

As we have seen, father-and-son relationships are often at their best with extremely gifted boxers. Your Mayweathers, Calzaghes and Trinidads don't come along every day. They have also been taken to the gym from a very early age. The kids are almost born into it, and with so much amateur pedigree behind them, there is a good chance of a rosy future for the family.

It's also true that, on the whole, these trainers have far less success with their other fighters (with the possible exception of Enzo Calzaghe), many of whom obviously come under the trainers' guidance much later than their own children. So does it need the natural talent of the son blended with the correct bond with the father for the partnership to gel?

The problems of father-and-son relationships seem to stem from the emotional bond; they also veer off track through greed and ego when the sons get to the top. The son might also feel that the father is not capable of advancing him to the highest level. Obsessed fathers can actually stunt their sons' growth, as they live their lives through them in a highly manipulative and selfish way. Then there are the hundreds of sons who try to follow in the footsteps of their famous fighting fathers. Sometimes it works; often it doesn't.

One successful younger family member was the two-weight world champion Cory Spinks, whose father Leon, of course, beat Muhammad Ali to become the wearer of the world heavyweight crown in only his eighth fight. Cory's uncle Michael was a wonderful two-weight world king too. The 'jinx' had most certainly passed through the generations. So much so that Leon III has now embarked on his professional career.

The former two-time world heavyweight champion Floyd Patterson handed down vast knowledge to his 'son'; the difference was that Tracy Harris Patterson was initially an orphan. Adopted, saved and trained by his 'dad' Floyd, the Pattersons marched to almost a hundred amateur wins and, later, the world super-bantamweight crown. However, a dispute in the corner about whether or not to pull Tracy out of his defence against Hector Acero-Sanchez in 1994 led to a bitter split between the two. Floyd was dismissed and was devastated. Once upon a time this had been a sentimental tale of the power of the human spirit, then all that was crushed through boxing egos. Floyd Patterson is the family member who's remembered today.

Occasionally, though, the fathers are upstaged by their sons. Lenny Mancini was a super pro, but an injury in World War Two prevented him achieving his dream of becoming a world champion. Lenny encouraged his son along though, and Ray 'Boom Boom' Mancini was a colourful ruler of the world lightweight division. Bill 'Dynamite' Douglas was a decent professional, but his son did even better. James 'Buster' Douglas scored that monumental upset over Mike Tyson to truly shock the world. Harold Johnson was the son of a good-class heavyweight, Phil, but he went on to become world light-heavyweight champion. (Incidentally, the great Jersey Joe Walcott claimed a quite amazing 'father and son' double over the Johnsons. In 1936, Walcott knocked out Phil Johnson in round three of their fight in Philadelphia; and in 1950, he dispatched Phil's son Harold in the same round, in the same city!) Guty Espadas and his son Guty Jnr both became world champions, while Jack and his son Brian London were crowned British heavyweight kings in different eras. But that's not often the case. Big things were expected from Ross Minter when he blazed on to the scene, turning pro in 2001. Britain's popular former world middleweight champion Alan Minter was convinced his son had the perfect genes. I like Ross, because he knew he wasn't nearly as talented as his father, but he worked very hard, and was always jovial on the scene. However, the harsh reality was that he was levels away from Alan, and he achieved very little. The latest I hear is that Ross is involved in the small hall boxing scene.

The pattern that tends to repeat through the generations is that the kids struggle to come out of the shadows, and to live up to the name and stature of their awesome fighting dads. Imagine the pressure when they also share the same name. So many do, from the legendary 'Hands of Stone' Roberto Duran and his son Roberto Jnr to those clown princes Jorge Paez and Hector Macho Camacho and their sons Jorge Jnr and Hector Jnr. There's the three-weight king Wilfredo Vazquez and Wilfredo Jnr; the heavyweight great Larry Holmes and Larry Jnr; and Buster Mathis Snr and Jnr. The list is long.

One of the finest Mexican boxers ever, Julio Cesar Chavez, has watched his son Julio Cesar Jnr become a world champion, despite not having nearly as much talent as his 'old man'. The wonderful 'Hitman' Tommy Hearns passed the torch on to son Ronald, but he hasn't exactly made a startling impression. The son of that exciting former world light-welterweight champion Aaron 'the Hawk' Pryor, Stephan, is now on the scene.

This can be another troubling dynamic, which might well lead to fractured relationships in the future. On the one hand, the son of a big-name fighter gets the notice and attention other prospects are not afforded. On the other hand, living up to the achievements of one's more notorious and usually more talented parent makes it extremely tough for boxing juniors.

Sometimes you wonder how much the sons actually want it. Did Marvis Frazier fight mainly to please his dad? Marvis used to wear the same robe as Joe. He was crushed by Larry Holmes and Mike Tyson, but Joe was still the proudest dad standing. How tough it must be, because it's not just in the genes, but in the blood and in the heart. So many try. Sons often want to emulate their fathers, but the father's responsibility is to provide for the son's future.

Two of our most famous fighters are very much still involved in this respect. Barry McGuigan was heavily against any of his children taking to the ring. My good friend and colleague in the studio was always telling me how adamant he was about that. That's probably why he's worked doggedly hard to give his four kids the best start in life. However, his son Shane has got the boxing bug, and has already excelled in the amateurs. I've seen how emotional Barry gets at ringside, even when he has only a loose interest in prospects.

So too one Christopher Eubank. The son of the original eccentric won the Nevada Golden Gloves in America, then his first professional fight in November 2011, so like Shane McGuigan he is getting a good grounding. It will be fascinating to see how the junior versions fare on their boxing journeys, and how much presence their totally contrasting fathers will have.

*

Boxing is a sport where, in some capacity, fathers will always be linked with their sons. Some fighters like having their fathers involved. There's no rigid right or wrong as to how or where that influence and help should best be directed. What is necessary is common sense to make calm decisions that best benefit a son, without smothering him. Splitting the roles of father and trainer, or even father and manager, might avoid splitting loyalty. Many boxing dads fail to identify the barriers between protection and proving how tough one's son is. Some sons yearn to do what their fathers have done before them, even if they have not been blessed with the same skills. Every situation is fraught with difficulties, but it can also be very rewarding when the connection's spot on.

Joe Calzaghe and Floyd Mayweather. The best fighters of their time. Both groomed by their fathers. Both single-minded. Both fiercely dedicated. Both with bundles of talent, and both proof that natural gifts ultimately prevail, because neither took on another trainer outside their family to improve them. That's where the similarities end. On one side of the Atlantic, there are egos and jealousy; on the other, there's unconditional love, and unflinching support.

The impact on fathers and sons in boxing together is deeper and more complicated than in any other sport. Often born out of convenience, it can become a habit. What of their home life, the father's status within that home? How tough are they? Can they accept the truth? Will they be blinkered by confidence, or are they secretly plagued by fear? How far will emotions become distorted?

Egocentric dads can be mixed with distant, rebellious sons. There are strange interactions; inner and pathological conflicts; levels of machismo and pride to negotiate. Will the father let the boy grow up, go out and live as a man? Will the father respect him as a man or just keep him as a son? Can the boy ever fully leave the father's protective embrace? Tony Tucker's dad Bob admitted that he never wanted his son to face Mike Tyson. Neither would most fathers – or for that matter sons!

Ultimately it must be a question of whether the professional relationship can benefit the boxing without impacting on the personal relationship. I have witnessed many fathers and sons fall out in boxing, and surely in most cases it is safer to say that if a father is involved, he shouldn't run the corner. It's not natural to be involved in these kinds of situations; but each individual's different. It depends, as I said, on strength of character, and one's arsenal of talent. I do, however, feel most strongly that fathers should be 100 per cent involved in the background. Promoters might disagree, but it is not their sons who are taking punches for pay.

The father-and-son team who are smiling every single time I see them are the Schwers, Billy Snr and Billy Jnr. They constantly remind me of all that is wonderful about this particular relationship. Billy Snr was an Irish amateur champion who could so easily have trained his son and immersed himself in the quest for glory. But he left the coaching to Jack Lindsay while remaining a major support, set back, out of the limelight. The likeable Luton lightweight Billy Jnr narrowly missed out on world honours, but the Schwers remain popular within the boxing community because their relationship was infinitely more important than any prizes won. The way it should be.

So, lately, more fighters are choosing – or in several cases are forced – to have serious paternal involvement. It is spreading to the promoters too. Frank Warren was hugely against his children even going into boxing promoting, let alone the ring itself. Francis and George are, however, determined to continue the dynasty, leaving Frank to say, 'I wish they didn't want to do it. But it's their choice, and I will support them. At least I can trust them. The only people I probably can fully trust in boxing!'

Likewise, Eddie Hearn has got the boxing bug. Badly. The young, dynamic son of the entrepreneur and long-time sports tycoon Barry has relit the pugilistic fires at Matchroom headquarters with his natural enthusiasm and passion. It's obviously in the genes, and we welcome the new generation, the new blood. Will they be as successful as their fathers? Could there be some 'in-house' competition? Will it even work? Carl King, for instance, hardly had the flair and extraordinary personality his father Don had, and never looked at ease in the spotlight. At least these senior promoters know that though their sons are always in danger of getting outsmarted and done over in the complicated financial world of boxing, they certainly won't be getting knocked out in the ring any time soon. That will allow them to sleep easier at night.

I have always been close to my dad, but I never had any intention of following him into the retail world. The closest I came was a summer spent sorting out children's clothes in Marks and Spencer's flagship store in London's Marble Arch for holiday money. So although my father expected good things of me, and drilled home tough and important messages, there was never going to be fractious rivalry between us in terms of my desire to enter broadcasting.

From early fear, to total respect, to great friendship. My dad always knows best. Yet only since becoming a father to a son myself can I really understand some of the deep emotions involved.

Oscar is nearly five. How would I feel if he wanted to follow me into the world of boxing? Moreover, what if he even chose to lace the gloves on? I'd be horrified probably; it would certainly give me a serious quandary. Much as I would want to teach him the discipline and fitness benefits boxing has to offer, how could I be in his corner? My son would, as ever, receive unconditional support, but I would most certainly leave the training to the experts. I guess I'm lucky that although Lil' Oscar throws the odd left hook, and at the moment he has more interest in watching his sister Jessamy at ballet than in talking to me about boxing.

Saying that, though, James DeGale started off at the Barbara Speake stage school in Acton, just two minutes from our home, and guess what he really loved doing as a child?

Yup, ballet.

Three

BROTHERS IN ARMS

7

Heavyweights from the East

Reginald Kray: seven fights, seven wins, two knockouts, no defeats. Ronald Kray: six fights, four wins, four knockouts, two losses. Inked in the boxing annals for ever.

The most notorious brothers of all began their journey as professional fighters. Many might not know that today. Yet their time in boxing was cut dramatically short due to the dark temptations of the underworld.

What might have been? Why aren't we celebrating the achievements of two talented boxing brothers instead of remembering perhaps the most famous criminals of all? For when they were young, there were only two career paths the twins wanted to follow: they vowed to be either villains or boxers.

Ronnie and Reggie Kray, of course, went on to terrorize London's East End in the 1950s and 1960s as perpetrators of organized crime, from armed robberies and protection rackets to cold-blooded murder. Despite their atrocities and uncontrolled violence, the Krays were highly respected and mixed with global celebrities from Frank Sinatra to Judy Garland. They were recognized as cult figures who frightened yet lit up London.

It could all have been very different. Throughout history,

boxing has saved many young terrors on the streets who were rapidly heading for a career in crime. Maybe these two were just always going to be beyond guidance and help. Fighting was very much a way of life in the early to mid-twentieth century, deep-rooted within the rough-and-tumble, poverty-stricken East End. Furthermore, boxing was engrained in the Kray family. Both of the Krays' grandfathers had been celebrated local fighters. 'Mad Jimmy' Kray was a hard and vicious brawler, while Jimmy 'Cannonball' Lee was a famous East End boxer and quite a character. One of his party tricks was apparently to put a white-hot poker on his tongue for as long as possible. Cannonball won plenty of shillings from his bare-knuckle fights on Sunday mornings and used to recount the tales to the twins. He became known locally as the 'Eastern Southpaw', and if his left hook landed, it would be good night, God bless. Ronnie and Reggie were fascinated.

Also, Cannonball's daughter, Aunt Rose, was one of the meanest and scariest female fighters in Whitechapel. She had a big influence on Ronnie and Reggie; it was she and Cannonball who taught the brothers how to fight. They were taken to the Robert Browning youth club and were passed around the amateur scene, even spending time at the infamous Repton Boys Club.

It was in the boxing booths that Ronnie and Reggie really earned their reputation. A travelling fair once came to Bethnal Green, and the twins stepped up. They fought each other with ferocious intensity for seven shillings and sixpence. Elated with their winnings, the boys now believed they were proper prize-fighters. This adoration of combat developed swiftly into brutal wars with various gangs. Ronnie and Reggie loved to fight with anybody and soon became known as the hardest teenagers on the streets. With them, too, it meant double trouble.

Cannonball continued to try to steer them towards boxing, and the twins' elder brother Charlie was setting something of an example. He won eleven of his eighteen professional fights, and this seemed the right path to follow. Ronnie and Reggie worked hard in the gym and loved the excitement of the ring, proud too that they were following a family tradition. Both became school-boy champions in Hackney. Ronnie won the London Junior championship, but it was Reggie who exhibited more talent and went on to the final of the Great Britain championship. Charlie once said, 'As boxers, the twins were quite different from each other. Reggie was the cool one with all the skills of a potential champion, and importantly, he always listened to advice. Ronnie was a good boxer too, and very brave. But he would never listen to advice, and had a mind of his own. Unlike Reggie he would never hold back, and would go on and on until he dropped.'

They made an impressive start to their professional careers, rattling off victories at traditional smoky venues like The Arena, Mile End, Lime Grove Baths and Manor Place Baths. Boxing people firmly believed that while Ronnie was hard and ruthless, the unbeaten Reggie already looked like an experienced boxer and was a champion in the making. Ronnie was increasingly worried that he would lose his twin down another road. He was fiercely dependent on the support and outlet Reggie offered him.

Two things happened at that time. First, the brothers were involved in a nasty brawl outside a club in Walthamstow and were shopped to the police. Professionals weren't allowed to fight outside the ring, and Reggie had his licence withdrawn. His welterweight dreams appeared over before they'd begun. Then in March 1952 Ronnie and Reggie were called up for National Service, and were assigned to the Royal Fusiliers. They were always in trouble, deserted several times, found themselves constantly thrown into the glasshouse, and after more outrageous actions were dishonourably discharged. This meant they could no longer box, so the twins turned to crime, beginning by running protection rackets out of run-down snooker halls and nightclubs. Later, arson, robbery and murder were the Krays' game.

Although Ronnie and Reggie were very close, they would often row and scrap toe-to-toe with each other, before kissing and making up. You see, they never lost their ability to fight, and ultimately battled and killed as one in their working lives.

Professional boxing could have been an escape from that world of crime. It was such a shame, as they obviously loved the drama of the ring. Yet they were tempted and lured into an altogether more dramatic and devastating scene.

Ronnie and Reggie weren't quite boxing brothers in arms, but they were, literally, always, brothers in arms.

Brothers enjoy a unique bond. A closeness, a warmth, a loyalty. They can talk regularly, or speak rarely, but there is often a natural comfort and understanding between two brothers. Elders can tease their youngers, but there is usually a cocoon of protection that will then develop into a lifelong friendship. From childhood to adulthood, these boys have been through it all together. There is an escapist element with brothers too; they find solace in each other away from parental interference.

Sibling relationships can survive the passing of parents, outlast marriages, and offer companionship through the waves of emotional turmoil that life dishes up. On the flip side, there is a far more intensive rivalry with brothers. Adolescent boys fight to get attention, and there can be bad moments. Relationships with the opposite sex in particular can cause stress and jealousy. Another issue is favouritism, by parents and grandparents, uncles and aunts. It can be a natural tendency, depending on the way different humans identify with different people, but it is up to the parents to love equally. Brothers need to be treated as individuals and to be shown a unique affection. The more confident each feels, the less jealous he will be of a sibling who on the surface might appear better-looking, brighter, more athletic and more sociable.

All these problems tend to lessen over time. Most siblings have a deeper relationship with each other later in life. I have read that at least 80 per cent of people over the age of sixty describe themselves as enjoying close ties with their siblings.

Brothers tend to have plenty in common. It's just different having a sister. Brothers tend to adore competition; they constantly try to gain the upper hand, even in jest. Yet as much as they want to beat each other, they are also always there for each other, often providing unconditional support, especially when the chips are down and times are rough. Every family has issues to overcome; every fighter must endure obstacles through his career. It sometimes makes things a little less painful if there's more than one of you tackling the same thing.

Brothers are littered through sporting history, from football and rugby to motor-racing and cricket. In all sports this is a result of parental direction, genetic talent, a love of following in each other's footsteps, simmering rivalries. If Jamie Murray hadn't liked tennis, for instance, it's possible that younger brother Andy would never have pursued his chosen career path, and become one of the finest singles players in the world. Jamie has seemed content to be a top exponent of men's doubles, while leaving his moodier yet more talented sibling to power towards the highest echelons of a notoriously tough sport.

The Murrays may have had an intensive rivalry as junior players, but the Bryan brothers, identical twins Bob and Mike, were forbidden to play against each other in competitive matches. Just imagine how tough it is for the Williams sisters to meet, as they often have, in the final at Wimbledon. The Bryans are now number one in the doubles world, and they are virtually inseparable. Same school. Same university. Same fraternity. You name it. They come as a complete unit; one brother can't exist on court without the other, and they have always said that there is a better chemistry and more family pride because they are twins. They even celebrate winning points by chest-bumping each other.

Yet boxing surely draws brothers closer than any other sport. Passion, dedication, determination, love – all are made more intense through the joy and pain the pugilistic world can dish up in rampaging measures.

One of my favourite songs is 'Blood Brothers' by Bruce Springsteen.

> We got our own roads to ride and chances we gotta take.
> We stood side by side, each one fightin' for the other.
> We said until we died we'd always be blood brothers.

I love these lyrics. When I was constructing a music preview piece for Sky some years ago, I thought these would be the ideal words to accompany the outstanding boxing brothers who may well go down as the most successful in the history of boxing.

Vitali and Wladimir Klitschko are the first brothers to hold world heavyweight championship belts at the same time. Heroes in Eastern Europe, the Klitschkos are imposing physical specimens, elite athletes, ideal role models and excellent ambassadors – not just for boxing, but for sport in general. They epitomize virtually everything that is good about the fight game – and that is possibly the highest praise one can bestow on the pair.

Vitalii Volodymyrovych Klychko was born in the old Soviet republic of Kirghizstan in 1971 and Volodymyr Volodymyrovych Klychko in Kazakhstan in 1976, and they came from a combined military and educational background: their father Vladimir Rodionovich Klitschko was a colonel in the Soviet Air Force, and their mother, Nadezhda Ulyanovna, was a teacher.

The Klitschkos settled in Ukraine, where they were both stand-out amateurs. Vitali was initially a successful kick-boxer – a six-time world champion, no less – but he also managed to compile a boxing record of 195–15 with eighty KOs, and struck silver in the worlds. However, it was Wladimir who really caught the eye. With a slate of 134–6, the younger brother was generally regarded as being the more skilled of the pair, and achieved the ultimate amateur accolade when he took the super-heavyweight gold at the Atlanta Olympics in 1996.

At Sky, we have followed both of their careers since they turned professional, side by side, on 16 November that year. Today they stand together as a core part of what we do. Their universal charm and natural grace even won over British fight fans in the build-up to the crucial clash between Wladimir and David Haye. The Klitschkos conducted themselves with utter professionalism throughout. English may only be their third language, but boy can they laugh at each other, and at others, with a wonderful understanding of our language and even the nuances. They are unique. They really are. And we should all enjoy them while they are reigning over the heavyweight world.

I came across 'the brothers' fairly early on in their profes-sional rise, Wladimir first. Both of the Ukrainian giants have long been based in Germany, where boxing is a far bigger sport and the promotional ties are far stronger than back in their homeland. The intelligent, multilingual Klitschkos slotted right in. Vitali has even been rewarded with the Federal Cross of Merit – Germany's highest award.

In September 1998, I was sent to a rather dark, pretty depressing part of the Rhine-Ruhr valley, to a place called Oberhausen. I hate to say it, but shooting GVs (general views) around town made me think of the gloomy surroundings in that classic modern movie *Schindler's List*. The Sky cameras were in this industrial heartland to see how Britain's Mark Prince would fare in his world title crack against the superb light-heavyweight king of the period Dariusz Michalczewski. Mark had travelled with the smallest entourage one could ever find in boxing: he spent the week in Oberhausen with just his trainer, Carley Carew. Mark didn't even have an overcoat, and it was absolutely freezing out there. I ended up lending him my Sky Sports jacket!

Unfortunately nothing was of any great assistance to Prince that week, and he was beaten for the very first time, outclassed in eight rounds by a formidable champion. It was a shame for British boxing really because Mark Prince was a rather eccentric and fascinating guy. It was also the beginning of a story that was to end in more family horror. Allow me to digress briefly.

Mark's son Kiyan was on the books of QPR. An aspiring teenage footballer with the world at his feet, Kiyan was nicknamed 'The Bullet', and some likened him to Wayne Rooney. Yet Kiyan fell victim to a horrific attack with a pen-knife, while intervening to prevent the bullying of another boy. Tragically, the wound Kiyan suffered on 18 May 2006 was fatal.

Mark was told the news by his daughter, the eldest of his five children, and his world of course changed for ever. This was now by far his toughest fight. After hearing his son say 'Please don't let me die', Mark confessed, he had dreadful panic attacks and then felt a desire to 'destroy' the guilty lad in question, 'to hurt him with every ounce of power in my body'.

How does one come to terms with such a waste of human life, particularly a family member, killed in such a cold and calcu-lated way?

Despite suffering from constant emotional and mental pain, Mark Prince has since set up the Kiyan Prince Foundation to 'educate the youth against gang and knife culture, so they can be aware of the consequences of carrying and using knives, and the effect it has on the communities they live in'. Mark's focus is entirely on his family and his work for the Mobile Intervention

Team, which travels into areas where gang activity is rife. Mark also started the 'Put the Knives and Guns Down' campaign and has become an important spokesman against crime, as he passionately explained to Johnny Nelson and me when he came on to *Ringside*.

In quiet moments of reflection, I'm sure Mark wonders whether Kiyan could have become the next Rooney, or Jack Wilshere, or even if, like many other teenagers before him, he'd've elected to swap football for boxing. Follow his idol, dad Mark, by lacing up the gloves. How cruel that Kiyan was taken away without anyone actually knowing what would have happened if he'd had the opportunity to hone his talent. It makes of Mark Prince's long, painful fighting path to provide a better life for his son such a terrible waste.

I have been in many bad places during my long boxing journey, but this has to be one of the saddest chapters. However brave one is in the boxing ring, street bullies and shameful cowards can extinguish everything.

Let us return to the Klitschkos. For deep on that German undercard we found early evidence of how close and tight-knit the brothers are. The spotlight was on Wladimir, then one of the most exciting prospects in world boxing. As he climbed into the ring to face Nashville's hard-hitting journeyman Steve 'Storm' Pannell, I remember thinking how enormous this man was.

In many ways, this was our first introduction to the new age of colossal Eastern European giants who were about to change the guard in the glamour division, with the rather antiquated American heavyweight scene fast fizzling out.

Yet Klitschko was decked heavily in the very first round. He fell right in front of me at ringside, and I couldn't believe the force of it. Cries of 'Timber!' and 'He fell like a big oak tree!' have long been clichés associated with boxing. Well, this was as close as you can get to that. What surprised me even more was the fact that Wladimir got up. And rapidly knocked Pannell out.

Quick, exciting and memorable. Yes, his chin had been badly exposed, but I went away thinking that even though he looked rather robotic, this type of heavyweight had a decent heart and that crucial will to win. Critics began writing Wladimir Klitschko off. I felt that he'd show the kind of courage and commitment that might take him far.

I have always found the Klitschkos to be accessible; then it was even easier. I went backstage and peeked through the door of their dressing-room, which was slightly ajar. The brothers were embracing. They were having a quiet moment to themselves after the short, savage battle, and even as an outsider, one could feel the love between them.

I watched and waited. Sometimes, moments both inside and outside the ring are captured in silence. Not often of course, but here was one. The image engrained for ever. Fighting each other's corners.

You see, that is really how the Klitschkos have run their parallel careers. One performing under the lights, the other attempting to coolly observe his brother from ringside, working in the corner. I say 'coolly', because that is how it appears on the surface. Watching Vitali's reactions in the long build-up to Wladimir's battle with David Haye made me realize how each brother would die for the other. Vitali was quietly seething, and I'm not sure that anger would have been kept inside if, for example, he had stumbled across Mr Haye down a dark alley.

Vitali is older, steely, and certainly more ferocious. There is more to worry about when Vitali's blood is boiling. Wladimir is laid-back, approachable and easy-going, although his nerves of steel were really tested when Dereck Chisora disgustingly spat water in his face before that challenge to Vitali in February 2012. But of course Wladimir can turn it on in the ring, whenever he needs to. Both know and understand the game. With growing maturity, the Klitschkos are a real pleasure to be around. Critics rarely select a favourite. They see them 'together', flipping off each other, supporting each other – delivering the art of the sweet science.

After Vitali had won his first twenty-seven, Chris Byrd inflicted on him his first ever defeat. Just months later, Wladimir exacted revenge for his brother by beating Byrd. The favour was returned by big brother Vitali when he stopped South Africa's Corrie Sanders after the sharp-shooting southpaw had blown away Wladimir in one of the biggest heavyweight upsets we've seen on Sky.

In June 1999, the Klitschkos pitched up in London, and this time it was Vitali's turn to show us his credentials, as he challenged our moody but talented little heavyweight Herbie Hide. Vitali had already taken out British opposition in the shape of Julius Francis, a likeable domestic fighter most famous for having the soles of his boots sponsored the night he took on Mike Tyson. Safe to say it was an advertising coup, with five 'product' flashes in two ridiculously one-sided rounds.

Now the European champion, Klitschko stepped up and on to the world stage. He duly dispatched a poor, wide-eyed Hide in two ruthless rounds. Many of my colleagues had little time for the notoriously difficult Norwich heavyweight, and there was a feeling that Britain almost adopted the Klitschkos that night. Certainly Vitali, and then the more gregarious Wladimir, who returned in July 2000 to take on Monte 'Two Gunz' Barrett on the big Lennox Lewis–Frans Botha show in the capital.

Here were two forces of nature, but also two of the most down-to-earth sportsmen one could meet. In addition to their language skills, both had mastered chess, even playing simultaneously against the greatest of them all, Garry Kasparov. Vitali is also a friend of another world champion, Vladimir Kramnik, although he admits he can't quite get the better of him on the board.

I have long had a passion for chess as well as for boxing, and strategic planning and out-manoeuvring one's opponent, step by step, is how the Klitschkos think. They have similar qualities, and in many ways similar fighting styles: technical, tactical, upright, even mechanical. The long orthodox jab, overhand right and even short uppercut are the Klitschkos' most potent weapons. Most of their fights follow a familiar pattern; they know what they can do, and they are thoroughly effective at carrying out a plan once in control of the ring. Their physical stature and their ring smarts – their craftsmanship – are obviously vital to measuring distance and inflicting the necessary punishment to notch up another victory. Vitali is known as 'Dr Ironfist', is 6ft 7½in, and has a reach of eighty inches; Wladimir is 'Dr Steelhammer' and is 6ft 6 ½in with an eighty-one-inch reach.

Yet, as I was to find out, the brothers are certainly not clones. They have both long had their strengths and their weaknesses in the ring. In boxing terms, Vitali is the more dependable, consistent, rugged and sturdy; powerful, but at times slow and hittable. Whatever his limitations in fluency, though, Vitali does still boast the highest knockout percentage (94 per cent) of any heavyweight champion in total fights. Pretty impressive. Wladimir's the flashy slickster, with better ring movement, but his vulnerability is far more glaring than his brother's. A brittle chin can be the Achilles heel in so many fighting generals. Wladimir Klitschko has been floored eleven times, and stopped on three occasions. Vitali has only ever lost on account of injuries.

They may be the tightest of 'blood brothers', but they also possess different make-ups in terms of character and personality. Vitali, who idolizes the 1930s world heavyweight champion Max Schmeling, is the more serious, and in many ways the calmer and more settled brother. Almost five years older than

Wladimir, he's married to former athlete Natalia Egorova, with whom he has three children: Yegor-Daniel, Elizabeth-Victoria and Max. Vitali is quiet, mature and sensible, although he can be a touch volatile if provoked. He has campaigned to be the mayor of Kiev, and in April 2010 he became the leader of the Ukrainian Democratic Alliance for Reform. Wladimir is far more of a 'celebrity'. He loves the high-flying lifestyle, and once told me that David Beckham is one of his friends. From movie acting (*Ocean's Eleven*) to music videos, from kite-surfing to pro-am golf, Wladimir has a wide range of interests and oozes charisma. He was also dating American actress and model Hayden Panettiere until recently.

The Klitschkos often frequent Los Angeles, and we had the luxury of some time with them in 2003, just as Vitali accepted a massive fight with Lennox Lewis at less than two weeks' notice. Both brothers were in camp.

Their state-of-the art gym was a far cry from some of the run-down tin-shacks we have witnessed over the years. It was hardly the 'Badlands' of Philadelphia, the dusty back streets amid the Mexican haciendas, or even that crumbling old relic in the Welsh valleys where the Calzaghes mastered their trade. My cameraman Cainey got a shot of me sandwiched between the gigantic pair. Then I interviewed them, Vitali first. Both opened up about their unique bond.

'We are the closest brothers can be,' Vitali told me. 'I will do anything for Wladimir. He is my little brother and I was always encouraged to protect him. That is the way our parents brought us up. Not that he needs much protection now!'

'Who's the better fighter?' I asked.

'Oh, Wladimir. Without question.'

I turned to Wladimir. 'Which one of you is the better fighter?'

'Vitali, no question,' Wladimir replied. 'He is much more superior, and he is a very big puncher!'

Wladimir was far more outspoken and revealing, reminiscing about the time when they used to spar together, and how he never wanted to hurt his brother. All the way through the interview I was impressed by the overwhelming importance of family above any sport or competition.

'Fight fans love mythical fights,' I said to Wladimir. 'Is there any chance that you and your brother will ever meet for real in the ring? Some people are saying that would be the most incredible match in boxing history.'

Wladimir flashed that smile. 'Our mother would, of course, not be so happy, and we can't have that. She is very small, but she would put us both over her knees! No, being brothers is special. Particularly doing the same business. We will never fight. But we will always be there, in the ring with each other, until that bell goes, and immediately afterwards.'

Smashing guys, they really are.

Commentating on their fights, though, has not always produced the most dramatic evenings of our lives. The ceasefire between Wladimir and Sultan Ibragimov in New York, for which my father paid hundreds of dollars, springs to mind; he said to me afterwards: 'Does one have to hit one's opponent in boxing in order to get paid?' So does Vitali's one-sided schooling of the dreadfully negative Kevin Johnson in Switzerland. At least we were in Bern, one of the most beautiful European cities, at Christmas time.

Still, this is what they are all about. Successful, exceptional sportsmen who often adopt safety-first tactics and virtually always win. Thousands turn out to see them, and it is a real family atmosphere – music, entertainment, food, and a sporting event to remember. When Wladimir stopped Ruslan Chagaev in June 2010, more than sixty thousand fans crammed into the Veltins-Arena in Gelsenkirchen. It was claimed to be the biggest indoor attendance ever for a fight in Europe.

The Klitschkos are a commodity, a delightful double act. With one comes the other. They are cult heroes in Eastern Europe, and the enormous amounts of charity and humanitarian work they perform through the UN is extraordinary, especially supporting the needs of underprivileged children in Africa and South America. The brothers also spend a lot of time educating youngsters in the ways of sport and physical education. They always seem to be in superb condition.

The Klitschkos are classy. It was a pleasure – a highlight, really – to welcome Wladimir on to the set of *Ringside* in autumn 2010. My colleague Johnny Nelson and I were spellbound. Rarely do you see a fighter of Wladimir's standing talk so openly and intelligently about boxing, life and the universe – and in English.

Once more Wladimir reiterated to us his love of family, his idolizing of his big brother, and his hope that their work can bring help to millions of troubled children. 'Vitali and I try to make a difference,' he told us. 'We are very grounded – although I live on a plane! And Vitali is the better fighter. He's more natural. He would beat me in the ring. It would be scary to take him on.'

When we asked him about 'dream' fights against the likes of Joe Louis, Muhammad Ali and other heavyweight greats from varying eras, he refused to be drawn in.

'Ali, Holyfield – these guys were our idols. I would never like to have fought them. Different times. I looked up to them so much.'

Wladimir's got a great sense of humour too. As we heaped praise upon arguably the leading heavyweight of the last decade, he retorted, 'Don't blow smoke up my arse!'

The major issue that has riled both Wladimir and Vitali is the behaviour of certain English fighters like David Haye. Now, the Hayemaker is a charismatic, personable guy himself, but he has constantly wound up the Klitschko brothers with his trash-talking. Wearing T-shirts featuring their dismembered heads was treated with utter disdain by the Klitschkos, who said that they were 'embarrassed that such a man is involved in our wonderful sport'.

They needed Haye of course, for their dream to hold all four world governing belts (WBC, WBA, IBF and WBO) at the same time. Politics almost prevented this showdown from happening, causing several delays, until finally the date of 2 July 2011 was set for the crunch confrontation. Johnny Nelson and I had even pushed Haye hard on a Sky *Ringside Special* in his Miami training base, asking him to consider 46, 47, 48 per cent of the pot, not just a fifty-fifty split, to try and make the mega-match happen.

Finally, sense prevailed, the match was fifty-fifty, and we quickly found out that the brothers retained their near invincibility in this generation. Haye was simply schooled by Wladimir Klitschko, but he wasn't knocked out. Some expect Vitali to try and line up for more Haye bashing, despite David's promise to stay retired after his thirty-first birthday on 13 October 2011. In boxing, though, you quickly learn that never does not necessarily mean never. After all, Vitali retired for four years – following that demolition of our own, very brave, Danny Williams – before coming back at the age of thirty-seven. David is a two-weight world champion with bags full of gold, but is he ready to sail into the boxing sunset just yet?

Despite the sogginess of that night in Hamburg, the fans turned up at the Imtech Arena in their droves. Wladimir once again executed a perfect game-plan to defuse the negative Haye and make a mockery of all the Londoner's pre-fight boasts and threats. The Ukrainian giant was exceptional, and even tried to help educate David at the post-fight press conference by pleading with him not to reveal that broken baby toe as an excuse.

The brothers did not like, or have time for, Haye's practical jokes and games. Those shirts with the severed heads on and the constant threats to 'decapitate Wladimir and send him to the hospital' were, according to them, 'way, way below the belt'. In Haye's defence, he obviously intended to wind Klitschko up so he would engage, but then there is a line that some don't feel it's right to cross.

'Imagine how your mother would feel, Johnny,' Wladimir told my *Ringside* co-presenter when the brothers visited the new state-of-the-art Sky Studios in west London shortly after the fight. 'Boxing is a sport of gentlemen. Family honour is vital, and the way we conduct ourselves as fighters, especially world heavyweight champions, is hugely important as role models to children who follow the sport.'

The brothers though are still cheeky, bright and infectious to be around.

'What did you make of the toe?' I asked Vitali.

'If it is the big toe, maybe one would just about understand,' he replied. 'The next biggest toe, er, OK. The middle toe . . . mmm. But the little toe, no. Just a big no. What was he thinking, the sore loser? Brother, I am so happy you beat David. But he angered me very much. I would like to fight him and put him to the floor.'

Vitali concluded by saying the only person who could hold his treasured WBC belt was his brother. Total love and respect, and that came largely from excellent parenting. Unfortunately, just two days after the interview the brothers lost their father. I never met Klitschko Snr, but he was obviously a fairly impressive individual.

The Klitschkos have been a double dose of trouble for almost all their opponents over the last fifteen years. Yes, the Americans might find them dull and predictable, but they are articulate sporting marvels who are, in truth, pure winners.

The image I always have in my mind is one fighting and the

other cheering his brother on. It doesn't really matter who is performing which role, for then they swap. And back again. While different languages are spoken in the corner, the two of them choose to converse in Russian. This takes them back to their childhood.

In March 2011, a trip to Cologne provided me with another indelible memory of the Klitschkos, even if again it hardly gave us one of those memorable heavyweight nights. The once-brilliant Cuban amateur Odlanier Solis continued to prove something of a professional flop, his body, after years of fluctuating weight and conditioning, failing after just three minutes on his biggest boxing night. One Vitali Klitschko right hand to the temple, one awkward fall, and Solis was dazed, confused and in agony from a serious knee injury.

What does stand out is the image of Wladimir sprinting to get into the ring both to celebrate with his brother and at the same time restrain him from venting anger on his beaten foe after Solis's all-too-easy capitulation. The interview conducted afterwards saw the two brothers laughing and joking, utterly comfortable with each other. Wladimir even suggested to David Haye that he 'was the weakest brother' and therefore the one to take! These precious moments demonstrate the unconditional nature of their brotherhood.

Critics will continue to dream of the two meeting in the ring. But remember, their mother would 'not be so happy'. And now their father is gone, it is the last thing they will do.

Let's just enjoy them. Despite some of their fights lacking gut-wrenching excitement, we will miss the towering Klitschkos when they go.

It is rare, you see, to have two brothers who are equally successful in the ring, with no hint of jealousy or bitterness.

8

Clans and Dynasties

Along with the Klitschkos, the Marquez brothers have been the stand-out siblings of my time in boxing. Like Vitali and Wladimir, Juan Manuel and Rafael are close and have enjoyed their own successes while sharing their joy.

I have got to know Juan Manuel well over the years, ever since he was chasing down Naseem Hamed; Rafael less so, but I admired his punching power and fierce will to win as he captured world titles at bantamweight and super-bantamweight, and endured those four thrilling seesaw fights with Israel Vazquez. It really was 'Once and Four All!'

As with the Klitschkos, the younger brother again has tended to fight and live with more carefree abandon. The elder, Juan Manuel, is more stable. Meticulous attention to detail remains so important for him within the ring.

Juan Manuel has been a sublime exponent of fabulous counter-punching skills. Defensively tight, he's virtually controlled the pace and feel of every championship fight he has competed in – except that wide, predictable points defeat to the sensational Floyd Mayweather, who while the most technically gifted fighter of my time in the sport also had a rather unhealthy weight advantage thrown into the mix.

Take nothing away from Juan Manuel Marquez though; his ease, bright smile and dogged determination to master correct English for his interviews won me over long ago. JM has given us supreme performances against fellow modern legends like Mexican rival Marco Antonio Barrera and Manny Pacquiao, especially their first encounter when he picked himself up off the floor an astonishing three times in the first round to fight out a twelve-round draw he can count himself particularly unlucky not to have won. Marquez and Pacquiao met to conclude their trilogy in November 2011 and the result, another points decision, was equally controversial. The scorecards of the three fights read Draw, Pacquiao, Pacquiao; I had it as Marquez, Marquez, Marquez. In my opinion, the Mexican has always had the Filipino's number.

In the spring of 2009 I took a trip to Mexico City to visit the Marquez brothers. In the sprawling metropolis of the world's third largest city I found their gym on the rough east side, where the streets are numbered but not named. Their place of work was sandwiched between the dusty Iztacalco and Iztapalapa *delegaciónes* (boroughs) of the city.

Juan Manuel and Rafael had grown up in very poor and extremely dangerous surroundings. Along with their six other siblings they slept on the floor or shared two tiny beds. Their father fought, and used to teach the two boys the art of the jab and of throwing hooks on pillows. When one split, another would be found.

'My first boxing memory was when I was eight. By the time I was thirteen, I was boxing in amateur tournaments,' Juan Manuel began to explain when we had a little time off camera in the office of his boxing headquarters, where famed Mexican trainer Ignacio 'Nacho' Beristain is based. He is a wise old man.

A touch grizzled. Certainly hardened. And a man whose English is limited.

Through a translator, Beristain added, 'When I first saw Juan Manuel and Rafael, they were little more than scrawny kids. But they listened. And they had talent.'

Of the twenty champions Beristain has trained – including his three Hall of Famers, Ricardo Lopez, Humberto Gonzalez and Daniel Zaragoza – he has a soft spot for the Marquez brothers. 'They had natural combinations and real ringcraft. You can't really teach that. I just nurtured them and refined their fighting styles. Intelligence is the word I would use.'

Juan Manuel is a clever man. He trained as an accountant and worked for the Mexican government. He boxes with brains. He's also gentle and modest. 'Rafael was never far behind me when we were young,' he told me. 'And he had the knockout power I could only dream of. He was better than me. Maybe he liked my skills. But his punches hurt so much. Drugs and deaths on the streets were part of an everyday occurrence for our family to deal with. Boxing saved us – that was our answer.'

Rafael then entered the office. I didn't want my chat with JM to end, but he put an arm around his brother, as if to say – it's time to work. The pair moved into another room which was heaving with gym members, gym rats, a media scrum, call them what you will. Hundreds packed into this tiny, sweltering sweat-shop to see the brothers at work.

They entered the ring and began shadow boxing. I was just inches away and I watched in awe as they went about their train-ing regimes with concentration and utter commitment. Like a duet. Almost in time with each other, so many years had they prepared side by side for battle.

If their talents had been moulded into one fighter, I thought to myself, we would have had one of the all-time greats. Even as separate athletes they had managed to conquer the boxing world.

Juan Manuel might be my favourite. As a person and as a fighter. I bet there are many who'll happily sit in the Rafael camp. Together they currently share an amazing ninety-three professional wins between them, seventy-five by knockout. And in this day and age, that's extraordinary.

Synergy. Symmetry. Sweetest science. All from the shady streets around the borders of Iztacalco and Iztapalapa. And all side by side.

Kids who mess around in playful physical games can easily develop them into full-blooded physical confrontations. Mass boxing clans have appeared around the world, sometimes with as many as eight or nine brothers claiming to fight in some capacity. Take the six Australian Aborigine Sands brothers. Safety in numbers, maybe, within the loneliest sport there is.

Every country seems to have had its own brand of boxing brothers over the years. The United States lead the way. Many you will have heard of, some you may not have. Mike and Tommy Gibbons ruled the roost in the 1910s and 1920s, and were Minnesota's favourite boxing sons. Mike, known as the 'Saint Paul Phantom', fought the cream of the welterweights and middleweights, beating the likes of Harry Greb, Battling Ortega and the exceptional Ted 'Kid' Lewis. Younger brother Tommy was a quick-fisted genius rather like Mike who also got the better of Harry Greb, and the brilliant Georges Carpentier; he was also the only boxer to take Jack Dempsey to fifteen rounds. After that world heavyweight clash which virtually bankrupted Shelby, Montana in 1923, Dempsey was heard to say, 'Nailing him was like trying to thread a needle in a high wind.'

Twins Jack and Mike Sullivan boxed in the 1900s, and their brother Dan was a very decent amateur. Max and Buddy Baer also made their mark. Max became world heavyweight champion when he floored 'The Ambling Alp' Primo Carnera eleven times in 1934. Max Baer was a fearsome fellow who had previously made his living slaughtering cattle for beef. He simply moved on to slaughtering fighters: two of his opponents died after facing him. While Max possessed one of the most lethal right hands in boxing history, younger brother Buddy was gifted with one of the most dangerous left hooks. One of them lifted the phenomenal Joe Louis straight out of the ring. But he ended up losing two title challenges.

The Baers were colourful characters, and movie stars. As is often the case, one brother outshone the other. Max is remembered as the family success in the ring. Of course the same applies to the Alis. Muhammad's elder brother Rahman has always lived in the shadow of 'The Greatest'. After a hundred-bout amateur career, he won fourteen professional fights. Rahman has, though, always maintained an extremely close relationship with his far more talented boxing brother.

The wonderful rivals Marvin Hagler and Tommy Hearns are of course etched in the annals for all time. Tommy may be a much-celebrated five-weight world dominator, but his younger brother Billy only had eight professional outings. 'Marvelous Marvin', one of the finest world middleweight kings of all time, had a half-brother. Robbie Sims was also steered by the superb Brockton-based training brothers Pat and Goody Petronelli, but could only muster a career record of 38–10–2.

There were the three Texan Ayalas – Mike, Tony and Sammy. Tony was the infamous one – for all the wrong reasons. Once one of the most sparkling hopes of world boxing, the ferocious light-middleweight had won all of his twenty-two fights, nineteen by KO, when he was sentenced to thirty-five years inside for a brutal sexual assault. He served sixteen of those years – not just a waste of a talent and a boxing career, but of a life.

Then there were the cult LA Baltazar brothers, Frankie and Tony. Also the Carbajals from Phoenix. Michael 'Little Hands of Stone' was the stand-out, capturing Olympic silver before becoming a four-time world champion. His brother Cruz did manage to pick up a WBO crown, but his record was plagued with eighteen defeats. The Canizales brothers from Laredo were pretty special, especially the younger, Orlando. Gaby might have been a world bantamweight champion, but Orlando won the IBF crown and defended it a record sixteen consecutive times.

Most fight fans have heard of Don Curry, the 'Lone Star Cobra' and one-time pound-for-pound king whom our own Lloyd Honeyghan stunned in 1986. Curry had won four hundred amateur and twenty-five professional fights before that dramatic night for British boxing. Don had two older brothers. One, Bruce, had his own triumphs. He won 315 amateur fights and became the world light-welterweight champion. The Currys were the first brothers ever to hold world titles at the same time. Graylin, though, didn't enjoy the same success: he only built a professional record of 13–6.

The American list seems endless. There were the Fullmers: world middleweight champion Gene, with brothers Don and Jay. The Lopezes: world featherweight champion Danny and world title challenger Ernie, known as 'Little Red' and 'Indian Red'. They were lighter-weight sensations and ever so fan-friendly. The McCrorys – not my friend and colleague Glenn, who had a fair few fighting brothers himself, but their namesakes: Milton was the world welterweight champion, Steve a world title challenger. The two Tom McNeeleys: Tom Snr, a light-heavyweight, and Tom Jnr, a heavyweight who fought Floyd Patterson (and whose son Peter was Mike Tyson's comeback opponent in 1995). Then there were the Mitchells – not Phil and Grant from *EastEnders*, nor Kevin and Vinnie from Essex, but the first light-welterweight champion Pinky, and Richie, who challenged Benny Leonard. And what about the Norris brothers? Former cruiserweight champion Orlin fought Mike

Tyson, but the more brilliant Terry was a three-time world light-middleweight champion. Or the Quarrys (Jerry, Mike and Bobby) and the Sandovals: Richie, a world bantamweight king, and his brother Alberto, who was a world title challenger.

One of the best-known Stateside families has to be the Weavers. Mike was the world heavyweight champion, and the older brother of the triplets Floyd, Lloyd and Troy. There were also the famous five Zivic brothers: 'The Croat Comet' Fritzie, who won the world welterweight title from the legendary Henry Armstrong and fought seven future Hall of Famers, plus Eddie, Jack, Pete and Joe.

In more modern times, the Americans have boasted the Judah brothers. 'Super' Zab is undoubtedly the leader of the pack, head and shoulders above his siblings. Fast, furious and skilled at his best; feeble, disappointing, even shameful at his worst. I was standing next to Ricky Hatton when Zab Judah met Kostya Tszyu to unify the world light-welterweight crowns at the MGM, Las Vegas. In a fascinating twenty-minute period, a very immature Judah was rocked into the ring alongside a vastly pumped-up Mike Tyson, duly dispatched in two rounds by the right hand of the formidable Russian-born Australian Tszyu, and then remonstrated with referee Jay Nady and, disgustingly, hurled a stool at the officials. It was not Zab's finest hour. Yet I always found him approachable, and with age, plus new-found religion, he became a nicer person, and a better all-round fighter. I have also never encountered much jealousy in the Judah family. Zab's elder brother Daniel was a light-heavyweight, his younger sibling Josiah a super-middleweight. The family patriarch, Yoel, has been quite a character on the scene, but as with the Mosleys, chopping Dad out of the training equation has been tough to do.

The two families from America with most historical boxing significance are the Mayweathers and the Spinks. Leon Spinks shocked the boxing world when he overcame Muhammad Ali. His brother Michael was a wonderful two-division champion, a fabulous light-heavyweight who climbed to the world heavyweight crown before he was sensationally blitzed by one Mike Tyson. The other Spinks boxing members included Leon Jnr (who boxed as Leon Calvin), Darrel and Cory, who enjoyed a reign as the undisputed welterweight king.

The Mayweathers, as we have seen, are a most famous trio of brothers, certainly in terms of charisma and arguably in terms of talent. Five-weight world king Floyd was preceded by his father Floyd Snr, who fought the magical Sugar Ray Leonard; Uncle Roger, who was a more successful two-weight world champion; and Uncle Jeff, who was pretty useful himself in the 1990s (he once fought Oscar De La Hoya). All three Mayweather brothers are now trainers. Never has there been a better example of a family enmeshed in boxing, however controversial they are.

Manny Pacquiao is one of the most famous fighters the boxing world has ever seen. The Philippines provided this six-weight king, who rose from living in cardboard boxes and selling doughnuts on the streets of General Santos City to thrill the world. The Pac-man has a brother, too: Bobby, who has always been in his shadow. Still, there is huge affection between the pair.

In the Philippines there was also the Penalosa trio: Dodie Boy, Jonathan, and the one I got to know, Gerry. There was a decade between them and they all fought for world titles. Both Gerry and Dodie Boy were two-weight champions. The boxing world has enjoyed the Donaire brothers, too – world champion Nonito and his older brother Glenn.

From elsewhere in Asia (Thailand) came the first twins to hold world titles together: the extraordinary Galaxy (or, by birth, Saenkham) brothers Khaokor and Khaosai. As with so many brothers, though, one shone: Khaosai. Currently there are the Japanese Kamedas – Koki, Daiki and Tomoki. Koki has won two world titles and is adored by the fans, and Daiki is also a world champion. If Tomoki wins a crown, they would be the first ever trio of world-title-holding brothers.

In Argentina, we've seen the Corros (world middleweight champion Hugo, and Osvaldo), the Narvaezes (world flyweight champion Omar with brothers Mario and Nestor) and the Baldomirs (former world welterweight boss Carlos, and Luis). Today we have the Matthysses, Lucas and Walter.

In Canada, the Gattis reigned supreme. The legendary Arturo we loved and remember. The former two-weight champion thrilled us in the ring, but was taken all too quickly outside it. His brother Joe wasn't in the same league but he still managed to challenge for the world light-middleweight title. Then there were the Hiltons. Dave was the world super-middleweight champion; Matthew made it to the top of the light-middleweight world. And we shouldn't forget the Vanderpools, Syd and Fitz, both of whom could fight.

I'm writing this section of the book in one of the most stunning parts of Ireland: Union Hall, a gorgeous fishing port in West Cork where, I am led to believe, Jonathan Swift once came to pen *Gulliver's Travels*. A world apart from my attempts, true, but Swift (and now Smith) came to the right end of the world. Union Hall is pretty, picturesque and serenely perfect, it really is. And so to the Irish warriors, because there are droves of fight fans in both Northern Ireland and down south.

The Collins brothers lead the family fraternity. Steve was the rugged, steely two-weight dominator, Pascal only an average professional. Likewise, Eamonn headed the Magee clan; Noel became a Commonwealth champion but had to play second fiddle, while Terry was no more than a tough journeyman. And what about the incredible Corcorans, an Irish travelling tribe featuring fourteen boys and girls? The Corcorans boasted no fewer than eight brothers who boxed out of the Stowe Amateur Club, with Billy going on to British championship class.

Plenty of clans and dynasties have cropped up in the rest of Europe, too. The Tiozzos – Fabrice, the two-division champion, and Christophe, who also ruled the world at super-middleweight – came from France. In Germany we enjoyed the careers of the Rocchigianis: Ralf was the world cruiserweight champion while Graciano, Ralf's half-brother, went one step better and became an outstanding two-weight king. Italy claims to have the first brothers to conquer the world: the Dundees, Joe and Vince. And there were the Steccas, Loris and Maurizio, world super-bantamweight and featherweight champions. Or how about the Brancos, world light-heavyweight champion Silvio and his brother Gianluca?

Mexico, of course, can boast one of the richest boxing heritages of all. In my twenty years in the sport I have become particularly fond of their fighters' machismo, and I have been fortunate enough to commentate on three future Hall of Famers in the fabulous Marco Antonio Barrera, the superb Erik Morales and that bright defensive genius Juan Manuel Marquez.

Now there is another star on the horizon: Saul Alvarez, 'El Canelo', the ginger Hispanic who looks like he could be straight from the Emerald Isle but is Mexican to the core. Rather like the former five-time world featherweight champion Manuel Medina, who turned professional at fourteen, Alvarez began at fifteen and he has already, incredibly, packed in thirty-eight fights. The Mexican people are right behind him, he seems to be the next media darling, and he is steeped in family fighting history. In 2008, Saul and all of his six brothers fought on the same card! Saul is the world light-middleweight champion; Rigoberto, Ricardo and Ramon are the others with real talent.

Jorge Arce has been a super character at the lighter weights.

With his cowboy hat and lollipops, Arce has provided fun, drama and excitement. A world champion at four weights, Jorge has a boxing brother, Francisco. It seems to be the Mexican way, just as we saw with Juan Manuel and Rafael Marquez. The Arredondo family consists of world light-welterweight champion Rene, world super-featherweight champion Ricardo, and Roberto. Marco Antonio Barrera – a three-weight world king, and still fighting – has a brother Jorge, and they are exceptionally close. A quite delightful visit to Casa Barrera in Mexico City demonstrated to me that the family rates each brother as highly as the other, despite their differing ring achievements. If anything, there were more pictures of Jorge on the walls.

Castillo is yet another well-known Mexican boxing name. Jose Luis was a rugged world lightweight champion and his brother Ricardo did well at super-bantamweight. Jose Luis gained much of his experience by sparring with the amazing Julio Cesar Chavez, a wonderful three-weight king. His brother Roberto boxed, as do his sons Julio Cesar and Omar. Erik Morales has won world titles in three divisions and is looked after by father and former fighter Jose. Erik's brother Diego became a world super-flyweight champion, while Ivan is an undefeated prospect.

Then there were Antonio, Julio and Joel Diaz; the incredible world strawweight ruler Ricardo Lopez, who defended his title a record twenty-one times, and Alonso; the Paez crew; the Romans; and of course the Ruelas brothers. The Ruelases have provided exceptional entertainment. Gabriel was the world super-featherweight champion, while his brother Rafael ruled at lightweight and dealt a harsh lesson to our brave Billy Schwer. In 1995, the Ruelases were the first brothers to retain world titles on the same show, Rafael stopping Schwer to keep his IBF lightweight crown, and Gabriel retaining his WBC super-featherweight crown by halting Fred Liberatore in two.

We can add to this list the Solis brothers: world light-flyweight champion Ulises and brother Jorge. Plus the Zarate family – the huge puncher Carlos, the former bantamweight champion, while his son, nephew and other family members all boxed. Two-weight king Fernando Montiel is one of five brothers (Alejandro, Pedro, Manuel Jnr and Eduardo are his siblings), and their father Manuel trains them all.

Along with Mexico, Puerto Rico, a gem of a Caribbean island, has long dished up wonderful fighting fraternities. Wilfred Benitez was a boxing legend; his brothers Frankie and Gregory are hardly ever mentioned. Hector 'Macho' Camacho was one of those eccentric entertainers from whom Chris Eubank and Naseem Hamed must have learned a trick or two. His ring costumes were lavish and always different. A boxing legend, Hector had a brother, Felix, who challenged for a world crown.

One of the most famous names in recent times is Cotto. Miguel Angel has been a superb champion, his brother Jose a tough but limited and rather forgotten fighter. Currently there are the Arroyo twins who have lit up the amateur scene, and the Bisbal boys – again, well known in the unpaid ranks and hoping to hit heights as pros. And there are more Solises: world bantam-weight champion Julian, and former world challengers Enrique and Rafael.

Let's begin to draw this list of boxing brothers to a close with a look at some less high-profile nations. Thailand boasted tiny champion siblings Ratanapol and Ratanachai Sor Vorapin. Trinidad and Tobago brought us the Noels: world lightweight champion Claude and his lesser-known brother David. Venezuela have given us the Espanas: both Cristano at welterweight and Ernesto at lightweight were champions. The Cermenos were also useful, Antonio a two-weight king and recently Nehomar. Colombia has provided the Cardonas: Ricardo was a WBA champion and Prudencio won world honours at flyweight.

The Dominican Republic have produced a world lightweight champion in Carlos Teo Cruz, and his brother Leo won honours at super-bantamweight.

And to finish, we find ourselves back in Britain. Between 1937 and 1964, at least one of the Turpin brothers was active as a pro. Jackie, Dick and Randy racked up an astonishing 302 fights between them, with 225 victories. Randy was the best known – he upset the legendary Sugar Ray Robinson – while Dick became a European champion. In the 1940s and 1950s, Watford boasted the Buxton brothers: Joe, Laurie, Alex and Allan. All four won on a pro show on 27 September 1949. Not all boxing brothers spar, but the Buxtons did. Other famous fighting brothers of ours include the Finnegans: 1968 Olympic gold medallist Chris and younger sibling Kevin, who gave us many memorable nights.

Of the many McKenzies, three-weight world champion Duke was the most successful, but Clinton and Winston also won plenty. Duke is, however, always telling me that Dudley was the most talented. 'Dudley was amazing,' he said, 'especially as a youngster. We all fought over the breakfast table. We were meant to be fighters.'

British heavyweight champion David Pearce was one of seven brothers; six boxed professionally. Pearce shunned the big-money offers to stay with his father and the family he adored.

Of the Eubanks, Chris might have been 'simply the best', but his brothers Peter and Simon also boxed. The Walkers were famous in and out of the ring, largely due to Billy's popularity as a fighter and older brother George's colourful life as an entrepreneur. And we'll never forget the Cooper twins: Henry, of course, a darling of UK sport, and George, on whom he doted.

Certainly brothers are a crucial relationship within a family. They tend to fight side by side – a fact which has long been evident throughout boxing history. One generally overshadows the other (or others), but, as with the Cooper twins, it rarely if ever matters who is the finer fighter. The fraternal bond matters most.

9

Hats Off to the Battlers

The name 'Hatton' will always be engraved on British boxing history. Richard. Ricky. The Hitman. The boy next door who captivated us on his way to the top of the light-welterweight division with his loveable personality and swashbuckling fighting style. Meanwhile, for the best part of his life, Ricky's younger brother has been well and truly lost in the shadows. How does the 'lesser' boxing sibling cope with the lack of attention, talent and bank balance?

'Magic' Matthew battled away, and after a long, arduous journey he captured the European welterweight crown; he even went on to challenge for a world title against the sensational young Mexican Saul Alvarez.

'Wrong weight, out in LA and against the hottest prospect in world boxing – isn't that mission impossible?' Johnny and I asked Matthew on the *Ringside* set.

'He who dares wins,' he fired straight back at us.

Hats off to Hatton Jnr. Yes, Matthew was outclassed and soundly beaten, but he did go twelve rounds, showed plenty of bottle, and earned respect in defeat.

Matthew wasn't born with nearly the same amount of natural

boxing ability or class as Ricky. He's a different personality, and of course hasn't enjoyed either as sweet or as successful a rise, in sporting or financial terms. Publicity-wise, Matthew just hasn't been as marketable as Ricky, despite the fact that boxing brothers obviously have appeal. But they get on great, they're close pals, and are from a very tight-knit family. Mum Carol and Dad Ray have always treated them as equals, and rightly so.

Ray told me, 'Richard might be a world champion, but I'm just as proud of Matthew, whatever belt he wins. Carol and I get as nervous watching Matthew at ringside as when Richard boxes. All we care about is that our boys come out safe. As for Richard, he's much more worried watching his little brother than he is about his own fights.'

They're hugely supportive of each other, but have plenty of independence and are often seen as contrasting characters. There is a quiet air of sensibility about Matthew; as a result people often feel he's not as engaging as Ricky when they first meet him, that he's therefore harder to get to know. What Matt does have is a steely resolve. He is also thoroughly dedicated and disciplined. Almost 24/7. In many ways far more than his big brother. Matthew can appear more secure too – maybe because everything has been that much harder a grind.

The love of the good life and the yo-yoing of his weight is part of Ricky's make-up. The depression and the binges escalated when he failed to come to terms with the devastating loss to Manny Pacquiao. Ricky flirts with danger, and those tabloid headlines from the now defunct *News of the World* made for unpleasant and damaging reading.

'I'm so sorry I let everyone down,' Ricky revealed to me when he travelled down to my house in London to film his official retirement interview. 'I apologize to the fans, and most importantly to my family. Depression is a very bad illness. I was out of control.'

Matthew found it tough to watch the downfall of his beloved brother. 'Despite all his world title wins, Ricky was so low after the Pacquiao result, and it was horrible to see my brother like it,' he told me. 'I am always there to help, but he needed professional assistance. Fortunately he's come through. Fame has its downfalls, and Ricky and I are different characters. But I would do anything for him.'

Matthew has needed to be very strong, and extremely structured in his approach to life and to his chosen career. For what he lacks in raw ability, he has had to make up for in dogged determination, sheer bloody-mindedness and a fabulous work ethic. That is now being honed by Bob Shannon, an intense, dedicated trainer who works his fighters – Wayne Rigby, Ali Nuumbembe, Andy Morris, Denton Vassell, Prince Arron, and now Matthew – very hard. (Bob has some family history too: he lost his father in a car crash when he was just twenty-one, and then in 2003 his own son Robert Jnr, who was the youngest ever cornerman at just seventeen, died in a car crash himself.)

The younger Hatton has long carved out his own niche. Even at home, Matthew's the odd one out. The City fanatics in the Hyde household call Matthew the 'runt of the litter' – he's a Manchester United fan. Just as Ricky had early success at Manchester City, Matthew too was very interested in football. Yet he turned down the opportunity of playing for Oldham Athletic to concentrate on boxing.

Matthew has always been competitive, ever since the days when he used to kick-box. I remember watching an old video of the Hatton brothers in an exhibition. They were just kids, but Matthew was far more aggressive, and seems to have always had that burning desire to battle his way through.

Ricky was a sensational amateur, a former national champion and thus the bright boxing spark of the Hatton family. Talent, pedigree, charm, charisma – Ricky had it all. Racking up quick professional victories, many of them in scintillating style, must have made it happy times for the Hatton household, but in private, surely particularly tough for Matthew. The little bro, you see, started relatively late, at fifteen. Matthew only had twenty-two amateur bouts, and never made the impact or carved out the sort of reputation his brother did in the unpaid ranks. He did win an ABA novice title, but decided to turn pro in 2000.

A quite painful rise over a decade or so followed. Matthew was brought along very carefully, largely on Ricky's undercards. His unbeaten record was snapped at thirteen by David Kirk, a journeyman southpaw from Sutton-in-Ashfield who lost more than he won. It was a bad result, and maybe an indication that Matthew wasn't always going to get the rub of the green, despite his family connection. Matthew was also stopped on a cut by David Keir, and held to a draw by fringe contender Francis Jones.

At this stage the critics were, quite correctly, beginning to write him off, saying that it seemed Matthew Hatton had reached his level. Yet Matt was still young, and simply knuckled down. All credit to him. In March 2005, he settled the score with Francis Jones, and then outpointed Rob Burton over ten rounds to become Central Area welterweight champion. I remember the happiness etched on Carol's face when her little boy finally had a belt of his own to put on the mantelpiece. For the Hatton family, that win gave them as much pride and pleasure, maybe even more, as the night when Ricky shocked the world by dethroning Kostya Tszyu.

I guess it was almost expected that the Hitman would become the big success for the regular Hyde family who owned a simple carpet shop. What impresses me most about Matthew is that he didn't mind. No hard feelings, just happiness for his big bro, to this day, as he continues to chart his own, very different, path in boxing. In many ways Matthew Hatton has had a broader education in life.

Having beaten Burton again for a second Central title, Matthew blew a British title eliminator against the naturally lighter Alan Bosworth, when ahead on points – he was disqualified for repeated infringements. It was another hurtful loss for Matthew, who was then forced to fight on against the backdrop of the Hitman express. That can't have been easy. He did so, often in America thanks to Ricky's adventures, and got good wins against the likes of Frankie Houghtaling, Edwin Vazquez and Frankie Santos.

Then, once again, just as his form was improving, there was a major setback. Unfortunately Matthew's big night in the open air at the City of Manchester Stadium in May 2008 (on the undercard of his brother's homecoming win over Juan Lazcano) fell flat when his challenge for Craig Watson's Commonwealth title ended in a wide points defeat. It really looked like Matthew had well and truly found his boxing level.

However, we've learnt never to write him off, for he comes back so well. This time there were wins over Scott Woolford, the dangerous but old and slow Ghanaian Ben Tackie, Brixton banger Ted Bami and Mexico's Ernesto Zepeda, which led to a clash with hardened Lovemore N'dou. Hatton had to make do with a draw in that one, which was a touch unfortunate again for the long-time trier.

Then, in March 2010, Ricky's new promotional base managed to secure him a shot at the European welterweight crown. Matthew boxed carefully, steadily and sensibly against the ageing former champion and world title challenger Gianluca Branco and finally had his night. Hatton showed fast flurries, patience and good footwork to win over twelve rounds.

Matthew then needed all his experience and cool mind to rise from a first-round knockdown against European challenger Yuri

Nuzhnenko, who had a strong amateur record of 110 wins in 142 bouts and had briefly held the WBA 10st 7lb crown. 'I could have stepped aside,' Matthew explained, 'but Nuzhnenko was my mandatory and I am a man of my word. Boxing's not full of easy options.' Hatton clawed his way back into the fight, and it was a classic example of the perseverance that has been crucial to his career.

Some say that Matthew Hatton has never been good enough, and of course he has been looked after by fighting regularly on Ricky's bills. Yet this is the hardest game, and you take every advantage you can. In his defence, Matthew hardly had the one-on-one treatment that Ricky enjoyed with trainer Billy Graham. There was never a great deal of time allotted to the rather unfashionable younger brother, who eventually moved to Lee Beard, and subsequently Bob Shannon.

On the one hand, Matthew's connections have allowed him plenty of opportunities, so despite the jealousy of fellow fighters, having a brilliant elder brother works; it even pays dividends. It is a business after all. On the flip side, while more chances may have appeared than if he wasn't a Hatton, Matthew has still had to make the most of them or the well really would have dried up sooner.

Think also, just for a moment, about how difficult it must be to be Ricky's younger and less successful brother. You're not as skilful, not as funny, not as popular – just not as good. Yet I have known Matthew for many years, ever since he was a teenager, and I have never witnessed a hint of jealousy. Not one iota. I have huge respect for him.

After losing to Kell Brook in March 2012, Matthew may find becoming a true world-beater beyond him. He certainly showed no signs in the amateur ranks, and he deserves enormous credit for sticking to the task and gathering results and belts way beyond any of our expectations. I didn't ever believe he was even British championship material.

Ably supported by all the Hattons, his lovely partner Jenna, his lively son Jack and baby daughter Lola, Matthew is settled and in a good place. He's been through his ups and downs and is now more mature, more seasoned. Following in his brother's footsteps continues even today, as Matthew recently moved into Ricky's old house. And this is the big brother who only moved out of the family home in his mid-twenties, venturing a mere fifty-seven seconds' walk away, and continued to take his washing home!

Ricky rightly bowed out at thirty-two after a long break following the Pacquiao loss. Matthew will have more longevity, but won't want to go on for ever. Maybe he will get another crack at a world title – a little nearer home, a little nearer his weight, a little more at his level. Maybe some will feel he doesn't deserve that. Well, I do. He's been through a great deal, and he has done ever so well not to get bogged down with antagonistic feelings towards his brother and his chosen field.

I have huge admiration for sportsmen who battle away. Like Sammy Lee, the bustling midfield dynamo who never possessed the flair of most of his colleagues but was a huge part of the Liverpool engine room in that wonderful team of the 1980s. Or golfer Justin Rose, who is a family friend. Justin burst to prominence at The Open back in 1998. As a seventeen-year-old amateur, he holed a dramatic shot from the rough for a birdie on the eighteenth to finish fourth. Yet when he turned professional the following week, Justin struggled badly. He missed twenty-one cuts in a row. But Justin never gave up fighting and has now notched up a handful of top ten finishes in the majors, secured a place in the European Ryder Cup team where he shone alongside friend Ian Poulter, and has won four titles on the US PGA tour. He still believes it is just a matter of time before he lands one of the really big ones.

In boxing, I never look beyond my TV partner Johnny Nelson.

He really is the prime example of extraordinary perseverance. After all, he followed his brother to Brendan Ingle's Sheffield gym to avoid being bullied and to make new friends. He certainly didn't need any more siblings: there were seven kids in the Nelson family – from six different fathers.

'I was absolutely awful, Ads. Useless. They really didn't know what they could do with me. I was the laughing stock of the gym. I lost ten of my thirteen amateur fights. Brendan told me that there was no point me carrying on, and that I might as well turn pro to see what would happen. Then I was beaten in my first three. They gave me five professional fights, and then out. But fortunately, I found a way to win those next two!'

This was merely the beginning of the fascinating Nelson journey. He was laughed out of Sheffield after completely freezing during a world title shot against Carlos De Leon. Then he went and did a similar thing out in Virginia, in the US, against James Warring. It looked all over for Johnny in his early twenties.

'There was only one thing left for me – to go round the world taking any fights I could. I started to believe I should have been the policeman I always wanted to be!'

The global voyage, and the 'have gloves will travel' attitude, proved to be the making of Johnny. During his 'exile', Johnny was forced to take fights in far-flung places like South Africa, New Zealand, Australia and Brazil, both at his natural cruiserweight or up at heavyweight, and often at just hours' notice, which all-rounded him as a fighter. He won some, he lost plenty, but more than anything he learned to look after himself. Johnny also mixed with the crooks and gamblers of the business who tried to force him to fix fights. There wasn't much he didn't witness during his travels.

So when Johnny returned to Britain, he was a totally different kind of animal. Never the most exciting, but he had the know-how, the confidence and the skill-set to clean up the cruiserweight world.

I knew he would make the perfect television analyst because of his intelligence, charisma and, most importantly, his vast experience. He has witnessed so many areas of the sport, seen it from all sides, felt the highs and lows, so I knew he would find it easy to relate to the majority of boxers.

He'd also gone full circle, righting the wrongs of throwing it away on the highest stage, and finally become a world champion. Beating Carl Thompson in March 1999 (ironically on the first bill I ever commentated on professionally for Sky) was the perfect conclusion. Yet Johnny Nelson wasn't even started. He went on to defend his WBO title an amazing thirteen times and retired (partly at my insistence) as an unbeaten world champion who had reigned for six and a half years. So Johnny's career really only came to fruition in his early thirties, and he ended up achieving far more than his brother ever did. The brother that Johnny felt was 'much, much, much better than skinny me'.

Matthew Hatton will never come close to matching Ricky's accolades, but it just goes to show that dedication, determination, a crop of defeats (which can actually bring fighters on) and an ability to deal with wild criticism can carry people a long, long way.

'I'd be lying if I said I hadn't thought of walking away before,' Matthew told me over a cup of tea in Hyde. 'No luck with cuts, the disqualification, the general rub of the green. The stream of criticism that I wasn't as good as Rick did affect me, Adam. But I always had belief. Ricky and my dad knew what I was capable of. It is unbelievable for our family, what we have achieved, because we are very, very close. Especially after both of us chose to fight, and not go into football. Natural competition and all that. Ricky has been a great success. I am so proud of him; there has not been any resentment. Ever. I just get down when I personally haven't performed. Everyone says I have come out of his shadow. I have never seen it like that. It's coming out of my own shadow. But I have to say, if I had any hair, I would have pulled it out years ago!'

It is tough being a brother at times, unless of course the individual is more than capable of dealing with rough, testing situations and carving out his own path. That most certainly sums up the genuine fighting man that is, and always has been, Matthew Hatton.

The same can be said about one of my favourite fighters, who is a real little cult character on our domestic scene.

There is just something about Nottingham craftsman Jason '2 Smooth' Booth that I have always warmed to. Jason has had an extraordinary journey. Once a talented prospect who quickly became a superb, skilful domestic flyweight ruler, Booth hit the darkest of places before climbing back in emphatic fashion to the brink of the IBF super-bantamweight crown: he lost a razor-close split decision on points to Steve Molitor in September 2010.

Moreover, there has long been double trouble, for the Booths are a terrible twosome. Jason has a younger brother, Nicky, who was a thrilling fighter and even crazier than Jason out of the ring. Nicky '1 Smooth' Booth was fresh, funny, but, as we were to discover, a real liability.

The Booths' journey has been compelling, frightening, yet ever so endearing. We at Sky Sports have in many ways grown up with the Booths. They had a rough start, with a rather wild home life in the tough Strelley area of west Nottingham. Jason had more raw ability and began boxing at ten, when his grand-father took him to the Radford Boys Club. According to Jason he was 'about four feet tall, and four stone in weight', but one of his earlier bouts, believe it or not, was against a far bigger and stronger Carl Froch. Jason's eighty amateur fights included a standout year in 1994 when he won a clean sweep of British junior titles.

I joined Sky that year and quickly heard about this young man's potential. Booth also made the European Juniors, and won National Schools, NABC and ABA youth accolades before turning professional in June 1996. Even though he carefully learned his trade on undercards, there was immediate interest in him because of his natural talent. And, of course, Jason had a sidekick: this cocky, confident brother Nicky, a fellow fighter just starting out, and a completely contrasting character. Nicky '1 Smooth' Booth and Jason '2 Smooth' Booth, the two loveable fighting rogues from the Midlands, quickly attracted a passionate fan base. They were certainly good value and a top crack at the time. (They were also for many years guided by another family unit, the father-and-son team of Mike and Jason Shinfield, whose name is steeped in its own boxing history. Mike's dad Billy and granddad Mias had spent their lives in boxing, and the Shinfield family folklore goes back to the bare-knuckle days.)

I always felt Jason had more ring guile than Nicky, even though he was the quieter personality. While Nicky was bragging about knocking out anyone from Mike Tyson to King Kong, Jason was nestling quietly in the background, happy for his brother to hog the limelight. The elder Booth brother actually taught himself how to play the piano and spent the rest of his time concentrating on learning new boxing moves.

Meanwhile, Nicky was hysterical. I remember talking to him at the weigh-in before his important clash against a heavy-hitting Colombian southpaw called Jose Sanjuanelo. It seemed a massive jump-up in levels to us, and I asked Nicky what he knew and feared about Sanjuanelo.

'I know diddly,' replied Nicky, laughing. 'I'm going to knock him out in five!'

But the Colombian puncher was rather good, and proceeded

to tear Nicky apart in nine torrid rounds at the old Wembley Conference Centre. It was a painful lesson for Nicky to learn. But I will never forget his braggadocio beforehand. Despite what happened in the ring, it really was a most amusing prediction.

Jason went about his work more subtly. He won his first fourteen, making good, steady progress before taking a gamble against David Guerault in a European flyweight challenge in Grande Synthe in May 1999. Booth lost the fight on points, but gave the world-class Guerault real trouble, and even floored him in the seventh.

Jason returned to capture the British and Commonwealth flyweight belts with a terrific performance against Keith Knox, and retained the titles with another excellent win over Ian Napa. Unfortunately two more attempts to lift the European crown ended in heartbreak: Jason was desperately unlucky not to beat Alexander Mahmutov in Spain, and on a second trip to France he lost a technical decision after cuts hampered his clash with Minoun Chent. Surely Jason Booth would have been crowned a European champion if one of those title chances had come at home. It's possible that while boxing analysts, fans of the pure sport, and certain fight promoters appreciated him, Jason just didn't possess the firepower and electricity both in and out of the ring which is always so vital in building boxing stars.

Still, along with Nottingham cab driver Jawaid Khaliq, who was a decent welterweight with a good crop of noisy supporters, the Booth brothers rocked their home city with some atmospheric and fun nights. They became the first brothers to hold British titles at the same time since the Feeneys from Hartlepool (John was a two-time British champion in the 1980s and George was the British lightweight champion, although his brother always referred to him as 'our George, that lazy git!').

They were the closest of siblings and the best of friends, but the Booth boys actually became a destructive influence on each other.

Stories began to circulate, and Nicky's downfall came fast and furious. The popular British bantamweight champion enjoyed a whirlwind of enticing victories, but then ended up in prison for robberies that fed his crack cocaine habit. Jason privately admitted to us that too much partying had become a problem, and one night in 2002, after several pints, he was set upon, viciously attacked in an alley. His life was beginning to spiral into chaos. Having drunk heavily from a fairly early age, and in a bad relationship with a crack addict, Jason was in dire straits. Big benders became a real problem; he was even drinking large quantities of alcohol in the weeks and days before fights. Amazingly, Jason admitted that he was actually drunk in the ring when he faced the Bulgarian Dimitar Alipiev.

In 2004, Booth had one of his sweetest victories, over Dale Robinson, but was then beaten by Damaen Kelly. His hold over British boxers gone, the former respected champion began hanging out on the streets with drunks and vagrants. 'I was rotten every single day for months and months and months. Booze led to drugs which led back to booze,' Jason told me in a quiet corner of one of his press conferences during his comeback.

He entered an abyss. He began to drink a bottle of sherry every morning. He hated Sundays, because he couldn't get a drink before ten a.m. Jason used to scour the streets for the dregs of cider cans. People watched his fall, and the story looked like it was going to have one of those tragic endings the boxing world sometimes produces.

The sport lost him for two years. A troubled young man, Jason was also deeply affected by the suicide of his eldest sister Deana. The brothers adored her, and had teased her rotten, like so many siblings do. 'I'm Nicky "1 Smooth" Booth, this is my brother Jason "2 Smooth" Booth; as for our sister, she ain't so smooth!' the boys used to tell us.

Losing his beloved sister hit Jason hard, and his money began running out fast, blown on his daily habit. He was waking up at five a.m. to have a drink. Wild spirits. Twenty-five cans of strong lager daily. Drugs. Doctors gave him two months to live.

Four people helped bring Jason back from the very brink. One was a girl, Sarita, who became his entire life, mainly on account of the fact that she had basically saved his. Sarita eventually encouraged Jason into detox, which was very, very rough. His body was falling apart. He had stomach ulcers, failing organs, constant shakes; hospital wards became a second home. A GP called John Cockerill worked out a programme and Booth went cold turkey. Wild hallucinations followed, but he fought valiantly, and got through.

Then there was Tony Harris, a former pro and friend, and Jimmy Gill, a local stalwart of the game. They took a risk. They wouldn't let Jason back into the gym until he turned up sober, and it was a long journey; it did not happen overnight. Jason still used to have a can of beer before he began his road work. 'They had so much faith in me, and the time they gave up – well, I can never thank them enough,' Jason told me. 'I'd known Tony for years, and he showed me what a real friend is all about. He picked me up from the gutter. If I hadn't got back into boxing, I would be dead in those gutters.'

'We were very tough with him,' added the wily old manager Jimmy Gill, with his instantly recognizable gruff voice. 'If he regressed once, he was out. He knew that. But Jase knuckled down, he really did. The talent that boy had is just unbelievable, and we've helped bring him back from very dark places. Nicky's off the wall with his addictive streak. Jason found a way out. Such a shame about Nicky, because he really looked up to Jase.'

With hard work, resolve and dedication, Jason somehow did it. He slowly began rebuilding his career and, more importantly, his life. After being lost in the blackest of holes, Jason Booth returned to boxing in November 2006, after twenty-three months out of the game. The ring rehabilitation was a long and carefully managed process. Tony and Jimmy were continually worried that Jason would fall dramatically off the wagon, and took training literally day by day.

'Slowly does it,' said Jimmy. 'We have to be sure he's ready, mentally and physically, for each test we give him.'

After a couple of low-key wins, Booth's new team grasped an opportunity, challenging Ian Napa for the British bantamweight title. Napa had gone through his own personal problems, but was further down the recovery line, and won the fight on points. Jason's body was not quite ready, his mind probably not in the right place either. But for the new-look Team Booth there was real relief that Jason had got to this point. The commitment had returned, the ambition to succeed was reinvigorated, and the will to prevail against all odds was of course the highest achievement of all.

Jason's recovery process was being played out against the backdrop of Nicky's wasted sporting career. Locked up and lost in the addictive world of crack cocaine, his fighting days were as fast as his fall. Nicky was virtually washed up as a boxer by the age of just twenty-three.

Meanwhile, Jason was sober, clean and rolling again. This second coming was testament to his fighting attitude. It was pretty special when Booth won his first title after recovery. After the Napa defeat he could easily have faded away again, but that fight was instead the beginning of a remarkable revival.

On 8 December 2007, all British sporting eyes were focused fully on the bright lights of Las Vegas, where there was a certain mega-fight between undefeated rivals Ricky Hatton and Floyd

Mayweather Jnr. Admittedly, I drew the short straw on the commentary front for Sky that night: my location was the Robin Park Arena in Wigan for a domestic supporting show which felt a long, long way from the hub of the boxing world. Still, there was business to attend to, plenty of fights to get through, and Jason Booth was right there in the middle of the lengthy bill.

The majority of his comeback was fought away from the little Nottingham fortress of home support which the brothers had enjoyed before their problems, and it was a bitterly cold night in the north-west when Booth tackled Welshman Matthew Edmonds for the Commonwealth bantamweight crown. With all the experience of those European title tilts around the continent, Jason was seasoned in tough twelve-rounders and prevailed to regain his first title since his drinking got out of control. It didn't really matter what it was, it was just a magnificent prize after dragging himself back from the depths of despair.

Jason stayed on for the after-fight party to watch the Hatton–Mayweather clash on the big screen that had been erected in the hall. I congratulated him, with his requested pint of orange and lemonade, and he then took immense pride in showing me this tiny notebook packed with spidery writing and phrases that obviously meant more to him than it did to anyone else.

'Since I started training again – clean – I have written everything down,' he explained. 'Absolutely everything. What I eat, what I drink, what goes into my body. The miles I run, the rounds I do in the gym. The whole lot.'

It was really quite moving. Jason had meticulously detailed every single part of his training regime, and all the fluids and food he'd had. Safe to say, alcohol was firmly a thing of the past. Jason was so proud of the fact that he had come back from the brink. And so was I. What a heart-warming story of grit, desire and sheer will-power.

I told him about some of my chats Stateside with Bernard

Hopkins. 'Jason, I have so much respect for you doing that. Hopkins would be very interested in hearing this tale. You're just like him, Jason! After years locked away in a Philadelphia penitentiary, Bernard has not smoked, drunk, nor so much as spat on the sidewalk. Hopkins monitors everything. If he eats food in a restaurant, he will make sure there is no sauce on his steak or his pasta. He's up at five a.m., hard training, bed by nine thirty, lights out.'

Jason listened intently and was amazed that I could even compare him to one of the greatest fighters of the modern generation. Now, I am not saying Jason Booth is anywhere near that sort of level, but there's every justification to tell his story, just as with The Executioner's.

It's true that Jason Booth's personally emotional victory was lost deep into the night amid far more important boxing issues (Hatton and Mayweather's fight), but the one and only thing I have taken away from my experience of 8 December 2007 is that little book. An achievement as big as anything Floyd Mayweather has ever done. It meant the world, not just to Jason and Sarita, but to Tony Harris and Jimmy Gill too, both of whom had invested so much energy into their project of bringing Jason back from the streets.

Yet as Jason's Indian summer got warmer and warmer, where was his once inseparable brother Nicky? Out of the nick, still in his mid- to late-twenties, and attempting to become a fighter once more, Nicky was apparently also on the road back. But where was he? He was rarely seen in the gym; there were just sporadic appearances at ringside to support Jason. We always wondered whether Nicky would be in a fit state even to record an interview about his brother. A pitiful shame.

Meanwhile, Jason defended his Commonwealth title, then took another risk, challenging for the British super-bantamweight crown when he was meant to be going down to super-flyweight.

And at just eleven days' notice! 'He's mad,' admitted Booth's promoter Frank Maloney. 'But he's saved the show. Never asked about money, just took the job. Total pro.'

Booth was even more of a revelation – he seemed almost a newcomer this time, not a man on the comeback trail – as he dismantled the unbeaten former Commonwealth Games medallist Mark Moran in style.

How Booth has since excelled at 8st 10lb, with his victories over Rocky Dean and the former world title challenger Michael Hunter, both a pleasure to watch. The British boxing community would have loved to see Jason Booth complete his recovery by winning a European or world title.

The big one actually came first, as Maloney engineered Jason a world title crack against the slick Canadian southpaw Steve Molitor, who had previous history on our shores. Molitor not only broke Hartlepool hearts when he destroyed Michael Hunter in their atmospheric Borough Hall, but more importantly to family Booth, the 'Canadian Kid' had outclassed Nicky a few years back, so revenge was firmly on Jason's mind.

In September 2010, just outside Sunderland, Booth fought a little behind himself. Calling the fight, I felt he was struggling with self-belief, lacking real confidence that he could prevail, as well as giving away a natural weight advantage to Molitor. It was very close though, and I'm sure Jason has been kicking himself since after watching the fight back on tape. So near, yet so far.

The next difficult title shot, the European this time, came out in Spain against heavy-handed Kiko Martinez, but Booth was stopped for the first time in his career – a sign that the wheels were beginning to come off, and the legs were starting to fade. Not particularly surprising after all Jason has been through. Then in October 2011 Booth lost his British title too, to hot hope Scott Quigg. If he can't dredge up another victory from somewhere it may be the end of the boxing road, finally, for Jason Booth.

But what a success story this has been. Jason won his biggest fight, that of survival, and one hopes that he has learned enough in the comeback to make sure he never has to do that again. With a little money in the bank, Jason should be much better off than he ever has been. Until a few fights ago, Jason had never earned more than £15,000 for any single appearance. That was still the going rate after seventeen twelve-rounders. Awful money maybe, but compared to a life on the streets . . .

Jason may still need guidance himself, but a possible route could be as a trainer and a mentor to the many youngsters out there who are suffering. His advice and stories would be invaluable. 'We want to get as much money in the bank for him and then get him his coaching badge,' Jimmy Gill told me. 'Keep Jason in the sport. Keep his life structured.' I couldn't agree more.

So, the fighting Booths. Same genes. Similar problems. Different outcomes. Why?

With Jason, it was all about the skills and ring savvy. He was a very clever fighter who picked opponents apart. He found the key using feints and classy moves, his body-punching and fast footwork his stand-out weapons. He had intelligence, too, and that seems to be the major difference. Nicky had the bigger character and maybe the bigger heart for an intense ring war, but he was never as slick or as bright. When both brothers had their problems, the smarter Booth came through. Just.

The good news is that Jason's happy, and he's still here fighting. His two children, Demi and Jayden, and his step-children, Cameron and Sharlea, keep him going, and his life is far more settled. He might need them when he retires, because he knows the demons remain and he is trying desperately hard to avoid going back to the 'old place'.

I have huge admiration for Jason Booth. There is a refreshing honesty about him, as we hear in virtually every interview he does. Good fighter too – a two-weight British champion who has the honour of keeping the treasured Lonsdale belt for ever. Jason's roller-coaster ride and life story is a real example of how boxing can save souls from the most awful and lonely of situations. I am sure he would tell you himself that he would have been dead without the sport.

There has been constant talk within the trade of Nicky attempting to mount a comeback, but he seems still to be fighting his own problems. How sad that his promising career was curtailed in a flash, but we wish him well. The worry is that Nicky will continue on the downward spiral. There seems to be hope, though – every now and then. Recently, when Nicky was kicked out of his latest lodgings, he turned up at Jason's with a hold-all, even though both Tony and Jimmy had been trying to keep Nicky away from Jason in the lead-up to fights. 'I checked Nicky's bag and I checked it again. Nothing. He spent the night at mine, and while he was under my roof he did nothing dodgy,' Jason told me.

That's a single twenty-four-hour spell. Good news, but underlying tones suggest there is still a long way to go. We watch with interest, hoping that Nicky can recover, and also that Jason doesn't fall away again. The Booths have given us, and their families, too many good memories for them to be flushed back down some drain alongside the cider dregs in a filthy Nottingham alley.

10

A Special Bond

The Booth brothers lifted Robin Hood country; the Hattons put Hyde on the map, for something other than evil Harold Shipman's lethal injections. Now the Murray duo are trying to motor in Manchester, the Heffron boys are fast stepping up to represent Oldham, and the Walsh trio are growing a fan base on the Norfolk coast. The four Smith brothers are really enjoying the sport's resurgence on Merseyside, while Amir Khan is of course leading the way for Bolton, and his younger brother Haroon, a decent amateur, is desperate to emerge from the shadows soon.

So, boxing brothers are in full bloom. It is more and more the done thing for families – siblings following each other into the squared circle. Healthy competition, important advice passed on, and camaraderie. The guys form their own entourage out of blood ties, and are not relying on outsiders looking to make a quick buck.

John Murray recently enjoyed the longest unbeaten run in British boxing history, until Kevin Mitchell burst his bubble in an astonishing lightweight tussle. Cheering their big bros on in Liverpool in July 2011 were fledgling pros Vinnie Mitchell and

Joe Murray. Of the two younger pups, Joe really looks the one to watch. A member of the successful Beijing Olympic squad, Joe has neat skills, a high work-rate and all the feel of a fighter destined to go places.

I have known John Murray for years. We spent time together in Tampa when he was gaining international experience, and he always told me that Joe was far better than him. Again, the brother displayed no bitterness, just seemed a real family supporter. 'You want to watch the little 'un,' he said after he'd impressed the Americans with a decent win over a tough journeyman, Johnny Walker. 'Joe Murray is absolute class and he's going to light up the pros. He's got the real talent in the family.'

Not that John has done badly winning the British and European 9st 9lb titles. Fiercely proud, with bundles of energy and aggression, he may still go on to achieve his dream of winning a world title.

They are good fighters the Murrays. More importantly, they are good friends, and great brothers.

From nearby Oldham come the Heffrons, whose dad Tommy once reached an ABA final. Ronnie was a former ABA champion and hit the pro ranks first, attempting to throw his left hooks à la Ricky Hatton. Unbeaten and exciting as he is, he may not be as good as brother Mark, who's following close behind. Again, there is no jealousy between this pair who are being brought down different routes by different promoters, so fight apart. It is an interesting idea which might have real benefits.

The Walsh tribe from Cromer are proving fascinating to follow. Elder brother Michael and twins Liam and Ryan are becoming local celebrities on the Norfolk coast. The three are closer than close, and are also right characters, as the Sky cameras discovered when we did 'A Day in the Life' with the brothers. It was madness. They live above an arcade on the pier, talk at a million miles an hour, are always trying to outdo one another, and are generally injecting real vibrancy into the boxing scene.

Liam is already a Commonwealth champion and looks the pick, but Ryan's a decent switch-hitter, and Michael has knocked out everyone he's fought. They even have fun side bets with one another as to who can win most impressively. From a television point of view, it's good having them on the same bill, and they have built quite a fanatical following which adds colour to any show they appear on.

All three brothers are unbeaten at the time of writing and remain interesting prospects. One wonders how they will react when the losses start coming in, as is bound to happen. Will they rally round? Probably. Will one or two of them even begin to drift away? Maybe. It will be intriguing to see what unfolds with those Walsh nutters!

Four brothers who always seem to be together are the boxing Smiths from Liverpool.

Here I must admit, as a passionate Red for many years and once a regular standing and swaying on the Spion Kop, I have a soft spot for fellow Liverpool fans. As a commentator it is important, as I have said, to remain totally neutral, and I always will when calling fights. I have, though, grown close to certain fighters; it is only natural given the amount of time I spend with them.

Paul 'Smigga' Smith is one of those. I first met him through Ricky Hatton when Paul was training at Billy Graham's gym, and I immediately liked the cheeky, chirpy Scouser who was fun to be around. When Hatton fought Juan Lazcano at the City of Manchester Stadium, Smigga was buzzing around the scene. I went to see Ricky in the City players' dressing-room afterwards, and his agent Paul Speak brought in a hold-all containing loads of after-fight party tickets – platinum, gold and silver bands, you name it. As soon as Speaky nipped off to have a shower and get his glam rags on, Smigga pounced, nicking as many bands as he could get into those puncher's hands.

'He never learns, Speak, does he!' Smigga said. 'There you go, Ad – how many do you need?'

The scally in full operation – mischievous, quick and amusing.

Paul Smith could fight too. I used to get so agitated at his lazy attitude, when he switched off both in training and during fights. Smigga had plenty of talent – he was the Commonwealth Games silver medallist, he was burrowing his way through the professional ranks, he possessed plenty of power – and he had a personality that attracted plenty. He's football mad, too. Mates with Carra and Stevie G. Races pigeons. DJs on the Liverpool club scene. Proper family man as well. Top, top boy.

Paul has three fighting brothers. Products of the famous Rotunda Club, they have won an astonishing twenty national amateur titles between them.

'So who's the best of the brothers?' I always ask Smig.

'Not me!'

Paul was the advance party in turning pro and lifted the British super-middleweight title from arch Liverpool rival Tony Quigley on Merseyside. Smith also turned back another Scouse challenge in a bloody battle with Tony Dodson, before he ran into the southpaw skills of Olympic gold medallist James DeGale and was stopped in front of his home crowd. Then he was surprisingly knocked out in just two rounds by George Groves.

'Swifty' Stephen Smith was hot on his heels as a pro. An excellent amateur with an exciting 'pocket battleship' style, Smith won the British and Commonwealth featherweight crowns after a couple of domestic crackers with steely Scot John Simpson, only to be dramatically taken out by Welshman Lee Selby. Still, Stephen has bounced back lately and is going to be in some really exciting fights. Meanwhile, Paul is always there, screaming him on from ringside, often working his corner.

The other two who make up Liverpool's leading boxing family's take on the Fab Four are young professional Liam, and Callum, a tall rangy amateur who like Paul won the Commonwealth Games silver medal. He's certainly another prospect for the future. Paul recently moved to rising trainer Joe Gallagher's stable. Stephen and Liam have followed suit. Now we just wait for Callum to join them.

The Fab Four: fun, close, and highly capable. They have added a real live energy to the rebirth of pugilistic endeavours in Liverpool. After the heroics of John Conteh, Paul Hodkinson and Shea Neary, the Merseybeat had stalled. The Smith brothers have helped bring boxing fire back to this famous sporting city.

Some, maybe all, of these brothers are good enough to become champions; other brothers enter boxing via a far tougher route. Take another set of Smith brothers, twins Billy and Ernie. Virtually inseparable, they grew up amid very difficult circumstances on a gypsy site in the Midlands. Their father wasn't really around, they pretty much had just each other for family, and they learned to fight the hard way. In the fields. Open and bare.

Ernie and Billy are the epitome of how important journey-men are to our sport. They were hardened, seasoned, capable operators who travelled the length and breadth of the country taking on all-comers at very short notice. They didn't win many, but they learned to survive, and if they lasted the distance, there was a bonus: they could fight the next week. Good little money-earners, fighters like these save shows, are crucial to promoters and their matchmakers, and teach the youngsters many old tricks of the trade.

The Smith twins ticked along nicely. Losing hard fights,

upsetting the odd prospect, giving their usual value for money, and well known to all of us in boxing circles. They never let anyone down.

I remember talking to Ernie early doors at one outside broadcast up in Halifax. He'd taken his fight on the day. Quite typical!

'Guys like you two are just critical for the game, Ernie,' I said to him.

'We fight to live. It keeps us in beer money – and lets me have the odd fag too,' he replied, lighting up, only hours before he was due in the ring. Not advisable, but this was a regular fighter. He knew the drill. He knew the business backwards. He also knew why he was there.

'I'll get beat tonight, but the kid will remember me,' Ernie told me. 'I am thinking of starting a landscape gardening business, which can tie in with the boxing. I have been going a long time now; maybe another couple of years, and then I can try something that doesn't hit me back.'

A little while later, there came a bolt from the blue. I was stunned and saddened to read that Ernie had killed himself. He was found hanging from a tree not far from the home in southwest Wales he had set up, near Billy, with his family. It sent shockwaves through boxing.

It is a cruel sport, and it is a cruel world. It was dreadful to read of the loss at the age of just thirty-one of that stalwart of British boxing.

Ernie only won thirteen of 161 fights, but he taught so many prospects so many things, and was a very capable survivor. He went the distance with some of our top fighters, like Nathan Cleverly, Kell Brook, Darren Barker, John Murray and Gavin Rees. I really enjoyed our brief chats at ringside.

Tragic.

And what of Billy, Ernie's twin brother, who was more talented in the ring and, if things had fallen a different way, may well have become a contender for titles? Well, if fighters can't sell tickets, have no promotional backing, and little pedigree, they often go down the journeymen route chosen by the Smith twins. There are still bills to pay. Billy had to fight on, and Johnny Nelson and I decided to travel to Wales to see how he was coming to terms with it all, and hear how he felt about continuing in these incredibly tough circumstances.

Johnny and I had an emotional day. Billy was about to get married to his long-time girlfriend, whom he had met in his day job of a carer. Ernie would obviously have been his best man, so it was a time tinged with extra sadness for the brother left behind.

'I miss Ernie every minute of every day,' he told us. 'We did everything together. He taught me boxing. It gave us a closer bond than normal brothers. Plus we were twins. He was found hanged down there.' He pointed out the fateful spot. It was in beautiful woodland that still makes up part of his morning run. 'I ask myself over and over again, why? Nothing was wrong. I just don't know, and it eats me up inside. Why did he just decide on that day? Life was good. What was going on inside his head? I was his twin so why didn't I know? That's the thing which will haunt me for ever.'

'How do you go on, how do you cope, how do you still function day by day when you were so close and fought alongside each other?' I asked him.

'You have to,' was Billy's reply. 'I will continue fighting, both for me and my family, but also for Ernie. I know he'll be taking the punches for me from up there.'

Billy showed Johnny and me around the neighbourhood which was the Smith twins' escape from the gypsy camps near Stourport-on-Severn. With new friends and support, it was meant to be a new beginning.

'Life will never be the same,' said Billy, welling up. 'I will miss his influence, his advice and his friendship every single day. I have a close bond with his son – my nephew. I am tucking away money each month. He's my responsibility now. Not his mother's. Mine. That's how much Ernie meant to me.'

Not many people know about Ernie and Billy Smith. But Johnny and I got the slow trains back to London and Sheffield humbled by our experience of the blood brothers who were ripped apart. Yet another boxing tale tinged with poignancy and sadness.

Hollywood loves boxing films. From *Raging Bull* to the *Rocky* series, there is something about pugilistic endeavours that appeals deeply to the cinematic world. In 2011 it was the turn of boxing brothers to be examined in the emotional, brilliantly acted and multi-award-winning film *The Fighter*.

The film tells the true tale of 'Irish' Micky Ward, a gritty and (at his level) exciting throwback fighter of a type that crowds love to see. Micky came from a strange brood of characters: a domineering mother, scores of peculiar sisters, and a drug-addicted half-brother called Dicky Ecklund. *The Fighter* chronicles their intense, close but fragile relationship, with much strife caused by Ecklund's crazy world of needles and night-marish behaviour.

Both brothers were fighters, and their mother tried her best to battle the politics of the sport for them while they took their skills into the ring. The film highlights how oblivious boxers can be to the fact that they are never going to make it to the top; that agonizing final realization that they're not what they once were; the dreadful pitfalls of fame; and the beautiful bond brothers have through both joyous and awful times.

Dicky Ecklund was a journeyman. He thought he was a star. He certainly was for a time in his home town of Lowell, Massachusetts, but Dicky got so wrapped up in his own ego, while getting higher and higher on crack, that he – and most of his unhinged family – believed American TV giants HBO were making a movie of his ring success and proposed major comeback. They were actually filming a documentary about the terror of drugs, and his crash into oblivion.

Ecklund had one notable fight. On 18 July 1978, he met Sugar Ray Leonard in Boston and managed to take the fighting legend the distance. Leonard also slipped at one point in the fight and Ecklund has dined out on this for years, claiming it was a knockdown. It wasn't really, even though Ecklund proceeded to step over Leonard's body. But yes, he did last out with one of the truly great boxers who have ever laced them up.

Ecklund fought for a decade between 1975 and 1985, during which time he won nineteen and lost ten. He then became his half-brother's trainer for twenty-six fights, from Micky's pro debut in 1985 until his first retirement in 1991, and was part of the camp pretty much through the remainder of his career. I remember Dicky well on the circuit. A fruitcake maybe, but an amusing one who usually had a smile on his face, and who would always mumble away with some old story or other. But the truth was that when Dicky's career finished he was heading for a five-year stretch for armed robbery, having been addicted to 'virtually everything', according to Micky. So the younger brother who had looked up to his elder actually learnt what he shouldn't do too.

I followed much of Micky Ward's career in the nineties, and enjoyed being ringside for some of his thrilling battles. He had his bad times, once losing six of nine fights, and was forced to work, paving roads. He also qualified as a prison warden. Yet his injured hands started holding up, and Micky Ward finally got going. Three of his bruising wars were voted Fight of the Year by the highly acclaimed *Ring* magazine.

I had the privilege of commentating on the first encounter

of that tremendous trilogy he had with fellow gladiator Arturo 'Thunder' Gatti. Their savage opener stands in my top ten list of great modern fights, both boxers having to go so very deep. Ward prevailed, but Gatti was to turn the tables by changing his tactics and executing a perfect boxing plan in their two other meetings. They found such a unity, sharing their spirits and bearing their souls over their three battles, that they became friends. When Ward retired (after the final Gatti fight on 7 June 2003), he helped train his old nemesis.

Micky standing at Arturo's side on those ring-walks in Atlantic City's Boardwalk Hall is one of those powerful images boxing often drags up. Another tragic and brutal ending was going to hit the sport though. Gatti was found dead, at thirty-seven, in mysterious circumstances when on honeymoon.

The Fighter stops rolling before the Gatti trilogy. In fact it ends with a fight I was heavily involved in during the early days of Sky Sports, when in March 2000 Micky Ward travelled to London to tackle his virtual mirror image, Jimmy 'Shea' Neary, a Merseysider who was as hard as they come. Both loved launching vicious hooks to the body and they dished up a sizzler, Ward's famed left hook to the liver eventually proving just too much for Neary. The fight was the support to Prince Naseem Hamed's four-round obliteration of South Africa's Vuyani Bungu, where most of the magical memories came before the first bell had even rung, after Naz floated to the Olympia ring on a magic carpet. How the purists would have been turning in their graves, I thought at the time. But it was sparkling television. Still, Ward–Neary was the fight of the night, and again, just typical of how much electricity the hard-hitting Massachusetts man brought to the ring. (Incidentally, Neary is now training his son, James Metcalfe, and they even spar together: 'The Shamrock Express' and 'The Mini Shamrock'!)

Mark Wahlberg, a regular at Freddie Roach's Wild Card

Gym, plays Micky in *The Fighter*. Mark trained for four years for the role, and physically looked magnificent. He mimicked Ward's stature and style perfectly. But Wahlberg, though good, is overshadowed in the film by the stunning Christian Bale, who rightfully won both a Golden Globe and an Academy Award for his portrayal of Dicky Ecklund. With his gaunt, haunting, mesmerizing eyes, it was one of those special performances. Amy Adams played Micky's girlfriend Charlene and was nominated for an Oscar, but the Best Supporting Actress went to Melissa Leo, who gave a fabulous portrayal of the brothers' mum, Alice.

The film superbly depicts the juxtaposition of Micky and Dicky's lives and boxing careers: one refusing to accept the inevitable end, the other wading away for any paydays he can get, to try to catch the eye of some high-roller or another willing to gamble on him, 'Irish' Micky Ward.

Dicky, once 'The Pride of Lowell', had been Micky's hero; during the film the tables turn dramatically as Dicky is left split between training duties and the local crackhouse. Their mum Alice and their seven sisters – Alice, Cathy, Cindy, Donna, Gail, Phyllis and Sherri – still look to side with Dicky, 'the family's golden boy', even though he is an ageing wannabe, and hardly the cash cow they all crave. Charlene stands up to the mob in support for her man Micky, and eventually the family come round. Meanwhile, Dicky finds some peace and harmony, particularly in terms of the all-important brother bond.

The Fighter went on to make more than $100 million.

I don't have any full blood brothers, but like Micky and Dicky, I found out early on that my two half-brothers are the real thing. We have a close bond, with friendly, almost joking rivalry. None of us has ever boxed. But if we had, we would all have been there for one another 100 per cent in terms of support, encouragement, help, you name it.

Brothers share secrets, trusts, and bonds. There is a symmetry with brothers, a natural relationship through which they can grow, mature and ultimately 'be'. Together they are responsible for the future welfare of their particular family. Brothers go out to work, brothers carry the family name. It is a vital relationship which can flourish and blossom into something very unique indeed.

I love boxing brothers. There are so many of them! Whether they are of similar standards, or one is superior, in my experience they generally get on and they are good for each other; each provides the perfect foil for the other to go through good and bad times together. On the whole, it certainly brings them closer. The elder brother can teach and the younger can listen; and if the elder makes errors, the younger can learn.

When they are both very good it brings such enjoyment to fight fans, who can then follow a double career path. Comparisons are inevitable. Sometimes it doesn't work, of course, but lessons are often learnt to assist the other sibling on his rise.

Take Devon Alexander, who became the WBC light-welterweight champion against all the odds. From the downtrodden streets of Hyde Park, north St Louis, Devon began boxing at seven. There were thirty young boys alongside him. Eight died; Devon remembers seeing bodies lying on the ground.

Writing this makes me recall my walk around Brooklyn with the very exciting former super-bantamweight king 'Poison' Junior Jones. When he took me around his neighbourhood, there were guys staring out of windows giving the old slitting-throat gesture. Junior told me of friends 'that got killed over there. One got shot just here. Another got hit by a bike there . . .'

Back in St Louis, ten more of Devon Alexander's boxing contemporaries went to jail, including his brother, Vaughn, who was fourteen months older and once a hot prospect himself. The boys had dreams, but Vaughn took the wrong road and was banged up for eighteen years for robbery. Another wasted talent.

As we have seen, there are many success stories, and it is likely that the more skilled and talented brother brings the best out not just of himself, but his brother too. We are compelled to find out who is better; we dream about whether they would ever commit to the ultimate fight (or sin) and tackle each other; we are drawn to following their individual and conjoined tales.

Strong belief, athletic genes and a desire to make better lives for their families draw brothers deep into the sport. Long may that continue.

Four

ABSENT FAMILIES

11

Streetfighting Men

Boxing brothers typically look after each other more than anything. Never has that been more true than with the Peterson boys. Lamont and Anthony were once abandoned and left for dead. They are the archetypal example of boxers being forced to cope with the 'absent family' syndrome.

'It was like living in hell,' Lamont told me as we approached Christmas 2010. There were no 'special' holidays, no 'festive season' for the brothers when they were growing up. Every minute of every hour was an act of survival. Ironically, Lamont and I were chatting in the plush surroundings of the Mandalay Bay, that Golden Tower at the end of the strip in the City of Sin. From survival in the slums to the bright lights of Las Vegas.

You see, Lamont and Anthony were kicked out of home. They had done nothing, and then they had nothing. The brothers spent their nights sleeping in abandoned cars and bus stations in and around America's political heartbeat.

Washington DC. A city I became very familiar with in the early nineties when I worked at the American news channel CNN. A pompous, rich, yet desperately deprived metropolis all mixed into one. A beautiful place with bloody awful patches. The highbrow flock to DC where they are surrounded by spectacular architecture and intellectual institutions. Yet turn a corner and you may be gunned down. No joke. Washington is a seriously wonderful but seriously risky city. Fabulous and frightening. Rather like boxing really.

The Peterson brothers grew up in horrendous circumstances amid drugs and guns in Joliet Street in the Bellevue area of south-west DC. I never ventured there, but I did experience the infamous 'Navy Yard' in the south-east part of the city. The sound of guns firing was my lasting memory.

With their father locked up and their mother both unable to cope with extreme poverty and harbouring dreadful personal demons, the Peterson kids were left on the streets to fend for themselves. By the time Lamont was ten and Anthony just nine, the brothers were cutting up crack cocaine to hand to dealers in the slums and robbing from drunks. Their life was virtually snuffed out before it had begun.

'There were seven boys and five girls,' Lamont told me. 'Twelve of us. I was pitched out with Anthony and we hit the alleys. We learned the art of stealing from the rich in areas like Cleveland Park, Adam's Morgan and Georgetown.'

These words hit home hard. Back in 1993, and before I worked in boxing, I was fortunate enough to be living with friends in a four-bedroom house in Cleveland Park. Little did I know that just a few miles away these kids were cutting crack simply to get through another day. Makes you think, doesn't it.

'My brother and I had nothing,' Lamont continued. 'Our parents didn't care. We were chucked out like the garbage, and yet supporting and helping each other, and with our mentor Barry Hunter, we came through. Somehow. Boxing saved us. I knew many, many people who are now dead. I have lost count. It was the way it was.'

Barry Hunter deserves enormous credit. He ran a construction business, and not only did he take the boys in, he also taught them how to box in his Bald Eagle gym. They gained discipline, learned rules, and had a new family to love them.

By the end of 2011, following his amazing points victory over Amir Khan, Lamont Peterson stood with an excellent record of thirty professional wins from thirty-two fights. His younger brother won his first thirty. They are both flitting around the world scene – an amazing achievement considering the journey they have endured. The Peterson brothers are well spoken, humble, and importantly they have forgiven those who have done them wrong. They have got back in touch with their father, and still continue attempts to reunite their splintered family.

The Petersons are a shining example of how this brutal sport can actually be beautiful. How boxing can save lives. There will always be the detractors who call for a ban on the sport. Yes, it is risky and full of potholes, hazards and occasionally devastating consequences. But plenty of young men are brought back from the brink through boxing. They are taught how to channel aggression through tight and programmed discipline, and are then educated in the science of the sport.

The Petersons are inspirational. Look at it differently: how fortunate was I to have a roof over my head, food on the table and companions to socialize with while I was a long way from home during that winter of 1993? Just stop for a minute and try to contemplate the treacherous surroundings of that ghetto on Joliet Street. Crackhouses. Shootings. Murder. Unimaginable fear for a couple of children. The brothers weren't much older than my daughter Jessamy, who is now six and constantly craves protection, like any small, sweet, nervous and immature kid.

If it wasn't for boxing, there is no doubt that Lamont and Anthony Peterson would no longer be with us.

'I count myself lucky every day,' Lamont told me back in 2010. 'On Saturday night I am in Vegas and living out every boxer's dream. What is particularly incredible about this fight [in December 2010] is that I am meeting Victor Ortiz. He knows exactly how cruel life really is. We have similar stories.'

I listened intently to the rather shy, calm and organized Lamont Peterson, and then I wandered over to the MGM Grand, heading for the tasty Mexican restaurant Diegos, where a dinner was being hosted by Golden Boy Promotions. Victor Ortiz made an appearance, and I fully discovered what Lamont had meant. Yes, I had heard the tale of Ortiz. Troubled background. Found a boxing soul mate. Polished skills. Could be a future gem. But then, you hear that with many fighters. Still, Ortiz's story was another enthralling voyage.

'Childhood in Kansas wasn't good,' Victor began. 'In fact it was a constant struggle. I was forced to pick alfalfa in Garden City as a child.'

Now, anyone who has met the affable, good-looking and approachable Victor Ortiz comes away with one firm impression. It's made by his smile, which is broad and beaming. For me, here in Vegas, there was no smile as Victor recollected his haunted past.

'I had parents but I don't care about them. They just left. Deserted. My mother vanished one day. My family was destroyed in forty-eight hours. My mother said I would never amount to anything, and years later my father told my brother exactly the same thing. I say "Fuck you". One time I drew my mother a picture of a rose and she hurled it at me saying, "What do I want that shit for?" My mother left when I was seven. My father got me into boxing because I was bullied for being in a choir, but then he became a violent alcoholic who ended up smashing up my sister Carmen and brother Temo. He also beat me after I lost an amateur bout when I was eight. When I was twelve, he left.'

So Victor was effectively an orphan before his teenage years.

Totally abandoned by his Mexican immigrant parents. But, as with the Petersons, there were knights in shining armour. Ignacio 'Bucky' Avila helped tutor Victor at the Garden City Boxing Club. He was the dad Victor never had, and although Bucky has passed away, Victor still rings his widow after each of his fights. Then former world champion and hot trainer Roberto Garcia became a role model. Finally, there was the Golden Boy himself, Oscar De La Hoya, who raves about 'Vicious' Victor. 'I love that kid,' Oscar told me. 'He has been through so much, and yet he is extremely polite, has the movie star looks, sparkling charisma, the dedication – and boy can he fight!'

Victor was forced to grow up young and fast. His home was a banged-up trailer where he lived in squalor, without gas or electricity. By ten he was winning amateur championships while dealers shadowed his every move. At ten. Just like the Petersons. Can you believe that? By twelve, he was working long days, illegally, in the cornfields. He was also in care.

Boxing was Victor's only structure, and he excelled at it, winning 141 of 161 bouts before turning professional. A hard-hitting right-handed converted southpaw, Ortiz's power, he told me, really came from his straight left.

Along with boxing, his sister Carmen came to the rescue by adopting him, and he went to Denver to live with her. But when Carmen was evicted, Victor moved on again. This time he ended up in Oxnard, California, where a boxing manager called Rolando Arellano hooked him up with Roberto Garcia, who became Victor's legal guardian. Arellano had spotted Ortiz's vast ability in the amateurs, as had the late former heavyweight Ron Lyle.

'Despite my parents constantly telling me that I would be a failure, I was good at boxing and I managed to get a diploma from Pacifica High School in 2005,' Victor said. 'I even majored in business at Oxnard College, but had to give that up when my career began to get serious.'

Ortiz's perfect professional record was blotted in 2005 by a strange disqualification for hitting after the break when in total control against Corey Alarcon, but his quick-fire wins and his exciting style tempted Golden Boy to come knocking. 'We always thought Victor could become a star,' Richard Schaefer told me on the phone from his LA headquarters recently. 'It's an unbelievable story. He is so brave to have come this far with no parenting. Fighters need their families for support. Victor's left him lonely and hungry. But it was the making of him. He is a beautiful guy, and we at Golden Boy feel like we are the family now. The family he never had. He is special for all of us here. We have basically adopted him.'

Whenever I see Victor Ortiz around the Golden Boy crew, I see exactly what Richard means. There is a really tight-knit bond. Promoters are often criticized for looking after number one and fleecing the fighters who take all the real risks, but after all Victor has been through, maybe there is something different here. Maybe. Money can of course change a lot of things, but it's good to see him being loved and cared for at the moment.

While problems have continued – he declared himself bankrupt a few years ago, and adopted his brother Temo only to see him walk out amid troubled scenes, as well as discovering that he had another sister, Aneli, who is blind – Victor Ortiz has persevered. His ring performances have sometimes been strange though; maybe there's deeper psychology at work due to the rocky road he's been forced to travel. On 27 June 2009, he faced the feared Argentinian puncher Marcos Maidana, who had won twenty-five of his previous twenty-six by KO. It was a barnstormer of a fight – and that is usually the case when Victor Ortiz gets into a ring. Both men were down in a dramatic first round. Then Maidana was felled twice in the second. It looked all over, but Ortiz then got cut, and was floored again in the sixth. He got up, was asked by the referee if he was OK, shook his head, turned away, and the fight was waved off. Some critics jumped straight on that ending, believing that he had quit. In the post-fight interview, Victor basically said that he didn't need to get badly hurt, implying there was more to life. It was so strange, because of the hardship he'd been through. We were left puzzled. Did he lack heart in the heat of battle?

It's possible that it's just one of those things big punchers go through. If they can't knock their opponent out, doubts start to creep in. Roberto Duran famously called 'No más' ('No more') against Sugar Ray Leonard, and there was no harder man than 'The Hands of Stone'. A similar thing happened to Nigel Benn in his clashes with Ireland's 'Celtic Warrior' Steve Collins. After all the powerful displays, it suddenly looked like the Benn tank had emptied.

Yet Victor Ortiz was young when he faced the music after Maidana. He had fired Roberto Garcia and his father after feeling they had humiliated him. So there were obviously major issues out there.

With plenty of things to sort out in his head, Victor actually decided to stick with the Garcia family and joined forces with Roberto's brother Danny. He was also desperate to have sole and undivided attention – unsurprisingly, after all he had been through.

He finally proved the doubters wrong when he rose from his natural light-welterweight division to rip the WBC welterweight crown away from and take the unbeaten scalp of Floridian powerhouse Andre Berto. On 16 April 2011, in a contender for fight of the year both men were floored twice, but Ortiz's fast hands and southpaw movement gave Berto real problems and the adopted Californian scored a sensational upset win by decision. An intriguing rematch is scheduled for June 2012.

The result proved that Victor Ortiz has huge heart, bottle and courage. But then deep down we always knew he did. Maybe the Maidana fight was a shock to the system, maybe it was just a mishap. As in most situations during his eventful albeit so far short life, Victor found an answer, and the multi-million-dollar prize was a fight with my pick of the modern greats, the supremely skilled Floyd Mayweather Jnr. Ortiz was not expected to win, and never really got into the fight before there was the most bizarre conclusion in the fourth round: Ortiz panicked and butted his opponent before apologizing profusely, dropping his guard, and getting knocked to the canvas by an angry Mayweather.

I have so much time for Victor. I like him. He lights up a room. 'I love my English fans,' he told me ahead of the Lamont Peterson fight, 'and you know what, I really fancy that Hermione from *Harry Potter*. Tell her I'm coming to London to find her!' That huge smile, the infectious charm. Emma Watson has a sugary sweet admirer. And a fighter for life. To the core.

So what happened when the battle of the lost children from broken homes was joined in the Nevada desert? Well, Victor got the early knockdowns with the blisteringly fast and exciting start we have come to expect, but Lamont then responded gallantly. The judges couldn't split them, the result was a draw, and it was perhaps the perfect ending to my fight week.

They were both left standing, just as in life. It is a testament to their extraordinary self-belief and survival instinct. Much like wild animals, they found a way to cope. But nicer, more professional athletes you couldn't wish to meet. If you were lucky enough to share a room or have a chat with either the Peterson boys or Victor Ortiz somewhere, some time, you'd be blissfully unaware of their ravaged pasts. Wonderful guys forged from the most horrific backgrounds imaginable. Their harrowing tales are a wake-up call to us all. How their natural families must regret every selfish, deplorable decision they made.

Families are all different. It's a fact of life. Many are close, some more distant, a few at war; there are those who have families who are dogmatic, difficult, even dysfunctional. But what the vast majority provide is a base. A solid foundation. We have a wooden swing in our garden inscribed with the simple but rather magical phrase 'For the generations to come'. I'm writing this while watching little Jessamy learning to swing alone. A playful, innocent scene; she is safe in the knowledge that there is always someone watching her. A number of family members are just a call away. Familiarity. Support. Comfort.

Once in a while we read about a family ripped apart by some shocking accident. Parents die young. Babies are left orphaned. Catastrophic news, and something none of us can conceive actually happening to us. Yet in those dreadful situations we tend to hear about some good, some positives coming out of the horror. Grandparents rally round. Uncles and aunts. A network begins to build a shell around the survivors. Natural mummies, daddies, big brothers or baby sisters can never be replaced, but at least there are people who care deeply, and strands of family, however distant, coming to the rescue. There is help, there is concern, and in time there will again be deep love.

But for some boxers, as we have seen, it doesn't take car crashes or sudden illnesses to be left alone. Members of their families have simply chosen to walk out.

Few people can understand what it's like to lose both parents, fewer still that these instrumental figures might actually opt not to be involved at all. Who do these poor kids turn to for help and protection? How on earth do they cope? How do they become successful, not just in sport but also in life, with this sort of destructive start? Who will relate to them, and whom will they relate to?

The pain of knowing yourself to be completely alone in the world must be a massive burden to bear. Who is there to genuinely, and I mean genuinely, care for you? Children are the most precious gift in the world. To desert them is almost unforgivable to me. Even if there is no money, there can still be love. But to dismiss your children and to protect yourself is possibly the nastiest, most abysmal call of all.

Imagine the fear, the anxiety, the sadness, the pain, the numbness, the anger those who are abandoned feel. Such emotions are surely too much to bear on one's own. Where will the advice and help come from? There is the argument that those who know no different learn to deal with their situations. But boy, it must be tough. Especially if you then find yourself attempting to cope physically and financially with the lies, scandal and general skulduggery that comes hand in glove with the hardest sport there is.

I have mates who have lost a parent, others who have fallen out with one, but the majority of my friends have been moulded by their fathers and mothers. For forty years my parents have been guiding me. I can't imagine how I would have done it alone. A support system is crucial, essential, for development. As children, we may not always agree with our parents' decisions, but we know they are always there for us. From birthday parties to Easter egg hunts to presents and stockings under the Christmas tree. Just for learning to walk, to talk, to dress, to feed ourselves. Schooling, sports, jobs – the list is endless. And most of us take all this entirely for granted. The fighters who feature in this section have had none of these things whatsoever.

The kindergarten years of life are critical for giving children confidence and for setting them up to handle the sort of issues that pepper adulthood: affording food and clothes, paying off a mortgage, paying the bills, health worries, you name it. Parents have a natural role to play in shaping their child. Some believe that those youngsters who have little or no contact with their parents in those early days are more likely to develop a mental health problem later in life, or resort to anti-social behaviour. Doctors and scientists often focus on the first six years of life, when in particular the mother's role is vital. This period forms the child's personality and sense of security within the home environment; it is the time when insecurities can quickly develop. Parental abandonment can also lead to extremely low self-esteem in children. Do they begin to feel that they deserved to be left alone? That they were merely an unwanted burden?

Many boxers from broken homes suffer throughout their lives as a result. Some are not as lucky as the likes of Victor Ortiz, to be looked after and to be earning very decent cash. Without guidance and education, more misery can befall these unfortunate souls. Tragic starts can lead to tragic ends – and fighters sometimes attract tragedy all the way through their careers.

'Absent families are not a good idea for this sport,' Richard Schaefer told me. 'Fighters need protection, they need a shoulder to cry on. It is a very hard business. If there is no one there, they cannot release their feelings, their emotions – and that is not healthy.'

Having people who support and care about you is very important. Trust is everything. Fighters from difficult backgrounds often find themselves a father or mother figure, or a girlfriend or wife by whom they can be almost entirely guided. But total reliance on someone outside their natural family can lead to disturbing and dangerous obsessions.

Trainers like Brendan Ingle in Sheffield and Freddie Roach in Hollywood dedicate themselves not just to steering fighters towards world titles, but to nurturing and bringing them up through a different type of education. In many ways, they provide schools for life.

'Take someone like my old stablemate Jason Collins,' Johnny Nelson told me recently. 'Jason was in a very bad way. He had a troublesome childhood, with no real future. When he arrived at Brendan's he had no confidence. But the old master is brilliant at making everyone feel like part of the family. These guys are not all going to be champions, but they learn discipline and are basically taught invaluable lessons. Jason made some money from boxing, learned skills, has found friends, and now he is in a much better place. Good job, nice family – it works.'

Brendan himself loves fairytales. 'Johnny Nelson is *the* product of my system,' he said. 'He was scared, useless, no confidence, nothing when he arrived. He was the laughing stock of my gym. Look what he achieved. Undefeated world champion. Beautiful family. No ego, and now you've got him, Adam – we are so proud of that.'

Over in the States, Freddie Roach is like the Pied Piper. Of course, success breeds success, and with the likes of Manny Pacquiao and Amir Khan spearheading the stable, other wannabes are attracted. But his basic, no-frills gym above a launderette in a seedy part of Hollywood is full of all sorts of waifs and strays. Tramps training side by side with boxing greats and movie stars.

'We call him Columbo, that one there,' Freddie explained to me one day at the Wild Card Gym very early on in our working relationship. 'He was homeless, lost an eye. Going nowhere. He begged me to take him in, and I gave him a chance. He sweeps the gym, in return for sleeping here. If he doesn't work, he goes. He knows that. Now they've got him in HBO's *24:7* previews! Columbo's a cult character of the gym.'

Boxing conjures up these inspirational figures who do so

much good, but they are not the fighter's blood family. Given a nightmarish entry into the hardships of the world, these boys who become men and fight are often bewildering and crazy yet absolutely fascinating and engaging individuals.

It is time to meet the maddest I have come to know.

12

Iron Mike

He was once the most recognizable sporting icon on the planet. Feared, ferocious, a frightening fighting menace. His helter-skelter rise and fall made headlines on both the front and back pages. As dominant inside the ring as he was destructive outside it, his story was pure movie material.

Everyone knew Mike Tyson. Virtually everyone had an opinion on him too.

A couple of years ago, my boss asked me to prepare an obituary on Muhammad Ali. It was a sad job to have to undertake, but unsurprising really given the decline in health of 'The Greatest'. Once the piece was cut, he asked me to do another. On Mike Tyson. Even though the youngest ever heavyweight champion of the world was only in his early forties, I understood exactly why an obituary should be at the ready.

At that time Tyson's most beloved companion was his big cat – his tiger. The man himself had lived at least nine lives through turbulent times. There were scores of appalling moments amid the obvious vast appeal of his boxing capabilities. So many managers and promoters came and went; trainers were also hired and fired at an electric rate after the collapse of the successful working relationship Tyson enjoyed with Kevin Rooney.

In the build-up to Tyson's long-awaited clash with Lennox Lewis in 2002, I travelled around America talking to many of those creative corner men. There was Richie Giachetti, whose training style was aggressive and vocal. The brilliant, unaffected Freddie Roach. The outspoken, fiery Teddy Atlas. The relaxed, cool Tommy Brooks.

'How will the story end?' I asked Tommy on a ride up from New York.

'Back in the gutter, I would expect,' came the reply, fired at me almost as quickly as those machine-gun-like combinations Tyson was famous for. 'Look at where he came from. Look at what he made. Four hundred million. All squandered. All gone. Who actually loves him? Who ever did? He was brought up in crazy conditions. Guess that's where he'll die. With a bullet through him, I predict. Such a shame. Such a tragic waste.' Tommy's voice was tinged with emotion.

Teddy Atlas agreed. He was even talking about Tyson back in 2002 as though he was no longer with us. 'Remember, I was in the Catskills when he was growing up. I knew what he was like. Mike Tyson will never be remembered as a great fighter. It was all way too short. Just like a shooting star. Brilliant – but then it's gone. Being great is lasting, not fading away.'

Tracking Tyson down was worse than waiting for Naseem Hamed. We knew where he trained in Las Vegas, but would he be there? How many heavies would be on the door? Would we be turfed out? What mental state would he be in? Had he taken his happy pills? You just never knew what to expect from this modern-day Dr Jekyll.

I used to take my colleague Glenn McCrory along with me. Not only is Glenn big and useful protection, he also has a distinct charm and can talk his way into places which are notoriously difficult to access. Plus Glenn had had the dubious privilege of being one of Tyson's sparring partners when Iron Mike was red-hot.

'He always respected me,' Glenn told me as we sat outside Tyson's boxing shed in about 120 degrees of Nevada desert heat and dust. 'I turned up in tight shorts and white trainers. I thought he was going to kill me. But I stood my ground, and he liked that. He used to wipe sparring partners out. Bloody brutalize them.' We chatted over supersized bags of Doritos, our sustenance while we were pawns in Tyson's game.

Not only did you never know what you were going to get, you never knew when you were going to get it either. One day Tyson's cheerleader Crocodile did that slitting-throat gesture that I had experienced on Junior Jones's Brooklyn streets. We were told to 'Get the fuck out, fast.' But we'd be back: given Tyson's dramatic, pendulum-swinging moods, we might be given the red carpet treatment the next day. He was utterly unpredictable.

I wanted to ask Mike many things on that trip, but mostly I was interested in how he himself would like to be remembered when all was said and done.

When I finally got the chance, interviewing him tested me to the full. It was tough not to be intimidated, but it was my job, and my responsibility to our viewers, to get the most out of our intriguing subjects as possible. Gently get them to open up, like a flower in the spring sunshine, and then fire in the arrows. Even at Tyson's cooperative best this required intense concentration; at his truculent worst . . . that didn't bear thinking about. So, what of that question on a lasting memory?

'I just want to be remembered as a good person, a humble individual,' Tyson told me as we came to the end of our chat on the edge of his ring, with over a hundred people crammed into the sweltering gym, listening intently to his answers. 'I want my children to be good citizens. To help old ladies cross the road.

To be respectful. To open doors and be good people. And I just want to go and find a lot of pussy to fuck.'

There was silence in the shed. A silence that Tyson broke with a bellowing laugh.

Inside the mind of a madman. Imagine the out words to that feature: 'Pussy to fuck'. Oh my God.

This was Mike Tyson. One minute he was kissing a baby, the next he was banged up for rape. He kept every single one of us guessing, and I am convinced these violent episodes were engrained deep in his atrocious childhood. Maybe those crucial first six years of his life.

The Brooklyn districts of Brownsville and Bedford-Stuyvesant were certainly eye-openers for me when I paid them a visit to see what Tyson had emerged from. I thought the badlands of Philly were rough when Charles 'The Hatchet' Brewer showed me the cardboard shack he'd once survived in. We didn't want to outstay our welcome in Bedford-Stuyvesant. Murals on grey walls pay homage to Tyson, but if the area had cleaned itself up of late one could only imagine what sort of carnage had surrounded little Michael Gerard back in the day.

His loving dad cleared off when Tyson was two. His mum was plagued with problems and died when Tyson was in his teens. He never got to have any sort of relationship with her, because he was way out of control long before he became a teenager. Mike bizarrely befriended racing pigeons, an obsession that has interestingly come back into his adult life. Maybe he only feels totally free and himself when he is with his birds. The flying variety.

By the age of twelve and a half, Tyson had been arrested over thirty times. He mugged old ladies, and despite his small size and embarrassing lisp, he was notorious on those Brooklyn streets. He tackled those who dared ridicule him. There he learned how to fight, destroying one youth who had yanked off the head of one of his beloved pigeons. Tyson would definitely have become deadly if he hadn't been saved by being sent to the Tryon School for Boys.

A juvenile detention counsellor, Bobby Stewart, saw the talent in Tyson and passed him to an eccentric old trainer/manager called Cus D'Amato, who had mentored former heavyweight king Floyd Patterson. Cus and his companion Camille Ewald took Mike to their sprawling home in the Catskill mountains. Cus was made his legal guardian, and became the father Mike never had. Cus taught him to listen and learn, he taught him to fight, he taught him life.

Cus also had a huge boxing library of all the old greats of the sport. I vividly remember Mike sitting with Britain's legendary boxing commentator Harry Carpenter going through many of his fighting idols, like Willie Pep and Kid Chocolate. Cus predicted that if Tyson stayed on the straight and narrow, his name would be added to that illustrious list.

After a decent but not phenomenal amateur career, Mike blazed into the paid ranks with a string of devastating knockouts. Once he'd pulverized his preliminary opposition with nineteen straight KO wins, an amazing twelve of them in the first round, it seemed D'Amato would be proved spot on.

Looking back on that early highlights reel now, it seems barbaric. Black shorts, black boots, the cold eyes in the face-offs, the twitching neck, the lightning speed, the awesome power generated. Despite weighing only fifteen and a half stone, and a couple of inches shy of six feet, Mike Tyson seemed unstoppable.

Yet his life has been plagued by loss. His mother Lorna died young, then his sister Denise was lost at just twenty-five. The most harrowing thing for Mike, though, was when he was forced to bury Cus before he had become a champion. Carrying the coffin really broke Mike's heart. 'Everything good I ever did was a result of Cus D'Amato. I loved Cus. He was my world,' Mike told me when we were catching up in London a while back. His manager Jim Jacobs also passed away. As recently as May 2009, tragedy struck hard when his four-year-old daughter Exodus was found dangling from an exercise treadmill cord. So you can understand why I was asked to write his obituary.

What we can't take away from 'Iron' Mike Tyson was his raw ability, menacing attraction, ring achievements and, for a time, that aura of invincibility. Armed with trainer Kevin Rooney, Tyson rocked the boxing world in 1986 by demolishing Trevor Berbick in two rounds. The image of Berbick reeling all over the ring, collapsing, rising and crashing back into the ropes sits in many fight fans' minds. What has stayed with me was the American commentary: 'And we have a new era in boxing.'

It was so true. After dedicating this stunning title triumph to Cus D'Amato, Tyson cleaned up, unifying the glamorous but fractured heavyweight division by capturing the WBA and IBF crowns at the expense of James 'Bonecrusher' Smith and Tony Tucker. He was still only twenty. Tyson's felling of Pinklon Thomas stands out for me; a ferocious thirty-second-long combination of hooks and uppercuts finished proceedings there. Several top heavyweights, like Tyrell Biggs, were dispatched in a similar fashion.

The peak was the destruction in June 1988 of Michael Spinks, one of the best light-heavyweights we'd seen, who had previously never lost a fight. Now settled at heavyweight, Spinks met Tyson in Atlantic City in a mega-match. There were reports of a frustrated Mike drilling a hole in a locker door with his fist when warming up in his dressing-room. He wasn't in the mood for hanging around, and obliterated Spinks in just ninety-one seconds.

'That was Mike Tyson at his most destructive,' Alex Stewart told me as he helped Oliver McCall prepare for his world title defence against Frank Bruno within the plush grounds of the

English health farm Champneys. 'When I met Mike Tyson, I got blitzed. Reason: when we came face to face I thought he was an animal. I admit I was terrified,' the very capable London-born American heavyweight revealed.

That is quite something, when a fighter admits to an intimate secret like that.

But Teddy Atlas was right: the shooting star didn't last. Cracks began to appear in Tyson's personal life, while his professional career lay in Don King's hands.

Tyson still defended his heavyweight crown nine times, proving far too much for the old, once supreme Larry Holmes and our brave and beloved Frank Bruno, before then spinning Tony Tubbs around in almost comical fashion out in Tokyo.

The return to Japan in February 1990 was, of course, the next focal point of the Tyson ring tale. By the time he met the unfancied James 'Buster' Douglas, his life was in utter turmoil.

Over the years, Mike has had eight children with several different women and been married three times, most recently to Monica Turner and then Lakiha Spicer. It was his first marriage, to glamorous *Head of the Class* actress Robin Givens, which was the most unhinged. There were constant allegations of violence. Givens told US chat-show host Barbara Walters that her life with Tyson was 'pure hell'. Mike sat right next to her during that interview looking sheepish, bewildered and lost.

Tyson, you could argue, was himself taken advantage of by Robin, and her mother Ruth Roper. There was apparently no prenuptial agreement between the two. Ruth and Robin bought a huge mansion in Bernardsville, New Jersey. Robin reportedly suffered a miscarriage, but Tyson said she was never pregnant and has claimed he was forced into marriage. Reports say that she received $10 million in the divorce settlement. Ironically, Robin Givens had also grown up in New York City and been abandoned by her father at the age of two. Not an absent family, but a hurtful one still has a major effect.

Tyson was fast becoming a manic depressive. He had a street brawl with former opponent Mitch Green, was hurling rocks at TV cameras, and when he crashed his sports car into a tree, many thought it was a failed suicide attempt. Iron Mike was unravelling fast, and despite many people claiming they were his friends and there to protect him, the truth was that, despite the terror he brought into the ring, he was an easy target. Uneducated, with no structure or family backbone, Mike Tyson was unable to handle either the fame or the vast amounts of money he earned. There was no true support system in place. Well, certainly nothing he could fully trust.

I was at university in North Carolina on the night Mike Tyson lost his heavyweight crown, and his aura, in Tokyo. I didn't see the unbelievable fight live, but word passed through the frat houses of Davidson College that Tyson had been beaten. No one could believe it. I saw one huge American football player sobbing in a corner. It was like the end of an era. Few could accept that this massive underdog Douglas had overcome the monster. The king was dead. It was a most sobering experience. When I woke up the next morning, I thought I must have dreamt it; I was completely unable to comprehend this most unexpected news.

The fight provided another picture postcard of the Tyson career. Scrambling around on the canvas, trying desperately to put his gum shield back in, almost like a baby who has lost his dummy. He knew what to do, but his body couldn't compute. It was shocking. I'm not sure he ever fully recovered from the Douglas experience. They tried to call it all a fix, that old Buster had survived a long count earlier in the fight, but the raw truth was that Tyson had been beaten. He was no longer invincible.

The freefall came fast. Despite two victories over Donovan

'Razor' Ruddock in 1991, Tyson was soon back at rock bottom. He was meant to challenge the new champion Evander Holyfield, who had swatted aside a timid attempt by Buster Douglas to retain his crown (it looked like Buster had been training in a burger bar). Yet with Givens gone, Tyson was on the prowl, and there was more controversy when he met a young lady called Desiree Washington at a beauty pageant. Tyson was accused and then convicted of rape. He was sentenced to ten years in jail, the last four of which were suspended. The fall from grace was complete.

Despite the fact he only served half the sentence, Tyson – much like Ali when he was banned from boxing over his refusal to go to Vietnam – lost some of his most potent years. Although, unlike 'The Greatest', the longevity wasn't there with Tyson, and despite the fact that I had loved that so-called ring invincibility of Iron Mike, I felt that the bubble had well and truly burst out in Japan.

Tyson read huge amounts of literature, and apparently reformed when inside, converting to Islam. His release was a nationwide event, and it was no real surprise to see Don King there to greet him. Then a right couple of characters in trilbys emerged, who claimed to be guiding the revival. It struck me that this was more of the same: people keen to get a piece of the action; Tyson a lost soul.

We all watched as Tyson obliterated Peter McNeeley in farcical circumstances, destroyed Buster Mathis, and then regained the WBC crown as he wiped out Frank Bruno, who had crossed himself thirteen times on the way to the ring for their rematch. Tyson fell to his knees after the three-round hammering, leaving our Frank to admit, 'He was on me like a harbour shark. I didn't know where the punches were coming from. I'm so sorry to everyone in England.' There was of course no disgrace in losing to Tyson, who then blew away WBA champion Bruce Seldon with some sort of phantom punch in a poor one-round spectacle.

Then, in November 1996, came the long-awaited clash with Holyfield. Sky sent me to see Evander at his training head-quarters in Houston. He had been written off by every single boxing critic apart from Ron Borges of the *Boston Globe*. Let's get this straight. Nobody believed he'd win. Most felt it was a stretcher job – Holyfield in hospital after one round. The form suggested this. In their trilogy, Riddick Bowe had taken plenty out of Holyfield, who had also been advised to stop boxing on account of heart problems after he failed to get past moody southpaw Michael Moorer.

At Evander's Houston house (not that one with 109 rooms on Evander Holyfield Highway in Atlanta, but a pretty nice choice for a boxing camp nonetheless) I wanted to know how he thought he was going to survive against Mike Tyson. That was when he spoke to me about his faith in the Lord. 'I'll be fine,' he told me. 'I'm not scared of Mike Tyson. I have known him a very long time and I am not scared.'

The next morning he was outside his gym waiting for us at 4.45 a.m. 'The early bird catches the worm,' he remarked. That remains one of my favourite sayings in life.

I returned home and had a small flutter on Evander. I didn't think he'd prevail, I just liked him and his fearless attitude. After all, if the bully can't out-bully, has he got a plan B?

And so it unfolded. Tyson was out-hustled, out-thought and taken out for the second time in his life, in the dramatic eleventh round. 'That's the biggest upset in the fight game bar none,' stated Britain's other legendary commentator, Reg Gutteridge. It was, again, a monumental shock to the system.

The multi-million-dollar rematch happened in the MGM, Vegas. My colleagues Ian Darke and Glenn McCrory told me there were gunshots flying around the casino. A most dodgy night. Certainly a dodgy, and unsavoury, ending when Tyson, arguably looking for a way out as opposed to taking another beating, bit a chunk out of Holyfield's ear. Tyson complained that it was due to the use of Holyfield's head, that as a result 'he went back to the streets', but it was disgraceful behaviour and it was plastered all over front pages around the world. He was banned from Nevada. More problems with the law. Again, this was Tyson at his troublesome worst.

Yet there was still a magnetism, a fascination about Iron Mike. This time music mogul Shelly Finkel and Frank Warren involved themselves in a comeback, bringing the iconic heavyweight to Britain twice in the year 2000. Just like Tyson's double-sided personality, the two appearances on these shores were like chalk and cheese.

When he came over in January to face south London's Julius Francis, Brixton traffic stopped for him. Then, for the fight itself in Manchester, it was again manic. He was smiley, friendly, a pleasure to be around. Ian Darke got a wonderful and revealing interview with him: 'Mike and Tyson. We're two different people. Tyson's the product. I'm just Mikey. A family man. Tyson – people treat me like the gum on the bottom of your shoe.'

The weigh-in was bizarre, though. Speculation flooded the Midland Hotel that Tyson wasn't going to fight and that the show would fall apart. In fact Mike remained cool, sitting on the stage, twirling his hair. There must have been two hundred cameras pointed at him. There was an eerie silence. No one wanted to say anything if there was even the slightest chance of antagonizing the star attraction. Another Tyson moment I will never forget.

After defeating the rather tame challenge of Francis, Tyson was back in a fiery and fractious mood in June to tackle the gigantic but rather limited American Lou Savarese on a rain-drenched summer's night at Glasgow's Hampden Park. We were under black covers at ringside for most of the bill. Despite the appalling Scottish weather, the hunter approached the ring seeking out his prey in typical Tyson fashion. Savarese was down within seconds, and the whole sorry and soggy spectacle was wrapped up in the very first minute of the first round. Referee John Coyle even tumbled to the ground when Tyson continued to fight after the contest had been waved off. The Showtime interviewer Steve Gray approached the victor moments later, and Tyson was in some rage. Like a caged animal. There followed the infamous 'I want his heart, to eat his children' line directed at Lennox Lewis.

So Britain had seen the good, the bad and the ugly sides. My colleague Sara Chenery witnessed more anguish when on a fleeting visit to Hawaii to film training shots in the build-up to the Lewis fight, Tyson stuck up a V-sign and hurled abuse at our cameras. Maybe it was all just getting too much for him. Maybe he needed stronger medication. Maybe he'd just had his boxing time. Deep down he was surely ring-smart enough to realize that his best days were behind him.

The Lewis–Tyson clash was almost twenty years in the making. Lewis had joined Tyson as a teenager in the Catskills, so they had known of each other for two decades. The big fights between Lewis and Bowe, and Bowe and Tyson, had never materialized, and the worry was that Lewis–Tyson would follow suit. But it eventually happened, in the Pyramid in Memphis in 2002. Too late for both men, really, especially for Tyson.

With all the money at stake, and Tyson at his most volatile, there was genuine concern in the final hours that Tyson would do something bizarre. His state of mind was extremely worrying. Ironically, when he turned up for battle, he couldn't have been nicer, kissing HBO's long-time floor manager Tami Cotel and looking anything but the menacing figure we had come to expect, and whom I had genuinely feared interviewing.

I'll never forget when he walked towards me after his

one-sided defeat of Denmark's cult heavyweight Brian Nielsen in Copenhagen in 2001. Brian couldn't cope with Tyson's power, but won the hearts of the fans for coming out to probably the most comically chosen ring-walk music I have ever heard, Monty Python's 'Always Look on the Bright Side of Life'. That remains one of my and Bob Mee's favourite boxing moments.

I was waiting in a room at the end of a long corridor for a post-fight interview. Suddenly Tyson's huge entourage of about twenty heavies began to head towards me. Tyson was in the middle of the pack and Sky's senior boxing director Mike Allen came through on my headphones from the gallery back in London: 'Remember you're a public schoolboy! Stand up straight, and you'll be fine. Sure he'll be very obliging.'

It really was the most terrifying situation. Tyson's posse stopped bang in front of me in an incredibly intimidating fashion. Despite his victory, Tyson was in a dark place.

'You got one minute, and we're counting,' bellowed Crocodile, or one of the other cheerleaders.

It felt more like a public execution than an amicable interview with the dominant winner of a fight. I quickly asked Mike a couple of questions about the Nielsen performance before saying, 'Have you enjoyed it in Copenhagen?'

'It served its purpose,' was the curt response.

'So, all smiles then,' I suggested.

Without a flicker, the reply: 'I'm not a happy, smiley kind of guy.'

And off they all stormed. The helpers, the hangers-on, and the main man of so many moods.

But he was a smiley kind of guy on the night he met Lewis. Until he got into the ring. A line of security guards stretched diagonally from post to post to prevent any possible altercation before the first bell. It was another totally surreal boxing scene. The legendary ring announcers Michael Buffer and Jimmy

Lennon Jnr worked in tandem, and the tension was extra-ordinary.

The fight, though, demonstrated Lewis's dominance and Tyson's demise. The myth had been exposed by Douglas, exploded by Holyfield, and now it was wiped out by the technical brilliance of our greatest ever heavyweight. Tyson was outboxed and beaten up. He looked an iota of his former self, and despite showing immense courage was forced on to the back foot – where he's always struggled – and knocked out in eight rounds. To be fair, he took his lumps and bumps, but his career looked finished.

But Mike Tyson had long become a kind of unmissable circus act that was going to be wheeled out, rebuilt and sold again to the public, who quite simply wanted to see what would happen next – as, if truth be told, had happened throughout his career. To us it looked like he was trying to break François Botha's arm in a clinch; he dispatched Orlin Norris after the bell; there was just a catalogue of infringements, and a series of bans. Outside the ring there were more alleged sexual assaults, drugs and road-rage incidents. There was most definitely a freak-show element to everything Tyson did, but post-Lewis it was an especially sorry and pitiful sight.

The strange comments continued to rattle out.

'How can I convince my girlfriend that you are really a decent human being?' I boldly asked Tyson when he was preparing in Phoenix, Arizona for his fight with Britain's Danny Williams.

'Tell her it's me, nice little Mikey,' was his reply.

Then, at the end of the interview, he looked straight down the barrel of the camera and started waving in an utterly odd, virtually psychotic manner. 'Say hi to your girlfriend now' were his final words, followed by a rather haunting stare. Jo, now my wife of seven years, and I still laugh about it. A touch uncomfortably though.

Despite Tyson's eroding skills, I thought he would destroy Williams, who was himself a rather strange ring performer with unpredictable tendencies. Danny used to be sick on the way to fights and could look dreadfully ordinary or flat, but when he was up against it and little was expected of him he could stun us all.

Only twice when commentating have I stood up during the climax of a fight. Once was to the astonishing ending to my favourite clash of recent times, when after a truly savage war Diego Corrales rose twice in the tenth round to stop Jose Luis Castillo. The other was when Danny Williams dislocated his shoulder twice in a British championship meeting with Mark Potter. Fighting on nonsensically, in agony, his right arm virtually unusable, somehow Williams found a left uppercut to floor Potter and stop him.

'Unbelievable!' I screeched. 'Danny Williams has won the British title – with one arm!'

'If you'd seen it in a *Rocky* movie, you wouldn't have believed it,' Jim Watt added.

The fight with Tyson proved to be another of those totally unpredictable Danny Williams displays. We thought Tyson would have put the fear of God into him. On one run with Danny and Jim McDonnell in New York a few weeks earlier I had tried to gauge his real feelings.

'Which Danny Williams is going to turn up?' I asked.

'I never know,' Danny replied, laughing.

I told him that Jim Watt gave him a seriously good chance of winning the Tyson fight. I can't actually remember if Jim had said that to me, or whether I was just instilling some confidence.

'Really?' said Williams.

'Yes, really.'

'No way.'

'Yes, *really.*'

To this day I am unsure as to whether Danny Williams really believed he would come through. However, in Louisville he passed every pre-fight mental test. He didn't lose it. He looked straight back at Tyson in the inevitable stare-down, and despite a torrid start he came firing back to knock out Iron Mike in four stunning rounds. It was Ian Darke's turn for a magical line: 'One of the biggest upsets in British boxing history . . .'

You see, every time Tyson was turned over it still felt like something almost incomprehensible, so much had he been repackaged and resold. But the cold truth is that Danny Williams, decent as he proved to be, wasn't nearly good enough to trouble an even close-to-peak Mike Tyson. Here was a shell of a fighter.

Sadly, Tyson carried on, but a terrible defeat to the average Irishman Kevin McBride, when Tyson virtually quit, proved there was absolutely nothing left in his arsenal. He retired in 2006, and despite many rumours of comebacks, particularly talk about what would be a farcical third encounter with Evander Holyfield, nothing has happened. Most of Tyson's estimated $400 million earnings have long since gone.

However, no obituary is needed yet. Mike Tyson is still very much alive, and actually looking good and healthy. I bumped into him recently, in a pizza parlour of all places, in Los Angeles. It was a regular restaurant, and he was sitting in a corner. We exchanged pleasantries, but he looked like a lost kid. I have always felt he has needed a real family around him to help support his fragile, highly delicate self. He admitted he was 'pretty much broke', but that he was beginning to find peace and to lead a far more balanced and sober lifestyle.

Johnny Nelson has become quite close to Tyson – they dished up a fascinating interview a short while back – and he remains an enthralling character. Tyson has been in movies, most famously in *The Hangover*, as well as makaing other public appearances.

An excellent documentary film was made in which Tyson, in tears, admitted frailty and bitter loneliness. Most of his pain, I believe, generates from that absent family syndrome. He is beginning to spend more and more time with those racing pigeons again – the one, if not the only, escape from the horrors that littered his childhood.

Some tired of his antics long ago, but for many Mike Tyson remains an irresistible draw. Part of that fascination is generated by the web of controversy woven out of such an exposed and utterly unstructured individual. As he once said, 'I'm not Mother Teresa. But I'm also not Charles Manson!'

We've had other such pearlers, from all sorts of press interviews, like this: 'One morning I woke up and found my favourite pigeon, Julius, had died. I was devastated and I was gonna use his crate as my stickball bat to honour him. I left the crate on my stoop and went in to get something, and I returned to see the sanitation man put the crate into the crusher. I rushed him and caught him flush on the temple with a titanic right hand. He was out cold, convulsing on the floor like an infantile retard.'

Or this: 'I paid a worker at New York's zoo to reopen it just for me and Robin. When we got to the gorilla cage, there was one big silverback gorilla there just bullying all the other gorillas. They were so powerful, but their eyes were like an innocent infant. I offered the attendant $10,000 to open the cage and let me smash that silverback's snotbox! He declined.'

And, maybe most tellingly, this assessment of his character: 'I'm the most irresponsible person in the world. The reason I'm like that is because, at 21, you all gave me $50 or $100 million, and I didn't know what to do. I'm from the ghetto. I don't know how to act. One day I'm in a dope house robbing somebody. The next thing I know, "You're the heavyweight champion of the world." Who am I? What am I? I don't even know who I am. I'm just a dumb child. I'm being abused. I'm being robbed by lawyers. I think I have more money than I do. I'm just a dumb pugnacious fool. I'm just a fool who thinks I'm someone. And you tell me I should be responsible? Everyone in boxing probably makes out well except for the fighter. He's the only one that's on Skid Row most of the time; he's the only one that everybody just leaves when he loses his mind. He sometimes goes insane, he sometimes goes on the bottle, because it's a highly intensive pressure sport that allows people to just lose it. I'm a man. I lived it and I'm not afraid to die, but when I die I'm going to paradise and I'm not worried.'

Extraordinary stuff, and we may never quite see his like again. We remember, a long time ago, for far too short a window, that Mike Tyson was one of those supreme heavyweights whom we as fight fans can't get enough of. Maybe even for those ninety-one seconds against Michael Spinks, one of the best any of us has ever seen.

Some agree that the streets gave Tyson his ruthless nature and made him that fearsome predator in the ring. Yet imagine how great he could have been if his family hadn't been absent.

13

Into the Ring

Stories of fighters emerging from ghettos and next to no infra-structure are common, and there is no doubt that Mike Tyson is the most obvious example of the modern era. Yet there are one or two other amazing figures who are not nearly as famous but whom I have come across over the last couple of decades, and their tales are every bit as compelling.

There's another Mike who has travelled a crazy road, Michael Gomez. A fighter whose endearing journey was captured pretty much from start to finish on Sky Sports.

'Gomez – mad. Completely insane. But I love him,' Ricky Hatton told me when we were watching him skip rope in the old Phoenix camp one bitterly cold winter's afternoon.

'No one like me,' piped up Michael. 'Where I came from, nothing. I am a fighter to the core.' And he didn't stop preaching for as long as he was skipping. Which was at least an hour. Me, Michael Gomez, against the world. I am the hardest man, believe me. No one cared. I am a survivor and a gladiator. Watch me go. When I'm right, I'm unstoppable. Me, Mike Gomez. Unique.'

On and on he went. I listened intently, because there was

something intriguing about him. He made you want to be around him. He was infectious, laid bare.

His real name is Michael Armstrong. He was born in a clapped-out banger somewhere in the Irish countryside. Michael's mother was driving, went into labour, and his partially sighted father then crashed the car. Michael was born on the back seat. A rather interesting introduction to life – in fact only the first chapter of what was to become another of those vivid picture-book stories. (Ironically, my late friend, former fighter and fellow crazy man Diego Corrales, who much like Michael fought with his heart on his sleeve, had delivered one of his children in similar circumstances. Sometimes car seats are just fine.)

Armstrong's Irish gypsy family – Michael was one of ten children – drifted from Longford to Dublin. The obstacles and difficulties were only just beginning. His father was virtually blind by the time they moved to Manchester, when Michael was just nine. Rather like Tyson, Gomez was surrounded by tragedy and loss. His younger sister Louise died from sudden infant death syndrome – for which Michael got the blame – and then his mother left the family to shack up with another woman. Not much stability, then, for a youngster, whose family were according to him 'hardly the kiss and cuddle type'.

Much of his youth was spent in children's homes. Michael Armstrong began to learn the streets of Manchester, and he turned to crime. His mother had encouraged him to master the art of stealing. A right little Artful Dodger Michael must have been. The football team he sometimes turned up for tired of his constant scraps on the pitch, but as in many cases, boxing saved the out-of-control youngster.

Enter another father figure who has done so much good for kids, in this instance in and around Manchester. Brian Hughes has recently retired from boxing, but did wonders for many years. He always reminded me of a Father Christmas type of figure. He had a lovely warm gentle nature, always had a smile on his bearded face, and taught many tearaways the value of discipline and commitment, and ultimately gave them a career. Scores climbed the jagged steps that led up to Hughes's boxing hideaway, from world champion Robin Reid to that exciting if limited warrior Anthony Farnell (whom I'll never forget having ballet lessons!). There was a comedian and quite talented slickster called Thomas McDonagh and serious sluggers like chunky, powerful Matthew Hall. As with Brendan Ingle's Sheffield sanctuary of talent, many of these Manchester youngsters were groomed into strong professional fighters.

Michael Armstrong fitted snugly into the Collyhurst and Moston Gym; he enjoyed the banter between fellow cheeky reprobates, and he could obviously fight. Hughes and his assistants Karl Ince, Mike Jackson and Pat Barrett became guiding lights for Michael, who badly needed structure in his life.

He also met Alison. Now if there's ever a lady who deserves only good to come to her, it is Alison. The two youngsters had met in one of the children's homes and related to each other early on. Since those troubled days, she has been Michael's rock, his support through absolutely everything. 'Without Alison, I would be dead,' Michael told me during one of our many interesting interviews, this time up in Scotland. 'No question. What she has had to put up with, well you'd never believe it. Sometimes I shudder to think why she's still with me.'

'That woman is an absolute saint,' Ricky Hatton agreed. 'What she has had to endure with Mike – extraordinary. My Jennifer has been a huge support to me through bad times. But as for Alison . . . something quite different with Mike.'

In Ricky's old house (now Matthew's), he had a pool, darts and trophy room which doubled as a late-night bar with little fridges full of his favourite tipple, Guinness. Ricky and I still laugh about the time when Michael came over for a session, crashed out on a chair, and when he woke up thought he was in a real pub. A proper paying boozer. He tried to order drinks, looked for the staff, and was lobbing cash to all corners of the room!

'One time, I left the house on a Monday morning to go to the local shop to buy some bacon and eggs,' Michael admitted to me. 'I left Alison, said see you soon, and shut the front door. I didn't return for a week.'

'God only knows what happened,' commented Ricky.

Alison has, though, stuck by through thick and thin. Thankfully. And the boxing chums Michael made, like the Hattons, Farnell, and latterly the Smith brothers, have in many ways become the family he never had. Michael never reeled in massive money, and squandered plenty along the way, but there is always that sense of hope with him because people genuinely love him. Not his real family, but an adopted, muddled together, rather caring one nonetheless.

Michael and Alison were teenage parents, and Michael chose to turn professional at the tender age of seventeen. Many Mexicans do that, not many Brits, but Michael was fairly hardened already and he fought much like a Mexican too. When not out robbing and abusing people as a street urchin, he had another hobby: he loved watching old fight footage. Maybe, like Tyson, he found connections. His favourite boxer was the great Wilfredo Gomez, and because there was another Michael Armstrong, the British Board of Boxing Control asked him to fight under another name, and 'Michael Gomez' was created.

He quickly began to make some real noise. With his mariachi-band ring-walk music, Gomez's faithful turned up wearing sombreros and calling him 'The Manchester Mexican'; he also went by the ring nickname 'Predator'. There were Irish links too: Gomez often had a shamrock shaved into his head, and he wore the longest boxing shorts on the circuit, decked in the Irish colours.

Again, there are similarities to Mike Tyson, who always talks about 'Michael' and 'Tyson' being two very different folk: 'Michael' is the family man, 'Tyson' the media creation, the monster. Here 'Gomez' was the act and 'Michael' the very vulnerable young man inside the heavy clothing.

And there were battles to overcome. Rather like Johnny Nelson, Gomez had a very poor start, losing to three journeymen in Chris Williams, Danny Ruegg and Greg Upton. He was going nowhere fast. His desire and bad lifestyle were already being questioned, and it looked all over when in 1996 Michael was charged with murder. Yes, murder.

There had been a brawl outside a Manchester club, and Michael was attacked. He retaliated and floored a man called Sam Powell, whose head hit the pavement. He died. Michael 'Gomez' Armstrong faced a life sentence, but because the blow was eventually viewed as self-defence, the verdict was reduced to manslaughter, and he actually, and rather sensationally, walked free.

This awful incident made Michael knuckle down. He worked hard at the Collyhurst gym, rebuilt his career and started to gather real momentum.

We loved going to Manchester for Gomez nights. There was always antagonism at the weigh-ins, where Gomez would try to wind up his opponent by putting his head in for the face-off, constant reprimands and controversy, electric atmospheres, and this swashbuckling, no-nonsense style. He was simply enticing television. No one quite knew what Michael Gomez would do next, or how far he could really go. He was pushed down the 'intercontinental' road but soon began to headline shows and put bums on seats.

Gomez enjoyed a successful and popular run, undefeated

for three years. In September 1999 he won the British super-featherweight crown, destroying Liverpool's seasoned Gary Thornhill with his trademark left hook in two rounds. This helped bring Michael the award of Young Boxer of the Year, as voted for by the British Boxing Writers' Club. Top-notch stuff.

Gomez was on a march, and keeping him busy (and out of trouble) was key to his success. He defended his British 9st 4lb belt in a good battle with Coventry's underrated Dean Pithie, who had beaten Naseem Hamed in the amateurs; scored an emphatic knockout of all-round Midlander Carl Greaves; and then comfortably triumphed over Scotland's Ian McLeod.

A bump in the road, though, was never too far away. Gomez was meant to easily brush aside a pretty basic Hungarian southpaw called Laszlo Bognar in 2001. Despite being on top early, Gomez didn't look himself; he seemed lethargic, weak, and possessing little strength in the legs. His debates in the corner with Brian Hughes began to intensify, as if the trainer knew more than he would let on in front of our cameras. Was Gomez fit? Why did his tank begin to run dry? Eventually Michael was stopped in nine rounds. It was a big upset, and Frank Warren was rightly looking for reasons. One of his most decent ticket-sellers and quirky fighters had been severely derailed. Gomez blamed it on flu. Maybe. Maybe not. There could have been some darker reasons. Yet what was really brought into question was his reliability.

One criticism that most certainly could not be aimed at Michael Gomez was any lack of pride and passion. He personally called for a rematch, and in Manchester in July 2001, Gomez–Bognar II was a thriller. There were early scares for Gomez, when it looked like the reflexes might already be starting to slow a touch: the Mancunian was down in the first and second rounds. However, he sorted himself out, showing courage to rebound and floor Bognar twice in three short but dramatic rounds.

'I went back to the drawing board,' Michael bellowed at me in a typically fiery but honest post-fight interview at ringside. 'I was getting taxis to the nightclubs, not the gym. I only have myself to blame. I was in a bad, bad place. But I am back. Watch out. And Alex Arthur – I want to burst that fake bubble.'

This was the fighter who went by the nickname AAA – Amazing Alex Arthur. Fast, skilful, good-looking, unbeaten and highly marketable, Arthur was being touted by some as the finest boxer to have come out of Edinburgh since Ken Buchanan. But Gomez had other Scottish business to attend to first, defending his Lonsdale belt successfully against Craig Docherty.

He was on track again, but not for long. In June 2002, enter Kevin Lear, a talented Londoner who systematically outboxed another out-of-sorts Gomez. He was so poor that Brian Hughes pulled him out after eight lopsided rounds. Hughes advised Gomez to retire before he got badly hurt. Gomez refused to wilt, though; he split with the patriarch of the Collyhurst gym and moved across town to Billy Graham's buzzing stable, headed of course by Ricky Hatton.

Personal problems continued to rear their ugly heads – street brawls, barrels of booze, numerous drink-driving convictions, and one incident that almost killed him. Michael was knifed, and his heart actually stopped beating on the operating table. 'I flatlined for thirty-eight seconds,' he told me. 'I was gone. But I am a fighter. I refused to give in. Something in me. Deep inside.'

So Michael Gomez had escaped facing a life sentence, and now he had escaped with his life. All this time Alison was there. Alison and the Phoenix camp – his new boxing family.

Remember, Billy Graham had this office in the back of his Denton gym. It was his treasure chest. Billy would puff away there, get his mind sorted while playing with his beloved array

Above: It has been my privilege to interview some of the all-time greats of boxing. Here (*left*) I get the inside track from Evander Holyfield and (*right*) from Emmanuel Steward.

Below: Vernon Forrest was one of the most wonderful human beings you could hope to stumble across in the boxing world, and this signed photo is one of my most precious mementoes.

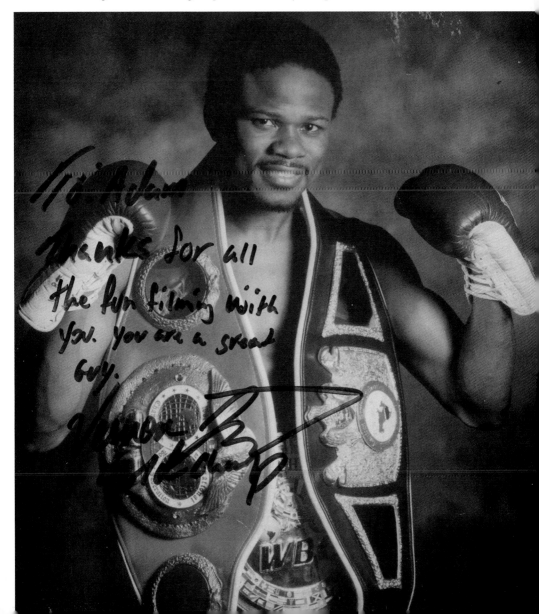

Top: Getting up close and personal with Floyd Mayweather Jnr, who has rarely been out of the headlines, like the rest of his family.

Middle: Cainey and I get some quality time with Sugar Shane Mosley ahead of his bout with Mayweather in May 2010. Mosley's son Shane Jnr is now training to be a fighter.

Bottom left: Bernard Hopkins: another incredible character and an inspiration to so many.

Bottom right: We had complete access to Lennox Lewis in his camp in the Pocono mountains in Pennsylvania. This was before his last fight against Vitali Klitschko.

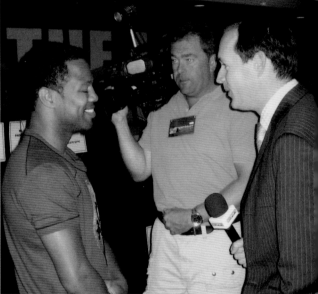

Top: Another from my signed photo collection: the great Freddie Roach. What an influence Freddie has had on the career of Amir Khan (not to mention a certain Manny Pacquiao!); here is my commentary sheet from the night Amir won his first world title, against Andreas Kotelnik in Manchester.

Bottom: Amir and me in Vegas before his fight against Marcos Maidana In December 2010.

Top left: Prince Naseem was the fighter I got closest to in the early part of my career. Here we are in his rented home in Palm Springs before his only loss, against Marco Antonio Barrera.

Top right: A still from the infamous interview with Naz at Prince Promotions in Sheffield. He laid himself bare, it was television gold, and we fell out for a while.

Left: Out on the road in Tenerife with Naz and his entourage Anas Oweida (*left*) and Maurice Core (*right*) before his fight with Vuyani Bungu in 2000. You have to be able to keep up to get the best scoops.

Bottom: With former fighter and now trainer Anthony Farnell. This photo was taken at Carol Hatton's fiftieth birthday party in Hyde Town Hall – what a night that was!

I loved nothing better than a game of chess with Lennox Lewis. This was in California's Big Bear mountains before his fight with Henry Akinwande.

Joe Calzaghe is one of the best examples of when the father/trainer and son/fighter relationship can really work

Top: Me and Ricky Hatton outside the MGM in Las Vegas in 2001. We were there to see the unification battle between Kostya Tszyu and Zab Judah, and what a crazy night that turned out to be.

Bottom: Ricky's trainer Billy Graham (here next to me and Cainey) could be pretty eccentric too. Billy was such fun to have around.

Opposite top: Ricky and me in Manchester after the announcement of the Pacquiao fight and the launch of Hatton Promotions.

Opposite bottom: The Hitman was not just a legend in the ring; I got to present him an award for his help with injured ex-servicemen.

Right: My role at Sky means a lot of work at press conferences ahead of fights. Audley Harrison talked the talk but does he know what's about to hit him?

Below right and below: David Haye went on to fight Wladimir Klitschko in Hamburg. It was one of the biggest fights I have been involved in, even if the night itself did not live up to the build-up. Will the Hayemaker get back in the ring with another Klitschko?

of frogs, toads and snakes that lived in a tank hanging on the back wall. You had to earn your way into that room. It was often closed and I longed to be a fly on the wall, or maybe one of those ever-present beasts! Billy didn't mince his words, and I liked that. He had opinions on all subjects, not just boxing, but it's safe to say that promoters got a fair bit of his bite.

When Ricky and Michael's careers were in full flow, I was invited into the office more and more. Often Alison would be sitting there in the background, shy and pensive. I remember asking her once what it was like living with Michael.

'Well, it's never dull!' she replied. 'You aren't quite sure when he's going to be home, but he'll always come back. We had similar childhoods, and I think that means we need each other to deal with the world. We're fragile, both of us. I love him come what may.'

What a great girl, and what was to come next was Michael Gomez's greatest hour. After seemingly endless taunts from Gomez, Alex Arthur finally took the bait. The cracking match-up was made, yet Gomez was seen as a massive underdog. Timing and levels are all I usually go by and to me an Arthur win was obvious. Yet boxing has a strange way of turning the world on its head. Add Michael Gomez's fire to the equation and we should have learned not to write him off. But, I admit, I did. Alex was the golden boy, given all the treatment – home advantage in Edinburgh, trained (albeit at a distance) by Freddie Roach, talk of marquee fights ahead. Many, including me, perceived Alex Arthur as one of the sport's future gems.

'I can't wait to shut him up, Adam,' Alex told me in the charged weigh-in room. 'I hate boxers who talk disrespectfully. He has no manners and no skills. There are many, many ways I can beat him.'

'I'm going to destroy him in front of his people,' boasted Gomez, who looked in magnificent shape. He was absolutely glowing. 'I forced him into this fight. I have had to come to the lion's den. I am better than him. Bigger heart too. I'm going to knock him out.'

In a spine-tingling atmosphere at the Meadowbank Centre in the autumn of 2003, Arthur and Gomez met, and it lived up to all expectations. The Scottish crowd sang; a few pockets of Gomez fans waved those sombreros. It was one of those nights that will live with me and with everyone else who was lucky enough to be there. The meeting was a classic. Gomez took the fight right to Arthur, who tried to use his polished boxing ability but was fast dragged into a war. It was a seesaw battle, both boxers having their moments, but both were soon in danger of falling apart.

Michael Gomez found out, in the trenches, that he was at last in the physical shape he needed to be in, and he was just too strong and too accurate, breaking Arthur up. The Scotsman was down twice, and despite showing real character, he made naive errors, such as laughing at one of our cameras as if to say he was OK. When Arthur crashed to the canvas for a third time, Gomez was declared the victor in five utterly absorbing rounds of action. Hats off to Billy Graham for whipping Gomez into the necessary condition to triumph.

Ironically, despite winning, it was Gomez who continued to call for a rematch (and a payday) for the rest of his career. Unfortunately it never happened. Arthur rebuilt and actually became a WBO champion, once he'd tightened his defence and learned those harsh lessons. The reliability factor, you see. Alex is still fighting today, has become a good analyst for us at Sky, and has ambitions to become a promoter. Bright, quick-witted and humble, he is a more rounded individual with a solid family base.

Gomez went on to win a pretty meaningless WBU title, in March 2004, when he halted the average Ghanaian Ben Odamattey in three. He took out a totally shot former classy world title challenger Justin Juuko in a horrific match, and then got an excellent win against the dangerous France-based Armenian Leva Kirakosyan. Yet the typical Michael Gomez yo-yo pattern continued. As soon as he was up, after prevailing in one of the domestic fights of the decade and putting some decent enough international wins together, Gomez was back down. Argentinian Javier Alvarez was too good, stopping Gomez in six, and there was a feeling within the fight fraternity that the wheels had come off. The snap and the timing weren't as good. The come-forward attacker suddenly looked particularly vulnerable.

Periods of inactivity followed, and then there was an extremely controversial fight in January 2006 in Dublin with Peter McDonagh. Gomez was desperate to fight in Ireland and should have brushed McDonagh aside, even at this stage of his career. The Irish lightweight title was on the line, and there was admittedly a strange build-up, with McDonagh enlisting the help of Uri Geller to prepare mentally for the fight. This was reminiscent of Steve Collins, who'd utilized a doctor that Chris Eubank felt was more of a hypnotist before their epic first meeting in Millstreet, County Cork, in March 1995.

In the fifth round against McDonagh, Gomez inexplicably stopped fighting, then walked back to his corner and retired. There was a major investigation with the betting companies, because apparently unusual patterns of money had been placed on a McDonagh fifth-round win. Some even claimed Gomez had placed £10,000 on himself to lose in five. Both fighters were cleared, after Gomez simply accepted it was the end of the road and said he needed to retire from boxing. Yet for such a gladiator it was a bizarre ending. Maybe he had indeed come to the end of the line.

Billy Graham seemed embarrassed about the whole thing, but in fact Gomez didn't want to go out like that. He joined forces with Graham's former assistant Bobby Rimmer, who had started his own camp. There were still fans who wanted to see Michael Gomez, and after some wins to ease him back, in October 2007 he tackled fellow pocket dynamo Carl Johanneson from Leeds in nearby Doncaster. In an entertaining scrap for the British super-featherweight belt he once held, Gomez was halted in the sixth round. He complained bitterly.

A decent payday was well deserved against the multi-talented Amir Khan, whom he even floored momentarily with a left hook. After losing in five, Gomez knew the adventure was close to a conclusion; but he was very brave in challenging Ricky Burns back up in Scotland for a Commonwealth title. Burns was too slick, fresh and organized for Gomez, and the Coatbridge stylist has gone on to become one of the best lighter-weight fighters in the world.

In the interview afterwards, Michael told me that he wanted a couple more 'easy' fights, to take his tally to fifty. Now, no match-up is easy when there is nothing left, but no boxer wants to hear those dreaded words, that it's over. I went backstage at the Bellahouston Leisure Centre in Glasgow to see our old friend. Michael was weeping on a bench and being consoled by none other than that rock in his life, Alison. I was so happy to see that she was still right by his side.

'It's over, isn't it, Adam,' Michael said.

Now Jim Watt has always told me that it is not our job to tell fighters when to retire for good. I don't disagree with Jim on many things, but I do on this. We have watched careers unfold from ringside. We have had a close look at how sharp speed slows, defences become more scattered, legs become dramatically bendy and the timing, for whatever reason, just isn't there. It can only be minor details. Bob Mee is so good at spotting them. I just felt it was time to tell Michael what I felt was the truth.

'Yes, it is,' I told him. 'Don't go on. Don't try to make fifty. It will only get worse.'

'They are making a movie about me,' Michael replied. 'And I could take your job! Boxing, and this lady, have saved me, kept my feet on the ground. Got me through the bad times. Given me direction, now I have a beautiful wife and three children.'

He hugged Alison, and I left them to it.

'Thank you for the memories, Michael,' I said to the fallen gladiator. 'I really hope our paths cross in the future. You have been fabulous, fun and box office – the whole ride.' I shut that dressing-room door, and the tears began to flow. I felt like it was the end of a relationship.

Maybe I am just attracted to these types of characters who have badly splintered and ripped-apart families but who, because of boxing, prevail. They don't seem to quite reach their potential, and I am never sure what will happen to them beyond the sport, but I just love watching the stories unfold, and in a small way playing my part in them.

It was a wonderful ride on a high-speed and, at times, runaway train. Michael Gomez brought brightness, colour and feeling to the fighting arena. He defied the odds again and again, and he guaranteed entertainment. Michael overcame a turbulent childhood to be a success. I just hope that poor long-lost Irish gypsy family is now immensely proud of him. Our boxing world hasn't quite been the same since Michael Gomez hung up the gloves.

I hope he's OK these days, and that he no longer takes quite so long to bring back those bacon and eggs.

If Gomez was wild, then one of the brightest and most eccentric fighters I have ever come across is Adrian Dodson. He is a real enigma of the ring.

Adrian was born in Guyana, hardened in America, and eventually settled in England. Blessed with an abundance of ring talent, Adrian fought in two Olympics, but while a useful professional, he never quite reached the heights he should have.

With his skill-set, engaging personality and rather odd attraction to the media, it's such a shame that Adrian Dodson didn't become a boxing star for Britain.

So why didn't it work for someone with his capabilities? Was it on account of his upbringing and a lack of family direction? Well, I believe this had a major effect.

There is of course no such thing as a 'normal' family, but Adrian would surely have benefited from sound guidance, structure, focus, purpose and balance, particularly as a youngster when so many vital components of a human being are formed. Instead, Dodson was a true individual and a signed-up member of the 'one man against the world' club. Yet, ultimately he didn't get it right. Adrian Dodson, quite simply, did not fulfil his potential.

He never really talked about his family; he certainly shied away from the subject of his parents. He initially fought as Adrian Carew, having taking his father Carly's surname. Yet Carly, who used to train Mark Prince in south London, never mentioned Adrian to me. His mother's name was Dodson, hence the change, but Adrian never talked about her either.

Was there enough love? Or comfort? Or protection? Or even some stability? Would things have turned out differently for Adrian Dodson if he'd enjoyed a more regular upbringing?

I kept a close interest in the career of this peculiar act from Islington, north London, because when I was growing up Adrian Dodson featured regularly in my local paper, the *Ham and High*. I actually did a few weeks' work experience there before I joined Sky Sports, and one of my first reports was on Adrian. I liked his supreme confidence, and he had a wonderful way with words.

Years later, as a young, overzealous reporter for Sky, I went to see Adrian as he prepared for a title fight. As usual I found him alone, working out in a back-street gym. He often liked it that way. For Adrian was a loose cannon who was notoriously prickly and difficult to deal with. He'd had spats with trainers, managers and pretty much anyone else who crossed his path. What Adrian did have was a natural intelligence, and he was suspicious of almost everyone around him.

Despite being in a minority as far as boxing critics went, I personally always enjoyed my time, my chats and my interviews with Adrian as the answers were controversial, thought-provoking, just different. On this occasion he had something in store for me. He was literally not going to let me off the hook before our time came to an end.

'Adam Smith, I'm only going to allow you to interview me if afterwards we box three rounds together,' Adrian announced.

He was off his head. If there's one thing I have learned from dedicating over half of my life to this sport, it is that I will never, ever become a boxer. I'm just not anywhere near hard or tough enough. It's not me. Genetically, mentally, physically, spiritually – no. No way. And in many ways, that is why I have such enormous admiration for any fighter who climbs through those ropes. Any fighter, of any standard.

Yet three things struck me about Mr Dodson's absurd suggestion. Firstly, I couldn't possibly return to Sky without the interview and footage for our forthcoming *Countdown* show to the latest Box Office event, which featured Adrian. Secondly, the closer I get to my subject matter, the better the result. Infinitely better. That's one of the main reasons I used to go running with the likes of Joe Calzaghe, Naseem Hamed, Lennox Lewis and Oscar De La Hoya. Attempting to keep up with the fittest of athletes is very hard, but the nuggets I used to prise out of them during that precious time were simply priceless. Finally, and most importantly, the experience would bring me much closer to the sport I am addicted to and admire more than any other. I might, I thought, just get some semblance of an idea of what these incredible men go through in the heat of battle.

As per usual, I was wearing a suit – a navy pinstripe if I

remember rightly – and I had absolutely no sporting attire with me, but I just had to accept his most gracious – or was that ghastly? – offer.

Fortunately, the rules favoured the journalist, not the highly trained prizefighter. Over three rounds, we were to go to war with a difference.

'Adam, you are allowed to hit me. Constantly, within the boundaries of the Marquess of Queensbury of course. I am simply allowed to defend myself. I can maul you around, make you work, frustrate the hell out of you, but I won't hit back.'

I was quietly confident that I would be able to do this for nine minutes. After all, I had trained for the London Marathon, played sporadic club tennis, and enjoyed what I thought was a reasonable level of fitness. I removed my shirt, but with no flashy boxing shorts my pinstriped trousers had to suffice. I must have looked absolutely ridiculous.

The first round began and I charged into him from a southpaw stance. I have no idea why – I am right-handed. It just seemed a good idea at the time. I threw bundles of punches, pretty much all feeble with minimal amounts of weight behind them, but plenty landed all the same. I actually felt OK, but it quickly began to dawn on me that I just wasn't getting anywhere, or making any sort of impression.

Suddenly, I started tiring. I thought I must be approaching the end of the first round, but one of those strange gym rats one tends to come across in virtually every boxing establishment yelled out, 'One minute gone, Adrian, and the kid looks in trouble already!'

That first sixty seconds had lasted an absolute eternity. This was fast becoming the most shattering experience of my life.

I carried on throwing punches. Adrian continued to hold me and physically drain any breath I had. There was no rhythm, no timing and no in-built clock to pace myself. They are such crucial ingredients in the make-up of a fighter, and areas I respect so much more now this Dodson torture has locked itself into the memory banks.

As the opening round eventually came to a close, I honestly thought I was going to die. Adrian had used his natural strength to mess me about, and I just had no energy left. To make matters far more embarrassing, I wasn't even getting hit. How pathetic an effort it all was. Puffing and panting like a chain-smoker, I somehow just about forced myself through the remaining two rounds. To say I endured this is an understatement – my life was flashing past me! It was seriously one of the hardest things I have ever done. The penny well and truly dropped: Adrian had just wanted me to appreciate one tiny iota of what a boxer has to endure, not merely what a journalist sees from the safe side of the ropes.

When I collapsed into his arms at the end, close to complete exhaustion, Adrian confirmed this for me in his unique but attractive concoction of Guyanese, American and English dialects: 'This day will live with you for ever. The best thing that'll ever happen to you as a journalist and broadcaster, Adam. Now when a boxer sits on his stool after seven or eight rounds, just think about your little taste of what we go through. Remember, too, what we, as boxers, have received through each and every round – you were allowed just to dish out. Incomparable really, but I wanted to give you a live situation. To make you become a better fight reporter.'

It was punishing beyond belief. I ached for days. Yet I am so pleased I had the opportunity of experiencing it. Not least because the favour was immediately returned: after our ring rumble, the inimitable Adrian Dodson gave me a quite spellbinding interview that went on until it got dark.

Now, one of the most wonderful moments in boxing is the embrace at the final bell. Weeks of animosity, minutes under the burning lights of attempting to dissect one's opposition, yet when the timekeeper tolls for the last time and the referee splits the combatants, the hardest of men simply hug like family. These experiences might be all the more important and heartfelt for those who don't have that family nest to fall back into. Sometimes mothers, fathers, brothers and sisters are even absent at ringside, when the fighter really bares his soul to the world. I'm sure Adrian Dodson was one such guy, and in a tiny way – one which might not mean much to outsiders – the Dodson–Smith connection would be a bond for ever.

Recently I was commentating at my favourite little boxing home, the York Hall, Bethnal Green. If you haven't enjoyed the delights and charm of this famous old spit-and-sawdust venue in east London, you really should do your best to get down there with a few mates. This traditional setting is where real fight fans converge to produce a smashing atmosphere time and again. We all have our special spot to see the action. Every seat, whether on the ground or up in the balcony, is a few feet from the ring. Each spectator is up close and personal to the thrills of thunderous action and spilling blood. To one's left is a bricklayer; to one's right is a City slicker. Crooks and lawyers sit or stand in perfect harmony. Some even have side bets for fun. There's nothing wrong with a little moonlighting, after all.

This was one of our Prizefighter shows, the enticing tournament that has brought in a new fan base and freshened up the sport. Eight fighters, seven fights: four quarter-finals, two semis and a final, with a juicy cash bounty of thirty-two grand up for grabs. All in one night. It's fast and furious and each bout is fought over the sprint distance of three three-minute rounds. Ironically, the length I did with Dodson. Well, in a half-hearted way.

I hadn't seen Adrian for some years. After he retired from boxing, we lost touch. There were a couple of rumours of comebacks, and I also heard he had become a father, and doted on his kids. Adrian was trying to make sure the next generation blossomed, possibly in compensation for his own difficult up-bringing.

Yet that night at York Hall, my colleague Ed Robinson told me that AD was in the building. At the end of the second round of the first quarter-final, I glanced to my left at ringside. There, leaning by one of the poles, was my old mate. A wry smile crossed Adrian's face; a wry smile crossed mine. There was that bond, the chemistry we shared, and as the prizefighters went out for their final three-minute session, Adrian knew that I had more of a feeling for what they were feeling in that sweltering ring.

Absent families. Fighting friends. You know what they say. Absence makes the heart grow fonder.

Boxing has long been littered with folk from lost families, and though there is no doubt in my mind that the sport has in many ways been a saviour, you always worry how each fighter's going to end up. We can only hope. Take Kassim 'The Dream' Ouma. How on earth did this little boy make it through to become a world champion and an idol of his country? 'The Dream' had the most nightmarish beginning. Treacherous, deadly, almost incomprehensible.

Kassim was born into appalling poverty in Maga Maga in rural Uganda in December 1978. The seventh of thirteen children. Of his seven brothers, only four are still alive. When Kassim was just five years old he was abducted from his village to become a child soldier. Yes, a soldier, at war, at the age of five. The rebel leader Yoweri Museveni was fighting a civil war against the dictator Milton Obote, and stole children for the cause.

'Kassim was snatched with his school class, blindfolded and herded into a truck – all the boys,' Ouma's long-time friend and co-manager Ron Body told me before Kassim's crunch clash with world middleweight champion Jermain Taylor in Little Rock, Arkansas, in 2006. 'Most never saw their families again. When the kids were woken, there were those who were crying, and those who weren't. The children who were crying were all just shot. Deemed not tough enough to fight for the cause. Luckily Kassim wasn't one of those. He joined the others in the bush where they fought with the guerrillas. We have grown up in middle-class England with a family, love and a life. Kassim's was ripped away from him at five.'

"They were told there were no more mummies and daddies,' added co-manager Tom Moran.

Kassim Ouma was trained as a fighter, a soldier and a killer in the National Resistance Army. He can naturally become un-comfortable when remembering his past. 'I don't really want to talk about it,' he told me. 'But it was like hell. I have no idea how many people were killed. One time I remember sitting on dead bodies.'

'He was ordered to shoot one of his best friends,' Body said. 'To see how hard he was. So he did. If he hadn't done that, he would have been killed.'

'Kassim had to do things no one should have gone through,' said Moran. 'He feels guilty for surviving.'

Kassim didn't see his family for years, but the Army's boxing team saved him. In 1998 he came to America to fight in a tournament, and defected. He knew this was the only way of supporting his family back in Uganda. He was lost, lonely, confused and broke, but he was determined. He travelled from Texas to Virginia and on to Philadelphia. With no visa, no social security number and no real help, Kassim was homeless. He managed to get a job delivering flyers for a pizza company, and with his earnings bought himself a bike. Amazingly, he began riding the major interstates in search of boxing gyms.

Despite run-ins with the law, Kassim ended up in Philly at 'The Dungeon', one of those dark boxing hideaways I have heard mentioned several times when around ringside. The word from The Dungeon is that only the toughest – and maddest – can hack it.

However, more turmoil and tragedy were to follow. First his father was killed by the Ugandan army, who were furious that Kassim had absconded. Then he was involved in a car accident, before being shot twice in a drive-by shooting in Florida in December 2002. Yet Kassim had courage, and talent. A heavy-handed if small southpaw, he amassed an amateur record of sixty-two wins, and went on to lift the IBF light-middleweight title in October 2004 by beating Verno Phillips.

The reign didn't last long – unheralded Roman Karmazin dethroned Ouma the following summer. He had obviously lacked focus and discipline. Kassim was threatened that if he ever returned to Uganda to see his family, he'd be arrested for desertion and executed. Fortunately, a pardon has since been given to him.

Problems continue to plague him, though. When Tom Moran's sister, 'Mommy Patti', passed away, Kassim was devastated. Death just seems to follow these guys. He has had financial woes, several partners, and is constantly battling political foes back home. He has children of his own and pays for the education of scores of cousins back in Uganda.

But Kassim is a natural born survivor. He has taught himself several languages and now wants to do missionary work for the UN, helping those African people he was forced to leave behind. His charity Natabonic provides pumps to bring clean water to desolate areas of Uganda. A documentary called *Kassim the Dream* has been made and was a notable success at several film festivals.

The child soldier. Just unreal, isn't it?

*

It is surely only a matter of time before the movie world also tackles the subject of Johnny Tapia. Most of us in the business have lost count of the number of times Tapia has 'died'.

This unique, tattoo-laden boxing character from Albuquerque, New Mexico simply goes by the name Mi Vida Loco – 'My Crazy Life'. Read this, and you'll think I'm making it up. Tapia's life story is one of the most hellacious I have ever heard about. Yet he has won a multitude of world titles and remains engaging and charming, albeit utterly, totally mad.

Born in February 1967, Johnny learned early on that his father had been murdered when his mother was pregnant with him. When he was seven, he was in a horrific bus accident on a hundred-foot cliff. The pregnant woman next to him was hurled to her death; Johnny survived. At eight, his mum Virginia was kidnapped, raped, hanged, stabbed twenty-two times with a screwdriver and left for dead.

'I remember the noise that night,' Johnny told me on a trip to England, when he fought at York Hall. 'I was woken by the screams and saw her tied to the back of a pick-up truck. I didn't dream it, but people thought I was just a crazy kid. No one believed me, damn it. She was found days later, dead. It was him, her married lover Richard Espinosa. Rot in hell.'

Johnny Tapia spent a large part of his life tracking down his mother's killer, 'to rip him from limb to limb'. In 1999, Johnny discovered that Espinosa had been run over by two cars and had died way back in 1983. That pushed him over the edge again, because he couldn't exact his own revenge.

We chatted on camera for over an hour in a darkened room. He was addictive and mesmerizing. 'Yesterday never happened,' he told me. 'Tomorrow never comes. I live only for today. For the moment. I have been clinically dead three, four, actually five times. Drug binges. My heart stopped beating on each occasion.

God brought me back. God and my wife Teresa, who has saved me. When Teresa's around, life's good, but she can't take her eyes off me. When she does, I go into very bad places. She tells me never to leave the house without her. I did one time, and I ended up left for dead in a gutter.'

Johnny was raised by his grandmother and began boxing at nine. He had some frustrations to vent, and discovered that despite being tiny, he had a bright ring future. He won 101 amateur fights and eventually became a five-time champion after turning pro in the spring of 1988, but he has been hounded by tragedy and toxic abuse. His early success led him to become a star, but it also brought him into the deadly world of cocaine addiction. 'Cocaine was like my partner, my calling,' Johnny told me. 'I couldn't resist it. My mistress – cocaine.'

There was anti-social behaviour, arrests, repeated positive tests for cocaine, bans from the sport, and many convictions. Apparently his criminal record grew to 125 pages! Suicide attempts followed.

Teresa Chavez saved him. But it took a lot of persuasion from Johnny, who pestered her, hounded her, and eventually got her. She became his manager, his wife, his rock. There was a time when Teresa locked the door of their apartment and forced Johnny to stay there for a month. It has been a constant battle for the two of them, and only through Teresa's resolve – and their faith – have they remained together. After all, Johnny did disappear on their wedding night to overdose. And almost die.

In March 2007 he was in a critical condition after another cocaine overdose, in New Mexico. His brother-in law, Robert Gutierrez, and Johnny's nephew, a young boxer, rushed to visit him in hospital the next morning. They were both killed in another automobile crash to haunt the Tapia clan. This almost broke Johnny and Teresa. He was jailed for drug possession.

Then Teresa's mother and grandmother passed away. So too did Johnny's grandfather. But Teresa has stood by Johnny. Maybe she's addicted to the danger, or just to him. They are reminiscent of Alison and Michael Gomez.

At forty-five, amazingly and incomprehensibly, Johnny Tapia is still fighting, and in the most recent ironic twist he found out that his father, whom he believed had died before he was born, is actually alive and well and – wait for it – a family friend. The plot just thickens at every turn. Quite how Johnny managed to become a world super-flyweight, bantamweight and featherweight champion God only knows. Boxing obviously helped channel him, keep him on the straight and narrow.

The heartbreak of his family situation and his erratic relationship with those of them who are still with us (many of his cousins still have nothing to do with Johnny) again leads me to those first few years of childhood. Yes, boxing may be the saviour, but it comes after a time when protection, nurture and family love are at their most crucial. While fascinating and endearing, fighters who somehow emerge from the ruins of absent families are not nearly as well equipped to deal with the fame and fortune of boxing, or the struggles of life. Full credit to them, and to the sport for turning wrecks of kids into future champions, but the lack of family support does undeniably unhinge them – witness the nuttiest boxer of modern times and the African warrior who fought as a soldier from the age of five, when most kids are playing with water pistols. Not to mention that baddest man on the planet.

Having witnessed up close the bizarre careers and lives of Mike Tyson, Johnny Tapia, Victor Ortiz, Michael Gomez, Adrian Dodson, Kassim Ouma, the Peterson brothers and many more, it's clear to me that each of these fighters is a most peculiar product. They constantly battle the demons of their past. They've all hit rock bottom. And for some reason they are all still standing. Without boxing, they most certainly wouldn't be.

But wouldn't they have done even better had they benefited from just some love and security at the right time?

Five

MOTHERING INSTINCTS

14

Something in the Genes

There really is nobody quite like a mum. 'A father may turn his back on his child, brothers and sisters may become inveterate enemies, husbands may desert their wives, wives their husbands. But a mother's love endures through all,' as the nineteenth-century American writer Washington Irving put it. And when Mama's gonna knock you out – in the words this time of LL Cool J – you're in big trouble.

A cult video, so infamous that no one really knows or cares who the actual fighters were, is posted on virtually every bloopers or funnies internet site. A boxer is under intense punishment and suddenly his mother climbs into the ring and begins to attack her son's opponent with a shoe. Mayhem breaks out. Have a look if you haven't seen it. Not only does it beggar belief, it also vividly shows how much devotion, dedication and unflinching, whole-hearted support a mother has for her son. It's a gut reaction, verging on the insane. Raw and real, from somewhere deep, deep inside.

Having carried the baby in her womb for nine months, and in many cases breast-fed it for a few more, a mother naturally has a profound initial physical and emotional connection with her child. Once the child is born, the mother is reborn too. She has to think twice, to double up – once for herself and once for her child. For now there is a more important person in her life. Not a partner, a lover or a husband but her own baby, who lies completely bare in her arms, for a period of time, like any living creature, utterly reliant on its mother to protect, love, nurture and develop it.

There is just something about a mother that a child will turn to. I am extremely close to my three young children, but when one is hurt or lost or pensive or worried, it is their mummy they naturally gravitate to and address first. Just human nature. Nothing less. Nothing more. And nothing as beautiful.

The primary role of a mother, above and beyond all else, is to raise children. Particularly early on, for as we know, the key part in the emotional development of a child comes in those crucial first few years. Strong maternal attachments tend to lay a strong foundation on which social skills can be developed. The children of mothers who choose to abandon their homes can become troubled – start hanging in gangs, abusing drugs, wasting precious years flirting with the anti-establishment.

Being a full-time mother is one of the hardest jobs there can possibly be. It is constant and truly testing. Mums must possess a blend of control and close affection. To be there for her child through thick and thin she must alternately be hard granite and silky softness, sometimes both at the same time. A mother is, after all, the truest friend many people can have.

On average, nature provides women with a longer life on this planet than men. Matriarchs of a family, mothers and grand-mothers, seem always to be around. The bereavement when they are lost is hard to bear as a result. That has happened both to my family and to my wife's. My father's mother, or Nana, lived until she was ninety-three; Jo's father's mother almost reached ninety-eight. Their passing was all the more difficult because of the

huge influence they had on family life through several generations. Women are extraordinary creatures, and the dependence
we have on them as sons, grandsons and husbands – as men – is
vital to our core.

Of course, traditionally a daughter is more attached to her
father, a son to his mother. A father can make his son strong
enough to fight and survive, yet it is his mother who usually
teaches him when and how to think from his heart. By nature,
mothers are fiercely loyal, unconditionally supportive and immensely proud of their children. Especially their sons. I know
mine is. Almost obsessively so.

In my case, after emerging from a divorced household, I took
longer to bond with my dad. He was often around, but because
he didn't live with my sister and me, our mum predominantly
brought us up. My dad cut more of a figure of authority whom
I didn't want to let down. It was only really in adult life that I
became close to him. Even now, though, the relationship is different. My dad is my great friend and adviser. My mum is my
mum. Always will be.

Mum – Veronica – has long been seen as posh and maybe
even bizarrely eccentric. One could imagine her lording it up
alongside the royals at Ascot, so comfortable is she on a public
stage, where her veneer of outer confidence propels her to
extraordinary levels. I still cannot believe it has taken her into
dark, dingy boxing gyms and halls. My mum would never have
previously chosen to associate herself with the shady, ferocious
sport of boxing. 'Absolutely ghastly' was her reaction when I
first dipped my toes into pugilistic waters, back in the nineties.
'Darling, what on earth do you see in it? People punching
each other, inflicting brain damage, there's just no place in the
civilized world for it!'

Yet, because of my immense passion for and devotion to the
sport, she followed suit. Because she's my mum. No other reason

– and mark my words, she would have done it for no one else. Not another man on the planet. Only for her only son. And boy has she immersed herself in it all. A regular at fights, she talks to everyone from the cameramen to the whips to the doctors! Mum's a right character, and however embarrassing she chooses to be, there she is, fighting my corner. Steadfastly. She'd attack an attacker with her shoe, have no doubt about that! She will always be cheering, hollering, shouting from the rafters. At the fighters and at me, even when I'm commentating or presenting. She is one of a kind admittedly, but a prouder, more supportive mum you couldn't find.

Take as well my adoration of all things red as a fervent supporter of Liverpool Football Club. Well, these days, Mum is more dedicated to the team than I am. A quite unique solo performance of 'You'll Never Walk Alone' which she sang, with just a harp as accompaniment, at my wedding is testament to that. If my wife Jo hadn't quite realized what she was getting herself into beforehand, she most certainly did when Mum reached for those astonishingly high notes on that summer's day in June 2005. Liverpool posters and songs filled the room, mixed, surreally, with an assortment of Ricky Hatton paraphernalia (the Hitman had been hitting the headlines with vigour following his awesome triumph over Kostya Tszyu, and images of Ricky's glory decked the walls).

Mothers and sons, eh? At least I didn't choose to become a fighter, but for the thousands who have, there is often a proud mum somewhere, whether she chooses to be visible or prefers to sneak off into the background, quietly praying for her son's health.

Working in such a male-orientated environment, I have long been fascinated by boxing mothers. The mothering instinct, after all, is to nurture and protect above all else; how on earth do they cope with, encourage, even accept a sport that goes totally against that natural grain? Their sons, their flesh and blood, steered not only into adult life and all the pitfalls that can bring, but deep into bloody battle and open to all the dangerous elements they have been sheltered from.

When the relationship between fighting sons and their mothers is explored, and cases revealed, it really does cut to the core of family life.

The name 'Carol' was originally a man's name with Germanic origins (derived from Carolus, meaning 'free man'). Now more commonly used as a woman's name, I have found there to be a continued sturdiness about Carols. There are three of them who may not be hugely familiar to fight fans, but they are every bit as important as their world champion sons. Three proud working-class ladies. Three tough birds. With three different tales.

Carol Hatton has been an ever-present along the Hitman's thrilling boxing voyage, and is never far from the line of fire. Constantly supportive of both Richard and Matthew, Carol became quite a feature in her own right. As is so often the case in boxing, media men like me are always seeking out a story. Little sub-plots. Engaging personalities. Carol hits the mark.

'To be honest, I never anticipated how well Richard was going to do,' Carol confessed. 'Never thought it would ever lead to this. We are just an average family from Hyde!'

Hardly. A former pub landlady and market stall holder, Carol Hatton's a right rip-roaring northern bird who says it how it is, is hysterically funny, and fiercely loyal. She towers over husband Ray, whom she met 'many moons ago' on the Hattersley council estate. 'Little men like big women,' Carol explained in her usual, brutally blunt manner. 'Where do you think Richard got his strength from? It wasn't his father. Look at him! Young Richard got hooked on kickboxing from the Bruce Lee films, and we converted the cellar in one of our pubs for his training. He never read a book. Boxing's what he wanted to do. I did all the washing and cooking over the years for the boys. When Richard eventually moved out of home – about a minute away – he'd be back all the time.'

I understood why that was. You always get a good brew and a bite to eat at Carol's.

'He'd been in his new place for a few months, and one day I went over. The instructions for the oven were still inside!'

Despite their difference in terms of culinary skills, there are actually many similarities between Ricky and Carol. Those inherited protruding eyebrows were an unfortunate hindrance when it came to dealing with savage cuts and the need to have 'God' (or Mick Williamson) in the corner. Matthew doesn't suffer to the same extent. He's more like Ray maybe, in personality too.

Carol and Ricky also love a laugh.

'I adore her more than anyone else, but she's a monster,' Ricky told me a while back. 'Her Rice Krispies don't go "snap, crackle and pop", they go "Watch out, she's coming!" A right handful!'

Jo, Mum and I all went to Carol's fiftieth birthday do at Hyde Town Hall. It was her all over. Unpretentious, real, and bloody good fun. She was so pleased to have such a turnout, and proceeded to make absolute mincemeat of the stripper! Many, many friends were there from all walks of life. Yet Carol can also mingle with the A-list celebrities. When her eldest tackled Floyd Mayweather on a typically glitzy Vegas occasion, Carol called Tom Cruise 'absolutely tiny', Sylvester Stallone 'pure ugly', and admitted that she wouldn't throw Brad Pitt out of bed. Ray just laughed.

'I don't want to be one of those celeb mums. I do like a celeb though!' Carol remarked.

But how did this Mancunian matriarch deal with the pain of watching her eldest suffer his two rare defeats?

'They were going down like bloody skittles,' Carol said. 'I

needed to be strong. No point in panic. It's only a loss. The Manny [Pacquiao] fight was worse. I was worried that he was down for so long. I just have to put someone else before me, and that's what I did with Jennifer. I need to be there. Ringside. Always. For Richard and for Matthew. Veronica knows, Adam. It's just the way it has to be.'

My mum commented, 'Carol always has a water bottle with her at fights. But there's normally something stronger in it – and I'm not surprised.'

Andy Murray's mother Judy is an ever-present at his matches. But Andy admits he has no idea how mums can watch their sons box: 'How on earth do they manage?'

Carol dreads being ringside but an inner desire to protect her boys compels her to be there. 'The one time I wasn't able to be with him was in Detroit. Richard was boxing someone called Quiros, or "The Animal". It was ten times worse not being there. I saw him cut, Billy Graham gave him one more round, it was so awful. The worst. Because I was not with him.'

Well, Carol Hatton has a most steely resolve. Through thick and thin, she has long tried to hold the Hatton family together. 'When Richard got beat by that Manny, it destroyed him. He put this bravado on, played his cards close to his chest. We said that people would look at his whole career, not just about one fight.'

Shortly after Ricky's cocaine binge was laid bare, Carol said to me, 'Thank you for your support with Richard and his problems in the papers.' We spoke at a charity function Amir Khan had organized in Bolton. She was bravely facing the world at a time when her eldest son was recovering in The Priory. 'Richard is very poorly, Adam, but he's in the right place now. And he knows his family's here for him. To me he'll always be Richard with his flip-flops and beanie hat. It has been difficult recently, but I will never stop being his mother.'

An emotional interview on Sky followed. Ray and Carol were sitting in their usual places on the Hyde household beige leather sofa; Ray always seems to be on the right and Carol on the left. Ray was struggling to hold it together, and Carol was gripping his arm and calmly supporting him through it. The domineering but soft-centred soul. Carol was convinced her son would win his biggest ever fight.

In recent months, not only has Ricky announced his retirement, he has become a father again, new baby Millie joining his ten-year-old son Campbell. Ricky also has his first training charges – Adam Little and Craig Lyon – and he has taken over the reins of Hatton Promotions. 'Ray has worked so hard over the years, and deserves to take things easy, spend more time with Mum,' he said.

Carol is always there to love and support, even though there have been rocky times to endure, and she remains addicted to the sport. As she made clear, though, 'The boys are never too old to get a clip round the ear. That's the way I have always kept them grounded. Richard can think he's the victim sometimes. I'm so used to it now with two sons doing it. I know the risks are always there, but then how many people win the lottery? Win or lose – we have a booze!'

She really is funny at times. After Ray retired and handed the promotional gig to Ricky, Carol told me that he now owns a small gym in Stockport so that he doesn't 'vegetate'. 'No more carpets. Only get laid once a month now!'

So what about the fact that she has two sons, both of whom chose boxing, but who have attained very different standards?

'I worry. Yes. To succeed, you must have that killer instinct. A ruthless streak. Matthew may not have that. Most people who excel at something are born with a gift. But Matthew went into boxing because of Richard. Don't bloody know why, but he was adamant. No choice but to support him. Just want him to come out with all his marbles intact. A loss is not some terminal disease. Richard wanted to be a fighter, but Matthew was far more into cricket and football. Adam, I always, always had to be there for them. Couldn't have done it any other way. In my mind, there is a need for me to be ringside in case anything went wrong. That was always important to me. I do like boxing. It's the hardest sport, but what I like is that you can be friends afterwards.'

She is an amazing woman.

One of the strongest, most fearless of the modern British fighting brigade has been Carl Froch. Few of our leading boxers have had more testing international runs. What a ride the Cobra's given us with seven straight world title fights in three years. Jean Pascal. Jermain Taylor. Andre Dirrell. Mikkel Kessler. Arthur Abraham. Glen Johnson. Andre Ward. And an eighth, Lucian Bute, set for May 2012. With only two home fixtures in Nottingham, Froch has taken challenge after challenge away from home, his faithful band of merry men following him to such far-flung places as Herning in Denmark – despite the ash cloud chaos of 2010 – and Helsinki.

Also making those long trips was Carl's mum Carol Weatherbed. Behind these hardened young men lie pretty tough mums! And it is blatantly apparent that this Carol also dotes on her sons, all three of them. 'Despite Carl's fame, I am so proud of Lee and Wayne too,' she told me during a charming phone call before she headed out to the Super Six Final on the eastern seaboard. 'Anything the lads wanted to do, I would have supported them. All three were into karate. For Lee, it was just another phase, and Wayne's not into sport. Carl wanted boxing. The great thing is that all three protect each other. Carl is very close to Lee. And to Wayne the pain! All three have to be there to look out for the others. It's instinct, and it makes me feel very reassured.'

'Were you happy that Carl pursued a boxing career?' I asked her.

'It was always going to be a concern,' she replied, 'but then we all know we are going to die some time. You just put the tragedies to the back of your mind. It is risky, but I believe in him. I couldn't be a weeping mother. Not wimpy or worrying the whole time. Now he has his son Rocco, he understands more. You want them to go to sleep, and you want them to wake up. At each stage with Carl, I have been more confident. It's his job. It's what he does. He has the pedigree. I'm not sure I would have let him box if he'd been a journeyman. We might all be nervous beyond belief. But he is a superstar. I'm fascinated by how he does it.'

'I know you have to be ringside,' I said to Carol, 'but how are you around the actual fight?'

'In the build-up, I always talk to him about boxing, and he'll always listen. We talk, talk, and talk. Then Carl will make the decision. But I won't speak to him on the day. He's not my son then. He's Carl. The Cobra. Yet I will jump around and scream at ringside. It's my way. I know how a swift uppercut should be thrown! Sometimes he'll even say, "Mum, that's exactly what I was thinking!"'

'Are you really not concerned about Carl being hurt, and being beaten? Tragedies can happen.'

'I once worried about him being hit, hurt. But as I said, he is an expert. We never have any discussions about losing. I am not worried. Even when that ash cloud came, and he was put on a tiny plane, he still went out and did his job.'

It was an absorbing chat. Carol was about to pack the warm winter clothes for the freezing Atlantic City boardwalk, so I wished her well. Her parting shot summed up the whole conversation: 'He's as strong as an ox, fearless. There's like an invisible wall with my Carl. He's going to annihilate Andre Ward on December seventeenth.'

Unfortunately Carl Froch very much found his match in that Super Six Final against the extremely classy Californian. He was outboxed, outfought at times, but like the true warrior he is Carl was still bulldozing away at the final bell. It must be something in that water from the Trent. Or maybe it's direct and pure, straight from Mummy's genes.

Our third Carol may not be as well known or as openly assured as her two namesakes. But she is every bit as resilient. Maybe more so. Few fighting mums can have had a more difficult situation to deal with than Carol Ingle – one that every mother must dread the day her little boy laces up his first pair of boxing boots.

If Carl Froch is the boxing pride of Nottingham and Ricky Hatton the famous Hitman from Hyde, then Paul Ingle was once the toast of Scarborough. Paul is forty this year and is now utterly dependent on his mum Carol. Once upon a time, Paul Ingle was a superb amateur, an Olympian, and the 'Yorkshire Hunter' became a world featherweight champion; today he needs constant care as a result of a devastating fight with the South African Mbulelo Botile at the Sheffield Arena in December 2000, which ended in a life-or-death dash to hospital after a blood clot on the brain. One of our most popular and fittest fighters underwent the ultimate battle, for survival itself.

I spent a great deal of time in Scarborough in the late nineties. Paul was a real working-class hero whom I admired immensely. He could really fight, and in many ways he was British boxing and Sky's next big thing. Paul was a throwback who used to train doggedly hard, even finishing stints with icy dips in the North Sea.

But to be honest, Paul Ingle has become a rather lost man in the last decade. There was once a fiancée, a life, real hope. But Paul's ring damage has led to a far more lonely existence than inside the squared circle. He has made a decent recovery, but he's not 100 per cent. I think the problem is that we – and I include most of the British boxing fraternity in that – have rather forgotten about him. Following a much-needed benefit night, when Paul was duly honoured in 2001, we left him to it.

After many years of absence, we belatedly went to visit him in 2011 for a shoot on *Ringside*. It was an emotional day for Johnny and me, because Paul was still very distressed about what had happened. Not with boxing. Far from it. He would do it all over again. But he was bitter that his career was cut off in its prime. He just can't seem to shake off the 'Why me?' He is almost obsessed with talking about the Botile experience – not that he remembers much of the build-up, or of course the fight itself.

Paul has also put on a great deal of weight. That is usual for ex-boxers, who are no longer boiling themselves down, but Paul admits he's let it go too far. He told us that he is careful about what he eats and wants to exercise, but can't seem to motivate himself. Two hernias have further restricted his movement.

Paul has issues with short-term memory but is otherwise very easy to talk to. Sharp and witty. Johnny and I immediately thought that he needed a personal mission, maybe completing a fun-run, or a half-marathon; or even helping to coach aspiring youngsters, putting his knowledge back into the game. He regularly watches boxing to this day.

It is the chicken-and-egg issue, as Paul desperately needs to get himself into shape before he can achieve any physical and mental goals. We took him down to the Scarborough seafront and he loved reminiscing about the spartan training and the features we did on him in this famous old seaside town. They call it 'the Queen of the Yorkshire Coast'. Well, Paul Ingle was once very much their sporting king. He now lives a remarkably different life with his devoted mum, a lovely lady who seemed particularly concerned about the attempts to get messages through to Paul.

Carol Ingle has given up her life to nurse her adult son. She was fascinating to listen to, so much so that I followed up our visit with a phone call. It was a harrowing hour; Carol laid her emotions bare. There was so much I wanted to ask her, but there were times when it just became very, very hard for her.

'Paul began boxing at nine. He loved his new hobby, and he became pretty good at it. I followed him all over as an amateur. I was a bag of nerves.'

'Did you continue on to see each professional fight?' I asked her.

'Absolutely not. I was terrified when he went pro. I only ever went to one fight – against Billy Hardy in York. Only one. So scared for him. I didn't even go to New York for his victory over Junior Jones. I used to go to some sparring sessions, and I was really worried about the Naz fight. I didn't think he was ready for it. That Naz was a bit of a beast. But Paul did so well. He never changed through his career either. I was proud of that.

'I would always sit at home waiting for the call, and then came the one that changed everything. After the Botile fight. My friend said that Paul had a bleed on the brain. It was fifty-fifty whether he would survive, and he would definitely have brain damage as a result. I rushed to Sheffield and spent seventy-two hours at the side of his bed. The medical attention was marvellous.'

Paul was treated in the Royal Hallamshire Hospital for six and a half weeks, under consultant neurosurgeon Robert Battersby, and then he went for rehab in Hull. He had a blood clot removed from the brain, and the side of his skull was cut out; in a later operation a titanium plate replaced the discarded bone. But here's an amazing thing about these fighters: Paul Ingle would do it all over again. If only he could.

'Tomorrow, Ad. Tomorrow. I'd take the risks all over. It is just one of those things,' he told me.

I asked Carol whether she in any way blamed herself for letting him box. She broke down at this point. 'No, I don't,' she finally replied.

I said that I had heard rumours that Paul had crashed his weight considerably, and at one point was eating just a couple of apples a day.

'No one really knows,' said Carol. 'I was told it could have happened in sparring, or in the first round. What I do know is that if it wasn't for his incredible fitness, he wouldn't be like he is today.'

'But you are a full-time carer now, Carol?'

'Absolutely. I am his mother, I am his protector. It's back to childhood.' By this stage she was finding it very difficult to hold back the tears. 'I'm sorry,' she said, taking a moment to compose herself.

I gave her all the time she needed, then asked her if she wanted to carry on.

'I just keep the emotions held in most of the time,' she explained. 'It is very, very hard. He has memory problems. Long term is fine. It's on the day that he won't remember what he's done. He's also blind in the corner of his eye. But like he said to you, Adam, he'd box tomorrow. He was only going to have that fight, and Naz again, and retire. I was happy about that. But I have absolutely nothing against boxing.'

At times like that I have to shake my head in disbelief. How can a mum who has gone through what Carol Ingle has gone through still back the sport?

'I really like it,' she said. 'I watch all the tapes and fights. We do together. It was one of those things. Might have happened to anyone, anywhere. I couldn't be more proud of Paul's achievements. I am his mother. This has been my life for the last twelve years. His fiancée left him. She found it hard to cope. I was bitter, but not any more. I am his mum. I have one other son, Dean, and I have to be there for them.'

It was a remarkably difficult interview, and in many ways I felt guilty for even pursuing the tough questions.

'If it wasn't for me, he would have no one,' Carol continued, weeping again, and setting me off too. 'That's how much I love him. A lot of his friends are gone. I can't get him into the gym. He's not bothered, but he must exercise. And diet. There is Neil, but he lives in Norwich. It's as though somebody needs to be with him. There is no other way.'

It is such a sad story, and one that makes it so difficult to defend my sport. Paul, though, is still with us. He retains his humour, but he needs the fight fraternity to take notice again. I promise we will do what we can to help get him up and running. After all the great memories he gave us.

It was a particularly emotional phone call I had with Carol Ingle, and one that made me think about agonizing chats I've had with a couple of other heroines. More of the truest and most admirable of fighting mums. Those who have quite simply been to hell and back.

Surely the most awe-inspiring boxing mother to have emerged through horrendous trials and tribulations is Joan Watson. This amazing woman has two sons – Michael (who you may have heard of) and Jeffrey. Like so many families from the Caribbean, the Watson family moved from Jamaica to England (Stoke Newington in north London) in the sixties, hoping for a better life. It could not have been tougher.

'Times were very hard,' Joan explained. 'I was pushing the boys' pram one day, a bus let me out, but the pram was hit by a car, which came from nowhere. Jeffrey received a brain haemorrhage and was paralysed down the side. Still, I counted my blessings that both of my sons were still alive.'

Joan has amazing religious faith. Just as well, as she soon had to deal with a fire blazing through the family home. She got the boys out, minutes before the place went up. They moved to the De Beauvoir estate in Islington, and Michael's dad returned to Jamaica.

'I've been through a lot,' Joan continued. 'With religion, strength and determination, I made it through.'

Michael said, 'She was a father, a mother, brother, sister – all in one. My entire life. She inspired me.'

At first Joan was surprised that Michael went into boxing because he was 'very soft, and would cry at the smallest thing'. Advised to learn something defensive to protect himself from bullies, Michael began boxing at the Crown and Manor ABC.

'He was really good at it,' said Joan. 'I used to cheer him on. Go on, jab and move, jab and move! I had to support Michael.'

Joan has a lovely way about her, especially for someone who has had so many issues to deal with in life. She talks of the 'horns, banners and music parties' after the sensational night in the Finsbury Park tent in 1989, when Michael upset and derailed the all-out army aggressor Nigel Benn.

In the first Eubank fight two years later, Joan remembers how proud she was of her son, despite the controversial defeat. 'Michael gave Chris a good beating!' she said, adding, 'Michael wanted to win the second fight so much.'

Virtually every sporting fan in Britain remembers that fateful night at White Hart Lane on 21 September 1991. Again Michael Watson gave Chris Eubank such a scare in their hugely anticipated rematch. But then 'The Force' began the biggest fight of his life. Stopped in the last round, Michael collapsed in the ring. Crucial minutes were lost as he was starved of oxygen. He was given virtually no chance of survival after suffering horrific injuries.

'I didn't know my son was so badly damaged,' Joan told me. 'When I realized how serious it was, I was in complete shock. I was told there was no way that Michael could lead a normal life. It looked for several weeks like he would die. He could only communicate by blinking. But I am a Christian lady and I had faith he would pull through.'

Michael Watson was in a coma for forty days and forty nights. He endured six brain operations to remove a blood clot. Joan slept in a box-room at St Bart's Hospital throughout. Consultant neurosurgeon Peter Hamlyn brought him back from the brink, while his Uncle Joe has been a huge support, and a childhood friend and carer, Leonard Ballack, is still Michael's constant, phenomenal sidekick.

'We had to start all over again – like a baby in everything,' Joan admitted. 'It was a long, long road back, but Michael and I believe that life's too precious to quit.'

Joan worked doggedly hard to help Michael in those darkest hours. This was even harder for a boxer's mum than having to go through what he did fight by fight, year after year. And Michael and Joan's battle has lasted far longer than a mere professional boxing career.

Our Sky cameras were there when Michael first walked again, six years after the accident, and also when he finished one of the greatest modern sporting feats, the London Marathon, in 2003, completing the arduous course in six days, two hours, twenty-six minutes and eighteen seconds. I had the honour of walking a small section of it alongside him. Joan said that seeing Michael with a medal around his neck was probably 'the greatest moment'. He received an MBE from the Queen, who told him that he was 'a remarkable man'. 'And you're a remarkable woman' was Watson's witty response!

Once again, there is no hatred of the sport from either mother or son. 'I love boxing,' Michael told me at a glittering gala testimonial function held at London's Dorchester Hotel in September 2011 in recognition of his immense achievements. 'It made me a champion. The best thing ever.' He is still so happy, after all that has happened. Chris Eubank and Nigel Benn gave him a guards' honour and hundreds of the boxing fraternity turned out to raise money for him.

Joan's so proud of him. 'Michael is just an inspiration,' she told me. 'Every mother's dream.'

He has no bitterness, no remorse, no regrets about what happened, and it is testament both to mother and son that Michael is the astonishing human being he is. In some ways they both feel that his injury was a blessing – it is what was written – and that life is much better now.

Promoter Barry Hearn summed it up best: 'He is a complete credit to mankind.'

I also think Joan Watson is a complete credit to womankind. Having had the privilege of visiting her home made me feel refreshed by the power of the human spirit.

But I have conducted one even harder interview over the years. It came following harrowing months for so many connected to the world of boxing, this world which can at times be terribly raw and painful.

15

The Darkest Night

Friday the thirteenth is not a date most people relish, and Friday 13 October 1995 will be forever etched in my memory, and that of the whole British fight game. For that was when we so sadly lost the brave James Murray in a Scottish ring.

A little background. I had been at Sky Sports for just over a year. It was a particularly exciting time because not only were we enjoying the pomp and circumstance of that ever-so-entertaining eccentric Chris Eubank and his 'world tour', but also Frank Warren had brought over his big-name stable from ITV. So suddenly the odd fight night was replaced with the likes of Bruno, Benn, Hamed and Collins, and through Frank's connection with Don King, the biggest name in the sport: Tyson. For a fledgling reporter, this was a great period to be learning the television trade.

One autumnal evening in 1995 we took our cameras to the Hospitality Inn in Glasgow for a dinner show that was headlined by a British bantamweight title fight between Drew Docherty and James Murray. I had gone up to Scotland early and spent a couple of days filming James. Despite one early defeat, the twenty-five-year-old had made decent progress to become the Scottish Area champion, and this was his first tilt at the Lonsdale belt. Murray was an underdog against the more seasoned Docherty, but the fellow Scot was coming off a fourth-round world title defeat to Ghana's classy Alfred Kotey.

James was just a year or so older than me, and we got on well. He drove us around Glasgow, relishing this big opportunity, and told me all about the first flat he'd managed to acquire with his girlfriend, as well as his extra work as a landscape gardener. This was a fighter with everything ahead of him.

The only slight concern I had was that he seemed very gaunt when tipping the scales at the weigh-in. In fact he looked fairly haunting coming in a whole two pounds inside the 8st 6lb limit.

When trying to assess dark nights for our sport, one observation is that the lower weight categories – bantamweight (8st 6lb), super-bantamweight (8st 10lb), featherweight (9st) and super-featherweight (9st 4lb) – are very tightly packed together. There are four classes there, just twelve pounds apart in all. Particularly back then there was a real craze for fighters to drag themselves down to fit into the lowest category possible. The idea was that by dropping pounds they would be the biggest and strongest for the weight supported by the rehydration period before the fight, which had recently been extended. It doesn't always work this way, though. Sometimes, but not always.

Anyway, the stage was set for an enticing all-Scottish affair. Unfortunately there was a peculiar, even unpleasant feeling in the air on that freezing Glasgow night. A supposedly civilized dinner show turned into a bit of a free-for-all, because packs of rival football fans who were standing at the back of the hotel banqueting suite had piled in to grab whatever free drinks they could. Bottles of red and white wine littered the tables. So, far from a calm black-tie affair, the atmosphere was fierce; at one point one of our VT trucks was attacked by a rampaging mob and we were very fortunate that it did not actually topple over.

Back inside the venue, it was hot. The fight itself? Brutal enough. Tragic outcomes, as we know, are extremely rare, but what often happens is that the stricken fighter tends to feel he can walk through his opponent's lighter punches and eventually takes too much. Just as with Michael Watson, and later Paul Ingle, Murray collapsed in the twelfth and final round. There were just thirty-four seconds remaining.

Dreadful scenes followed; the end of the fight seemed to be a cue for hundreds of fans to brawl. This severely hampered the effort to get crucial medical help to James Murray. The paramedics were badly hindered. I vividly remember my sense of utter confusion as that all-round boxing man, builder of rings and MC Mike Goodall was left calling for immediate help. John Morris, the board's former General Secretary, also appealed for calm.

It seemed an age before Murray was taken out of the ring on a stretcher. Drew Docherty, the victor, was in floods of tears. Murray's manager, Alex Morrison, was the next to break down. Referee John Keane had every reason to be inconsolable too. The well-respected official had been the third man eighteen months earlier when Bradley Stone ended up losing his life after battling Richie Wenton.

Now it was a young Scotsman who was left fighting for his life. James Murray was rushed to Southern General Hospital, but he was diagnosed as 'clinically dead' less than twenty-four hours after having a blood clot removed from the left side of his brain.

By that time I had left Scotland and was trying to prepare for a Sunday lunch party in Oxfordshire. I was distraught, and the news on Ceefax confirmed my worst fears: 'All signs of neurological activity are extinct. James Murray was confirmed dead at 0850 on Sunday 15 October.'

The bolt from the blue. Then the calls for boxing to be

banned. And I was about to attend a luncheon where I would be asked by older generations what my chosen profession was. Yes, it is television first and foremost, but my sport is boxing. In such circumstances it would be pretty hard to address that properly.

I still have an article written by the late, great boxing writer Harry Mullan, who mentioned the searing heat at ringside – not helped by copious amounts of cigar and cigarette smoke (which fortunately is no longer a problem inside boxing venues). The fighters surely suffered even more from the lack of oxygen. 'It was a volatile atmosphere which resulted in appalling scenes of disorder at the finish,' Mullan wrote. 'The television image of Murray on the canvas, his leg twitching in spasm while chairs and bottles crashed around the ringside does not sit easily with any perception of boxing as the noble art.'

For the next few weeks there was darkness around the boxing team at Sky. No one really knew what to say. My colleague at the time, Gary Norman, attended the funeral. The juniors among us were told to dig out every tape we had recorded, showing every possible angle for the police to sift through. It really was an unbearable time.

Meanwhile, Drew Docherty was a lost soul. He wasn't sure whether to carry on boxing, but eventually chose to stick with his profession, dedicating everything to the memory of James Murray. Unsurprisingly, he was never the same again. He lost five of his next (and last) six fights.

Docherty's promoter, Tommy Gilmour, initially wanted to walk away from boxing. And his family have been in the sport for generations. He said that he understood why some still felt boxing was indefensible, with its attendant dangers. Yet Tommy believed he had a responsibility to his stable of fighters so he kept going and continues to warn them all about the pitfalls and perils.

The British Medical Association stated that they had wanted a ban since 1982. James Murray's first trainer, Ally Gilmour, defended the situation, saying that James both needed and wanted boxing in order to get off the streets. His dad, Kenneth, believed that the people who were calling for a ban didn't know boxing, and he felt there was no reason for the fatal accident inquiry. 'Jim knew all the risks, he was a shrewd man,' he said.

Deep emotions. Knee-jerk reactions. We all needed some time. My appetite for the sport was strong, but I can't deny that I thought very hard about walking away in the months afterwards. But then I hadn't, by that stage, been around the world and seen all the good boxing can do.

There was one thing I really wanted to find out: how did James's mum now feel about boxing? Fortunately I got that chance.

On the first anniversary of James's tragic death, in October 1996, I was asked to travel to his family's home in Newmains, a tough area with terrible unemployment in North Lanarkshire. The steel industry had long gone, replaced by drugs and violence. I had also read that in Newmains there was a particular problem with shops selling a cheap but potent tonic wine called Buckfast to underage kids. It had got so bad that Newmains had been renamed 'Buckfast Valley' by locals.

The snow was falling by the time we landed at Glasgow airport. I made my way to Newmains to meet James's mum, Margaret. I was full of apprehension, thoughts flooding into my mind of that fateful night when Murray was felled, and his life was snuffed out so quickly, so cruelly. Would his mum even speak to a boxing journalist? Especially one who worked for Sky Sports, the channel which had broadcast the worst night of her life. How would she feel about the sport that took her son away from her? Bitter resentment and anger? Disgust presumably. I wondered if I could even look Mrs Murray in the eye, or ask her the most poignant questions. And if I did, how would I feel afterwards? Would I be able to carry on covering this beautiful but realistically bloody and brutal business?

We were welcomed politely, and to my surprise warmly, into the Murray family home, and shown into their lounge. That's when it really hit me. A huge portrait of James was on the wall, his eyes piercing; the mural seemed to take up the entire room. As I sat down, James's sister walked in. She was the spitting image of her brother, and that really sent shivers down my spine. It was a quite surreal and rather uncomfortable experience.

Margaret Murray obviously found it painful to talk about what had happened to her beloved son, but what shone through was how proud she was of James's achievements. 'I loved him to the core,' she told me. 'He was a good, good boy – so kind – and he was dedicated to doing something he absolutely loved. I was never particularly a fan of boxing, but Jim adored it. It gave him so much discipline, as a professional. I looked up to him.'

'It's been a year since you lost him,' I ventured. 'How on earth have you managed to keep going?'

'I haven't really talked about it. We just have to get on with it. It doesn't get any easier, but Jim died doing what he loved. He was so fit, so well, so happy. And however upsetting this is, I remember that. He did me proud.'

'Don't you just blame the sport for what happened to your family?'

Her response startled me. 'I don't blame boxing at all. Boxing didn't kill Jim Murray. Jim Murray could have died on the drug-infested streets round here. Jim did not die with a needle in his arm. Or up some alley. Boxing saved James Murray. That's the truth.'

Tears filled the room. There was huge sorrow.

'It was nobody's fault,' Margaret continued. 'Jim knew the

risks. That's the profession he chose. It was his dream. And he was living it.'

I looked up at his portrait again. You could feel the family pride in his accomplishments, in the knowledge that he'd done something positive with his life.

As an inexperienced journalist, I tried to keep it short and simple. This wasn't an attempt to use the Murray family for our own media interests; it was more of a personal crusade to discover what a boxing mother's true feelings were. Meeting Margaret Murray was a major turning point for me. In human terms, and with my highly sensitive hat on, I had started to seriously doubt whether I could make a professional career in this sport. As much as I adored so much within it, the loss of life was very hard to accept.

Yet if James Murray's own family, moreover his own mother and protector, could insist that boxing had saved him, I had to listen. There began my fascination with unearthing stories from around the globe where boxing has been *the* way out. It was all so far from where and how I had been brought up: the plush surroundings of Hampstead Garden Suburb, private education. No wonder it's normally the middle to upper class who call for the abolition of this sport. They have little clue. Come and meet the likes of Margaret Murray and then reconsider your stance.

Before I left Newmains, I went with Margaret to James's grave. It was another poignant scene. As the snowflakes tumbled down, she stared quietly at the resting place of her son. James was buried in his boxing gloves. That was his love, his life, and his dream.

'Am I right to be involved in the sport?' I asked Margaret, strictly off camera. 'How can I justify it when I see this scene?'

Mrs Murray reiterated her words: 'Boxing saved my son. Never forget that.'

And I never have, as I continue to ply my trade in this gripping sport. Thank you, Margaret Murray.

Out of the heartache came some good: Frank Warren established a 'Murray/Stone' fund to finance MRI scans for every British fighter, and the sport has become infinitely safer.

James Murray is the last fighter to die in a British ring. There is a bronze statue in his honour that stands in Newmains today. A fighting testament to a man who met his end in a quest to become a boxing champion. No needle in the arm. No life sentence. Just a good life that, tragically, was just way too short.

Owing to the increase in medical safety in and around ringside, Spencer Oliver is still with us today after collapsing in similar circumstances at the end of a European super-bantamweight title fight in May 1998.

It was meant to be the real launch of 'The Omen', a popular little bundle of energy from Barnet who was unbeaten in fourteen, with nine KOs. Spencer was lifted aloft in front of the famous organ inside the Royal Albert Hall as a choir sang him into an important fight with the light-punching Sergei Devakov. But Oliver's boxing world came crashing down around him with a tenth-round defeat, followed by a three-hour operation at London's National Hospital for Neurology and Neurosurgery.

Spencer's amazing. He made a 100 per cent recovery, largely due to the fact that he had a nurse in his corner who placed him into a controlled coma while still in the ring, so that his brain stopped swelling. The blood clot was removed within 'the golden hour needed', and over the following couple of weeks he quickly returned to 'normal'. Well, normal for Spencer, that is, who often jokes that the bump on his head did him good!

Just like Michael Watson and Paul Ingle, Spencer Oliver would do it all over again – he'd box tomorrow – possibly because his career was curtailed well before he reached his potential. Spencer still lives and breathes the sport, and is infectious to be around. 'I'd take the risks, every day of the week and twice on Sundays, Adam,' he told me. 'Boxing's my life, my passion. I love boxing as much today as when I boxed.'

Ironically, the Devakov disaster was the only fight his dad Jim couldn't make because of a trip to Vegas with a boys' boxing club. Spencer's brother Danny was out there too. Mum Anne was left in charge.

'We're right close, Mum and I,' my amiable Sky colleague Spencer told me. 'My mum did everything for me during my career. She was so helpful. She understood boxing because it had been in the family, but I'm sure she'll tell you that even if I could fight again, she'd never let me.'

So I tracked Anne down. Another right character along this journey.

'I was always supportive because I married into it, so I understood, but I never ever wanted to be there at a fight,' Anne told me. 'My role was to do the diet, make sure they all trained properly. And that they played by the rules!'

'So why not be there to cheer Spencer on from ringside?' I asked.

'It's a maternal thing,' Anne replied. 'You can't see someone throw a punch at your son. It's heartbreaking. I wish my boys had gone into something else. Like football. Or golf. That would have been nice. Anything that didn't involve violence.'

'Did you know how good he was?'

'No, only from what everyone was saying. Then his lifestyle changed. The limos started picking him up, and I thought, God, that's my son. I was so proud. But with each fight, I thought, here we go again. I used to have two friends watching next door, and I'd sit on my own. I'd hear the shouting behind the walls.'

'What about that horrible day back in spring 1998?'

'There was something strange,' Anne began, 'something that didn't feel right. I had to help him as his father and brother were away. I still stayed at home of course. I didn't know what had happened until lots of people came over the green at the end of my cul-de-sac. They said he'd been knocked out but was fine. Someone called a taxi for me, and I was heading to one hospital when it came on the radio that they had taken him to another. The neurological one. When I arrived, they wouldn't let me in. So I went round to the back and there were two, three hundred people. That's when I knew it must be bad. The doctors told me the extent of his injuries. It was a fight for life. Absolutely devastating. I stayed in the visitors' room for four days. Didn't move. I booked into a hotel for the next fourteen days. It was a long process, but I had to be there for him.'

'How did you possibly cope with those long days and nights?' I asked.

'It was desperately hard. We didn't know what state he'd be in. Would he walk again? What of his memory, his coordination? I was horrified he might be a schizophrenic. I would hate to see a mother go through anything like that.

'Meanwhile, his dad and brother were in the air for hours. What must they have thought? They didn't know what was going on. To be honest with you, I thought I was going to end up in a mental institute. I had five months of counselling and got a lot off my chest. Stuff about boxing that I couldn't talk to the family about. Like it being banned!'

'Obviously the most important thing was his full recovery, but do you now wish Spencer had done something else for a living?'

'Yes. I wish he'd picked up the golf clubs! I have eleven grandchildren now and four are boys. I dread one of them doing it. I would dread it. I still can't bring myself to watch a fight. If Spencer's highlights are on the telly, then I have to walk away.

I would like it if the sport didn't exist, but if it's in them, it's in them.'

'And Spencer would do it all over again,' I reminded her.

'I know! I told you – if it's in them, it's in them. He adores it. I am so thankful for Sky that he is still involved and so positive about life. He never knew anything else. He never worked. Well, apart from a few shifts on the building site. But then he'd come back cleaner than when he went out!'

'Are you proud of his achievements, Anne?'

'Of course. He's my son.'

I thanked her for being so open with me, but she wasn't quite finished.

'One last thing,' she said. 'He'd been asleep for four days in the hospital, and when he woke up, the doctor told me I could pop in and see him. The first thing he said to me was, "Mum, did I win the fight?" I said, "Spencer, you have just won the best fight of your life."'

Other mums have had to deal with adversity of a different kind: losing a boxing child, but not through the sport itself. Ironically, Anne Oliver and Jacqui Barker are virtually neighbours in Barnet. Their families are tighter than tight.

When Jacqui met future husband Terry, she knew he was a fighter, but didn't realize he'd won the top amateur title, the ABAs. She adored sport, her own dad loved boxing, and she had no problem watching Terry live.

The Barkers had three boys – Darren, Lee and Gary – and a daughter, Daisy.

'The boys were football mad, for Chelsea,' Jacqui explained to our Sky cameras. 'I thought they would go that route. Terry had put his trophies in the loft, out of the way, and I was really shocked that Darren picked boxing. He was such a sensitive kid and a very caring big brother. Darren wasn't winning much when he was at Finchley, so I thought he'd stop. But he went to Repton, where his dad had been, over in the East End. So I knew he was serious, and I was very proud.'

But what about watching Darren; was it as comfortable as being there when Terry fought?

'It wasn't a problem when he was young, as an amateur. I knew his coach Tony Burns very well. Darren travelled abroad, met people. It was good. But I didn't want to see Darren fight live as he progressed. My job was to get the kit ready, be a mum, stay on the backburner. For the final of the Commonwealth Games [in Manchester in 2002, when Darren struck gold], I was outside the arena. I brought all my nice clothes to wear!

'Meanwhile there were the others. Gary was very gifted. A southpaw. And Lee had this natural physique – he didn't do any training. Darren and Gary did the not eating certain things, and Lee said, "I can't do this, it ain't me!" Kids are all different, aren't they?'

She sounded to me like such a wonderful and loving mum.

'They never ever let me down,' she told me. 'Not in a million years. The way they came home from school. Picked up their training bags and straight off to Bethnal Green. They had to train when all their mates were out. Lose weight, not go out drinking. They were amazing, my two boxers, and you know what? No one cuts grass like Lee does.'

So was Jacqui always scared of what might happen?

'It's so weird, I really don't know what it is. It's not the fact that they might get hurt, because when your child falls over, you have to patch them up. I'm just not meant to be there.' She would always watch fights afterwards, but Jacqui's daughter Daisy was still young, and she wanted to make sure they had their time.

As talented as Darren was, the family and the amateur boxing world felt Gary Barker might go even further. By the age of nineteen, the cheeky, promising and very capable lightweight had represented England and Great Britain in several international tournaments, winning Junior Olympic gold in 2002. In October 2006 Gary won the London Amateur Boxing Association title and was one of Britain's major hopes for the Beijing Olympics. Tony Burns called him 'a special talent, one of the best we have ever seen at Repton – and a real nice kid too'.

Then suddenly, in December 2006, the Barkers' world was ripped apart. Following a charity boxing night, the family thought they had persuaded Gary not to get into his car, but a late-night decision to drive to Leicester to see his girlfriend proved fatal. Gary fell asleep at the wheel near Luton and was killed.

Gone was a beloved son and brother. 'The Fabulous Barker Brothers', a professional boxing dream team, had vanished for ever. Unsurprisingly, Darren went off the rails for ten months, wouldn't box, and disappeared into a dark hole of despair. Terry fell to bits too. Jacqui, despite being inconsolable, said she had to remain the family's rock.

Jacqui reminisced about the times when her boys sparred as she cooked. 'They would all box in the kitchen while I was preparing the meals. I have lost that amazing feeling of having everyone there. We just keep Gary's spirit alive.'

Gary's death altered Jacqui's attitude to being a boxing mum. 'After Gary, I was petrified that I'd lose another child,' she said. 'Darren stopped for ten months, but I went to his next fight live. I walked around in a daze at York Hall, but I had to be there. For Gary. I am much more concerned now when Darren boxes, but I do try and put it into perspective. Getting into a car is dangerous, as I know. Crossing the road is. Darren has a fantastic trainer in Tony Sims. I tell him, Tony, make him safe. I don't care if he wins or loses. Tony said he will, because he loves him dearly.

'I have to be realistic. This is his career, his life, and I wouldn't stop him from doing anything. But Darren adores his family. Everything we do is for family. So I just can't lose another son. The emotions Darren must have going into the ring, thinking of Gary. I don't know how he copes.'

Jacqui said she had to be out in Atlantic City for Darren's dream shot at world middleweight king Sergio Martinez in October 2011. Barker was a major underdog, but performed far better than critics had felt he would, before his brave challenge was finally halted in the eleventh. 'I was pacing up and down the Boardwalk – not the best place to be pacing up and down,' Jacqui joked. 'Everywhere you went there was a television, but you don't want anything to remind you, and you just want to switch off. Normally I have a routine. I usually work – in a hospital. I don't want anyone to talk about it. I have even done an essay on it at university. I don't want to know. If anyone speaks to me about boxing, I'll floor them. I just want a phone call to say he's safe. I don't want to hear bad news. The only bad news is if he's hurt. Because my emotions are so full of grieving and pain, it is all way, way too intense.'

Deep in the Welsh valleys there was for a long time another very worried Jacqueline. While Joe Calzaghe and dad Enzo were enjoying their unusual but highly successful boxing partnership, mum Jackie kept herself firmly out of the limelight. We hardly saw her, which was a shame, because she's a lovely lady. But she was so nervous, so scared, that she preferred the life of a boxing hermit.

Jackie rarely gave an interview, but with our family connections in Newbridge I was fortunate enough to speak to her on a few occasions, and I always got the impression that she just couldn't wait for Joe's career to be over. Jackie has two daughters, Mel and Sonia, but Joe's her only, cherished son.

'I never watch Joseph fight,' Jackie told me over a cup of tea one afternoon at her home in Pentwynmawr, when Joe was at his peak. 'Ever. I hide behind the sofa, or run upstairs when he's boxing. I always fear for his safety. What if he doesn't come back from work? I am his biggest supporter, but I have to do it from a distance. It really upsets me to watch it, actually even to talk about it. I hate it when he comes back with even a bruise on his face.

'Joseph was bullied at school,' she continued. 'Seems to be a theme with boxers.'

Jackie admitted that Joe had inherited some of her quick temper. 'If I went to one of Joseph's fights, I wouldn't be able to hold back if I saw him getting hurt. I'd be right in the ring with him. Just the way I would feel. I couldn't possibly go. And I keep asking him to retire, because I am so worried.'

Jackie Calzaghe never did attend a fight. Not one of Joe's forty-six unbeaten professional outings, although she half-watched his clashes with Mikkel Kessler and Bernard Hopkins at home. Joe told me she had to take Valium. Imagine if he hadn't been any good and still become a boxer!

'I'll always worry about Joseph,' Jackie concluded, 'wherever he is, whatever he does. It's called being a mother.'

So it doesn't seem to get any easier however high-profile and celebrated your fighting son is. One of the enduring memories of Amir Khan's shock knockout defeat to the then unknown Colombian banger Breidis Prescott was the reaction of his mum, Falak, on seeing him prostrate on the canvas. When you look back at the explosive minute that shocked British boxing to the core – with the commentary of Ian Darke and Jim Watt turned down, and the FX up – you hear one piercing scream. That of Falak Khan.

I remember leaving the MEN Arena that night of 6 September 2008, with the media pack debating whether Khan would ever recover, and walking past a group of Amir's family and supporters. They were tending to Falak, who was in shock backstage over what had happened.

Amir told me that his mother then tried to throw away his boxing kit rather than wash it, and to prevent his younger brother, Haroon, from fighting again by hiding his gear. It was only her husband Shah who persuaded Falak to accept that their two sons would box on. It's tough, of course, that both her boys want to fight.

'Mum thinks that I have achieved my ambition of becoming a world champion, and wants me to call it a day,' Amir said. 'She still doesn't like me fighting now, even though I will because I have the talent and I want to be remembered as a great.'

Rather reminiscent of Jackie Calzaghe, Falak Khan is also quiet and reserved. 'I don't like the boxing,' she stated to me after Amir's crushing win over Dmitriy Salita in Newcastle. I was at the Khans' after-fight party, and she seemed a very relieved mum. 'This is what my sons have chosen to do. I support them, yet I have fear. Family is everything to me.'

So Mrs Khan did recover, and is naturally extremely proud of Amir's quite superb comeback from the ruins of that Manchester night. But she will not be ringside any more. It has had a deep and lasting effect on her. On Amir too. 'My mum won't be at any of my fights now. She chooses to stay in the hotel, wait by the phone and pray. I am very close to my mum. She spoils me so much. I love being with her, and I love munching her amazing curries. But if she says jump, I will. If she says tidy your room, it had better be tidy when she comes back!'

Staying away from ringside is the choice of many boxing mums. One wonders what Amir's fiancée Faryal Makhdoom will decide to do. Interestingly, his sisters Tabinda and Mariyah come to the fights, and nervously pray at ringside. Amir tells them to stay at home, but they want to be there for him.

Mothers, you see, can be supported or replaced by the other ladies in fighters' lives. Girlfriends, fiancées, wives, even sisters are additional female influences. Ireland's popular 'Pocket Rocket' Wayne McCullough always had wife Cheryl right by his side. Robert 'The Ghost' Guerrero and his wife Casey are inseparable. She's the only girl he's dated since Junior High and was diagnosed with leukaemia in 2007. Casey was given a bone marrow transplant with a fifty-fifty chance of survival. Robert basically put his career on hold to tend to daughter Savannah and son Robert Jnr, and to travel miles to the best doctors around, at Stanford University. Casey's doing well again and is right behind Robert's flourishing fight career. A tale of life being so much more important than boxing.

Two women here who are as close as anyone to their fighters are Jennifer Dooley, loving partner of Ricky Hatton, and Rachael Cordingley, who spends her life supporting Carl Froch. Both have also become mums themselves recently.

Jennifer doesn't like giving interviews and shies away from any fame. She has become close to my wife Jo, is a great girl, and she's been an absolute rock for Ricky. Through good, bad and quite nightmarish times.

'I'm glad he's achieved what he has, but there are times when I think he should have carried on as a carpet fitter,' Jennifer told me in a rare 'on the record' chat. 'I've taken the rough with the smooth. The huge highs. The huge fall – when it was all taken away. In many ways that outweighs the good.

'We met just after the Tszyu fight. Really it was all completely alien to me. I didn't have Sky. If I ever saw boxing, I'd switch it over. I had no idea he was a world champion – or what it meant. We'd go out and there would be crowds around him. I am a naturally private person. I would have said thank you but no thanks to all the fuss. If Rick could have achieved his success without the spotlight . . .

'Don't get me wrong. We have a beautiful house and we are very, very fortunate. But it is like life in a goldfish bowl at times. We might be able to get the best table in the restaurant, but then everyone is looking at you. I'm uncomfortable with that.'

Those frightening images of Jennifer at the Pacquiao fight are what many of us remember.

'I wish he had pulled out. I didn't watch much. Jenna, Matthew's girlfriend, was there. I shut my eyes, stuck my fingers in my ears, to zone it all out. I didn't want to hear. I hated the crowd. They were singing things. They don't know me. Jenna told me when it was over. I looked up at the screen.

'I've never said this to anyone in the media, Adam, but I thought he had died. In front of my eyes. I collapsed, Jenna was dragging me up. The ambulance people said he's OK, he's OK. But I ran to the black curtain at the back of the MGM. The crowd are all shouting "Mrs Hatton". I collapsed again and I was carried like a baby by a security guard back to the dressing-room. I didn't want him to see me cry. Or any of that. I just wanted to be strong for him.'

'What of the aftermath, the tough realization, coming to terms with it all?' I asked.

'That was the hardest thing,' Jen said, her voice breaking with emotion. 'The Priory. It was a long time building up. After the fight, it was bad. And I can be a cold fish. People thought I was there for the money. Not my real and total love for him.'

I can personally vouch for that. Jennifer Dooley has been there through thick and thin for Ricky Hatton. Unconditionally.

'I thought he needed to be doing something,' Jennifer continued. 'Have a focus. A fresh start. Our own little family. Rick has his boxing interests, but now he has a daughter, Millie, as well as a son, Campbell.'

I asked Jennifer whether if she and Ricky had a son together, would she let him box?

'I used to hate it,' she replied. But not now. 'It brings immense dedication and I respect it, but would I want my son to box? No. Not if I could help it. I would try and influence him away.'

Finally, I wondered how Jennifer felt about her man.

'I can't describe it in words,' she said. 'Not just the boxing, but dealing with the Priory. Overcoming the bad times. He is immense.'

So Ricky had the support of both his mum Carol and his partner Jennifer. Likewise, Rachael Cordingley joins Carl Froch's mum Carol for every fight. Rachael also speaks in glowing terms about her 'man' who she adores being with. They were our Sky guests in Hamburg for the Haye–Klitschko match-up and were just a pleasure to be around. We all went for dinner one night and they were a thoroughly engaging couple: bright, focused, and fun to be with.

But how does Rachael honestly cope with what Carl does for a living? I caught up with her as she was packing Carl's case before his trip to Atlantic City for the Super Six Final.

'It's not nice watching him,' she told me. 'I get so worried. I just don't want anything to happen to him. But he's just so good, Adam. I am always convinced he's going to win. So that makes it a little easier. But no, it's not easy. Now Carl's a father, he's got more focus with Rocco and I. We have a really close family, and I just have to be there for Carl.'

I remember Showtime's *360 Degrees* programme, which had Rachael hollering so close to the commentators in Finland that they had to ask her to move. Would she hell! Choice lines like 'Carl, knock the fucker out!' or 'I've got a big mouth for such a little lady!' lit up ringside while her partner produced a master class against Arthur Abraham.

'Despite your cordial demeanour, you can be a little animated at ringside,' I joked.

'I'm not really like that, you know, Adam, but emotions are

running high in there. I have a loud voice. I am from Liverpool, and if I want to cheer him on, just try and stop me! The father of my child is in the ring – fighting for his life – and I'm right behind him. People who don't have partners in boxing can't possibly understand what we go through.'

Rachael had to go – to prepare her voicebox for the trip to AC maybe – but I had one final question: 'Would you let Rocco box?'

'I don't want him to fight,' Rachael said. 'I couldn't bear seeing him get hit too.'

And on that note, off she went to be Carl Froch's noisiest and most passionate fan. Well, maybe apart from mum Carol!

Danielle Rhodes has always been a steadfast supporter of her husband Ryan, who, by the way, just happens to be one of my favourite people in boxing. Always smiling, glowing even, Ryan was once that Sheffield 'Spice Boy' and Prince Naseem Hamed's best mate who ripped through the domestic light-middleweight scene to become one of the youngest ever holders of the Lonsdale belt, and the quickest ever to win one of those treasures outright.

After a number of setbacks, including a devastating knockout defeat to Jason Matthews in 1999, when Danielle was aghast, it looked like the Rhodes story had come crashing down. Yet with help from his tight-knit family, and two daughters Ellie and Lissie, Ryan rose from the ashes to win the British eleven-stone crown all over again, more than eleven years after he first held the belt. Superb wins over Gary Woolcombe and then Jamie Moore for the European title led to a mission impossible out in Mexico against future star Saul 'Canelo' Alvarez. He couldn't quite pull that one off, yet Ryan is still rolling along at thirty-five, and is a credit to the sport.

Danielle has been right by his side. The shots of her ringside willing her man on stand out in the Sky Sports library; but she hasn't been there as long as Tina Rhodes. Tina has been one of the most dedicated boxing mums on the British scene.

'Ryan had problems at school by the age of six,' she told me. 'Always getting into mischief. His dad was working away, so we needed to get him into a discipline. We knew Herol Graham who had a gold store, and he said bring him down to Brendan's. So we did. On Saturdays, then Tuesdays, then every day of the week. Brendan was excellent at teaching them to control themselves. Other kids were getting into trouble on the streets, so I am glad I took him. I wasn't like any other mother though! I would take them all on, on the bag, time them in the ring. I became the treasurer at the St Thomas's Club and drove the boys round the country. They all used to come to my house. Still do.'

So, having seen him rise from such a young age, how did she cope with Ryan actually fighting?

'Well, the night before his first amateur fight, I didn't sleep, then I couldn't eat on the day. He had this green gown and green sparkly shorts. The nerves on me were horrendous. I was very vocal so he could hear me in the ring. Very vocal! Lets my tension out.'

Tina has been through the ups and downs. For instance, Ryan was sensationally floored twice in the opening round of his professional debut, before rallying to stop Lee Crocker in two.

'Unless you are a mum that's got a son in boxing, you can't explain the feelings. I just couldn't be one of those mums who sit at home not being able to know. I just have to be there to protect him. I take and throw every punch with Ryan. I have never missed one amateur or pro fight. I understand how some mothers cannot stand there, because it is such an alien feeling to watch your son in a fight. It's not human nature. But Danielle and I have a system. We go together and I wander around. Ryan can always hear me. Must be near him at all times.'

'Mum still puts me in my place, even though I am thirty-five,' Ryan said. 'She stands out like a sore thumb at my fights! Mind you, she knows what she is saying. When I am looking at old tapes of the amateur and pro days, the one voice that stands out is my mum.'

'Tina was like everyone's mum in the gym,' Johnny Nelson recalled. 'She was always there for Ryan, and was a huge support to all of us.' Meanwhile, Johnny's own mum was the polar opposite. They have always been close, but she couldn't stand boxing. 'My mum never got it and still to this day doesn't get it,' Johnny told me when we were sitting on our benches on the *Ringside* set. 'I used to lie, say I was going dancing, not boxing! I was a mummy's boy, an ex-altar boy. She worked in a hospital, and was terrified of brain damage. She never watched it even if I won – never, never. When it happened to Michael Watson, she pleaded with me to stop.'

Johnny's mother also teased him for being a coward. 'When I got laughed out of Sheffield after I had frozen so badly in that De Leon fight, Mum asked me why I didn't hit him! Later she thought Carl Thompson would destroy me because he had mad eyes.

'I used to run in the morning near Mum – back and forth – as she walked to the hospital. It was early and it was at the time when the Yorkshire Ripper was on the loose. I needed to protect her.'

Johnny visits his mum whenever he's down in London, as he loves her old Caribbean cooking. But do they talk about boxing? No, he leaves that to us, or to when he returns to his favourite training home in Wincobank. Johnny may be long retired now, but he is still the father figure in the gym.

Not that new hot starlet Kell Brook needs him too much. Kell has a tight-knit group around him that includes step-dad Terry, and his loyal mum Julie.

'Kell is twenty-six this year and he still can't use a washing machine!' Julie told me. 'I do everything for Kell. All his washing. His kit, diet – different to the food we eat. You name it. My other kids have been great. They know that I've dedicated a lot of time to Kell.'

Did she really believe Kell was special from an early age?

'He was first in the egg and spoon race, first at running, whatever sport. He was a brilliant athlete, and went boxing at about seven. He didn't seem too bothered, just thought he could go to the gym as it was something to do.'

But Kell got the boxing bug quickly. He idolized Naseem Hamed, marvelled at those amazing back-flips over the top rope, and I remember going into the gym in the mid-nineties and Brendan saying to me, 'That kid over there? He'll be better than Naz.' Brendan made Kell do his party trick, walking on his hands all the way across the old gym floor. Kell must have been only ten or eleven at the time.

Mum Julie has been an ever-present, but strictly from the safety of her own home. 'My dad loved the boxing so I have always watched it. I knew it was dangerous. After his first fight, I have never been to any of the others. That one only; my hands were sweating and it wasn't an experience that I liked. So many feelings, it's hard to put it into words. I was so proud, but so frightened, and so nervous. I couldn't breathe. I was terrified of him not winning his first fight as it was the start of his dream.

'Kell always said, "I am going to be champion of the world." I never think he's going to lose, but watching someone hit him is not good for me. I just can't do it. He's asked me loads, but I've never been back. Before he goes to the fights, I tell him, Kell, you are taking my heart into the ring with you, so don't break it.'

Would Julie ever be tempted to be ringside and cheer her beloved son on if the stakes were really high?

'If it was a world title,' she answered, 'I'd probably have a couple of Valium and, yes, go. Mind you, my bottom lip once went blue when I saw him. When it's actually happening and I'm not there, I'm thinking, "I wonder how the first is going", "Now he must be in the fifth", et cetera, et cetera. I get texts saying "Don't worry, don't worry!" We do all watch it together afterwards though. When I know.

'I have a fantastic relationship with Kell. I was only nineteen when I had him so we're very close. I just worry so much for my boy.'

And in that, she is not alone.

16

Tough Mamas

For a parent, there is always the worry of something serious happening to your boy or girl. Thankfully, I don't know the unbearable woe of losing a child. And I hope and pray I never will. Jessamy, Oscar and Tilly mean everything to Jo and me.

Unfortunately I have experienced the pain of losing someone extremely close at a very young age, and it was shattering.

I had a tight group of friends when I was growing up in north London, and all of us are still great mates some twenty-five to thirty years later. From Shelvis to King Prawn, Iggy to J what a Lay, Chips to the Warf-Man, Chops to Kars, Bilgy to Jacko, Duck to Digits and so on. At the heart of the group was Dogger. His real name was Steve, but then we never really used our Christian names much. Dogger loved the dogs, he loved all sports – and he thought I had a dream job.

The last time I saw my fabulous friend was around Christmas 1996, when he asked whether I could possibly help him get into sports television in the new year. '1997 will be heaven' were, I think, the last words he said to me. Following a birthday party on the night of 3 January that year, Dogger went home in the early hours with a university pal, and they fell asleep. Unfortunately a cigarette had been lit. The ensuing fire was the first in that block of flats in Pimlico for some seventy-five years. Both were found dead.

Dogger was just twenty-three. His stepbrother and another of my closest friends, Hodges, had to identify him. Dogger's mother Patricia was naturally beside herself with grief. So were we all. It was the most dreadful time, and it seemed to last an eternity.

If any good has come out of losing one of our best mates at such a horribly early age, it is that the rest of the group bonded for ever. And we remember all those good times together.

Ironically, I am writing this on 4 January 2012 – on the fifteenth anniversary of Dogger's death. We are about to hold a memorial cricket match for him.

Time heals, but you never forget. We do, though, rest in the knowledge that Dogger was happy, never sad. He was a top guy, extremely sociable, and we lost him doing something he loved. Partying the night away.

Dogger's mum has obviously found it incredibly difficult to come to terms with the fate of her wonderful son. But Patricia is a strong lady and like us remembers the good in her little boy.

Talking of lost Stephens, in recent times the Stephen Lawrence case has dominated public thinking. It took eighteen years, eight months and twelve days to get Gary Dobson and David Norris convicted for murder – amazingly, one month and three days longer than poor Stephen had lived. Through the whole tragic ordeal, the light that has shone brightest is Stephen's astonishing mum Doreen.

When Dobson and Norris were given 'life' early in 2012, Doreen said, 'We thank the jury for their verdicts, but today is not a cause for celebration. How can I celebrate when my son lies buried? When I cannot see him or speak to him? Or see him grow up and go to university or get married and have children? Now that we have some sort of justice, I want to think of Stephen other than as a black teenager murdered in a racist attack in south London in April 1993. I know that's the fact but I now want people to remember him as a bright, beautiful young man who any parent of whatever background would have been proud of. He was a wonderful son and a shining example of what any parent would want in a child. I miss him with a passion. Hopefully now he can rest in peace.'

It was a senseless waste of a youngster who excelled at sport, and if that Eltham gang's thuggish behaviour had been channelled into something more constructive, there would probably have been a different outcome. Maybe Stephen, the teenager who was hoping to become an architect, would have been that promising father and son Doreen and Neville Lawrence so desired. Duwayne Brooks, Stephen's friend who witnessed the savage racial attack by that bus stop in south-east London, said 'it was like a lynching from the days of slavery'. What our sport of boxing might have done to help control the warped mindset and pathetic physical aggression those sad youths demonstrated on a night Britain will never forget.

Boxing provides positive discipline, dedication and, import- antly, structure. And there are far fewer grieving boxing mums than those whose lives are ripped apart by mindless violence, knife crime and the plague of shootings that still haunt our culture.

My wife understands my passion and commitment, but doesn't like boxing herself. She is surrounded by a large group of mums in west London who do the school runs together and work extremely hard to look after their homes and balance the enormous pressures generated by numerous children. An occasional treat is a coffee morning when the girls 'knit and natter', or 'stitch and bitch'.

It's interesting to test out my love of boxing on these lovely ladies, the Acton Mums. One or two conversations have descended into quite fiery debates. There's Suzanne, who can't tolerate it. She hates the thought of anyone hitting anyone, and she has her reasons. I have sat her down and explained my side – why I think the sport does so much good, especially for the underprivileged – but she would be horrified if her children ever laced them up. Then there's Sally, who's a paediatric consultant. She is fascinated about why I am a boxing commentator, and wants to learn more. Yet in medical terms, she tells me, it can't be good: 'Let's be honest, the aim is to inflict brain damage on each other, and every time a boxer is hit, he will get more brain damage.'

I try the 'it's not the most dangerous sport' argument. What about base jumping, speed skiing, scuba or even regular diving, bull riding, supercross, surfing, bobsleigh, motorboats, motorcycling, motor racing, horse racing, even ice hockey, skiing, American football and rugby? Compared to some of those both extreme and mainstream sports, the death toll from boxing in the ring is small. Our sport's safety record has improved; indeed it's now ranked seventy-fifth by the Royal Society for the Prevention of Accidents on its list of the most dangerous sports. Behind rollerblading and gymnastics, for instance.

Some of the Acton Mums may not necessarily agree, but boxing is also actually becoming more attractive to females, some rather influential ones too. Like Tessa Jowell, the Shadow Minister for the Olympics, who has dramatically altered her stance. Jowell admits she felt that 'twelve years ago, boxing was too dangerous to be seen as a mainstream sport. The BMA said it should be banned, but since then safety has dramatically improved.' Jowell now believes the sport provides things that other sports don't, actually 'getting rid of aggression, disengaging kids from gangs and carrying knives, from low-level crime to high- level anti-social behaviour'.

Then there's the engaging MP Charlotte Leslie, who is so passionate about the benefits of boxing that she has taken it straight to the House of Commons. Charlotte is close to David Cameron – apparently a boxing supporter – and is currently leading a major campaign. She heads the All Party Parliamentary Group that gives political and practical support to boxing.

Charlotte believes our sport can seriously transform lives. A hyperactive kid, she was hooked on boxing from the age of twelve, and took to the gym. A decent athlete, she has even sparred with top amateur Thomas Stalker. Johnny and I have spent time with Charlotte in recent months. She is always telling us that boxing offers the best discipline of any sport, boosting kids' self-esteem, encouraging them to gain a better respect for others, and also teaching teenagers that the solution is to walk away from a fight, not get into one.

Women's boxing will be included in the London Olympics for the first time in 2012. It is one of the biggest growth areas in sport. According to Sport England, more than thirty-seven thousand women are now regular participants. The number of registered female boxers has shot up from 50 in 2005 to more than 650 today.

I remember about fifteen years ago travelling to Llanelli to do a feature with Dynamite Dean Phillips, who actually sparred with his two sisters. That was virtually unheard of. Now so many more young women are getting involved, with fitness right at the heart of the decision.

A spate of daughters of legendary boxing fathers has helped put women's boxing firmly on the map. We've seen Muhammad Ali's daughter Laila, George Foreman's Freeda, Joe Frazier's Jackie and Roberto Duran's Irichelle. Then there was 'The Coalminer's Daughter', Christy Martin; 'The Preacher's Daughter', Holly Holm; glamour model Mia St John; plus world champion twins Cora and Dora Webber.

Women's boxing may not be everyone's cup of tea, but we should support what is going on, either in competition or just workouts like Boxercise, which take place regularly in many sporting clubs and gyms around the world. The former world title challenger Neville Brown runs one such class in Derby.

There are also more women promoters than ever before. Kathy Duva is the CEO of Main Events. She's a fascinating lady who left law school to run her late husband Dan's company. Kathy's a mother of three and has dealt with big-name stars such as Holyfield, Gatti and Judah. Also Stateside there's Lisa Elovich, a former Deputy Attorney General of New York State, and Assistant District Attorney of Manhattan. And how about Gladys Tsenene, a seventy-year-old grandmother hoping to resurrect boxing in South Africa for the sole purpose of getting kids off the streets?

Back home, most of us know the very popular Jane Couch MBE, the first officially licensed British female boxer, who's now a promoter and always flitting around the scene. Laura Saperstein, the corporate lawyer turned fighter, is also a regular at events. The Ingles have been a long-stay boxing family, and not just the men. Along with Brendan and hard-working trainer/ manager sons John and Dominic comes their mum Alma, who Johnny tells me 'took no prisoners and threw people out of the gym'. Alma has been a regular promoter at times too, and always Brendan's rock.

There's Miranda Carter, who was the head of the accessibility and equality unit of the Department of Transport. She now promotes small hall shows in London, having been gripped by the sport from an early age, when her father Frank fought in the navy and in unlicensed shows. Another mother of three. And what about the excellent long-time agent Geraldine Davies, who worked with Lennox Lewis and is still very much involved in the pugilistic world?

We have four women on our Sky team in director Sara Chenery, programme PA Sarah Hornsby, production coordinator Beth Taylor and presenter Charlie Webster, who lives and breathes the sport. Charlie had a hard upbringing and I think finds solace in the sport. She trains down at the famous Fitzroy Lodge ABC. That gives Charlie a real connection when she interviews fighters.

While I like to think of boxing as a sweet science, the aim to outsmart one's opponent rather than render him unconscious, I understand and appreciate those women who continue to have real concerns. One or two of the other Acton Mums are more open to it, and understand the virtues. But it is not a mums' sport. Ninety per cent of the Acton Dads get it. It just comes back down to those mothering instincts, which in my opinion makes boxing mums even more special. They have all got a story behind them.

Some of them are highly active, on both a personal and professional level. World-class lightweight Kevin Mitchell's mum Alice O'Connor and Olympic gold medallist James DeGale's mum Diane are in the thick of their sons' career decisions. Rightly or wrongly.

For all his talent and endearing cockney charm, Kevin has found himself in hot water on a few occasions, along with boxing brother Vinny. Kevin says his mum 'dragged him out of the pub' after a six-month drinking binge followed his devastating defeat to Michael Katsidis. He always seems to be conquering his demons, but swears by his mum, saying that she is the person to get him right back on track. 'Mum is my main ticket seller and my biggest fan,' Kevin told me at the annual British Boxing Awards ceremony in west London in November 2011. 'She never ever misses a fight, always in the front row shouting out advice. "Just keep your chin down!" [against Breidis Prescott]; "Don't have a war like you did against Carl Johanneson!"'

But even as I spoke with Kevin he was on a strict police curfew for being caught with a butterfly knife in his car. He got a hundred hours of community service, but told me that it was all alcohol-related and that he was now knuckling down to serious business, thanks in the main to his mother. 'My mum loves me more than anything. She is everything to me. She was there when I split up with my long-time partner. She takes all the punches for me. I'd be lost without her. I was in a real downward spiral and she's got me through it.'

A loyal supporter yes, but one or two question Alice's influence, and there is no doubt that the Mitchells are rough diamonds.

Kevin Mitchell is more mature now. He knows he should stand on his own two feet. But his mum, you feel, will forever be in his corner. Right there in the trenches. 'My mum would do everything for me,' Kevin told me. 'Whatever. I think she wanted me to be a ballerina, I was such a bad kid. But she took me to the gyms. She never misses one of my fights.' Whether that should be contained or encouraged may still be open to question. I have long had the feeling that Alice has made the career decisions. She has his back at all times.

Diane DeGale has a similarly intense and important relationship with her skilful son James, best known for capturing gold in Beijing. His professional career still has yet to ignite after that close defeat to arch rival George Groves, and some are at war with his attitude. He admits he is a bit like Marmite – you either love him or hate him – but I have always thought James possesses the right sort of electricity for television, provided he can make the right progress in the ring.

From a steady, stable and bright family, James is Mummy's boy. Like Alice O'Connor, Diane DeGale has had to drag her son out of trouble – albeit a long time ago. Boxing channelled James, and huge praise must go to Diane for that. But unlike Alice, Diane can't be ringside.

'She went to the very first one,' James's dad Leroy told me, 'when James was ten. The first and the last. She is normally in a hotel waiting by the phone, sweating and being sick. She can only watch James on a recording. Outside the actual fights, she does everything for him.

'We call her the Patriarchal Governor,' he joked. 'She looks after the lot. She does the diaries. She's the manager. She's the boss. She makes it all happen. I am her – and his – gofer! She's the boss – especially when James used to get into trouble. We were worried that he might end up inside, but I think his mum would have strung him up long before the judge had passed his sentence!'

Again, loyal to the core. You want your mum right behind you, but would the DeGales have even more success if they employed more experts?

The DeGales seem a sensible family. They have seen James's amateur career peak and obviously feel that his best interests can only be served by them. We'll discover in time.

Kevin Mitchell and James DeGale are entering very important periods for their boxing careers. Their mums are there for them 100 per cent. Remember those maternal instincts, though. Are they really the right people to be doing so much? Could they be just too close to their fighting sons? Then again, if the boxers feel comfortable, and having their mums guarding their every move makes them more secure, then maybe it can be said to be the right formula. It's a tough one, when blood is thicker between mother and son than in virtually any other relationship.

Fighters are hard men. Mothers give them the softest love. These steely sorts can often be very emotional, and the bond between boxing mothers and sons, as we have seen, is extremely strong. Some fighters have used their mums in different ways. Oscar De La Hoya doted on his mother Cecilia, and admits that she wanted him to be a fighter. It ran in the genes, for Oscar's grandfather Vicente, father Joel and older brother Joel Jnr all fought. 'She'd be at my fights, and really quite liked the sport,' Oscar told me. 'She was my number one cheerleader. Very noisy.'

Then his mum was diagnosed with cancer. For a while Oscar quit boxing so that he could visit her in hospital every day. She wore a championship ring her son had won at the Golden Gloves. Oscar said that on her deathbed she persuaded him to carry on boxing, that the Olympics was their dream. She died at just thirty-nine, when Oscar was seventeen. Oscar De La Hoya dedicated his life to her. 'I won the gold medal in Barcelona for my mother. She had told me to do it. I was so sad she wasn't there to see me triumph. It was our triumph.'

So Cecilia has been Oscar De La Hoya's inspiration and drive throughout his multi-title 'Hollywood' boxing career. Oscar has recently admitted to several addictions, vices and problems. I'm sure he wished his mum could have helped him steer a path through life; maybe he would have overcome his issues quicker if she'd still been around. How he misses his mum. How dependent we all are on our mothers. But in tragic circumstances, how their memory can be so evocative and powerful.

From one of the greatest fighters of the modern era to novice British pro 'Patrick' Liam Walsh, who uses his mum as a powerful supporting figure too, but in a different way.

Liam's is a harrowing tale of a web of drug addiction and family behind bars. He never had a Christmas when he was young and admits that the smell of heroin reminds him of childhood. Liam was even shot once, after a scrap with his mum's dealer. But he still loves his mum and says she's tried her best. Somehow she is still there for her undefeated fighting son. Amazing.

There are wonderful and wicked mums. Former world super-middleweight champion Robin Reid asks his mum (his foster mum, in fact) everything. Whenever we used to do features with the popular Reid, she always had a house full of contented children and was very supportive of Robin's boxing. Then there's the terrible tale of former world middleweight title challenger Edison Miranda. He was abandoned by his mother when he was one month old. Edison tracked her down when he was nine and she slammed the door in his face, leaving him to fend for himself on the Colombian streets. At just twelve, Edison was working in the plantain fields. Ghastly.

Some mums can watch, some cannot. Lennox Lewis brought his mother Violet to every training camp where she cooked, cared for and supported her champ, and she was always seen ringside. Margaret Smith, the dedicated mum to those four fighting brothers from Liverpool, has refused to watch them for fear of their getting injured, not even on a replay. Manny Pacquiao's mum Dionisia has only been in the arena for two of his blockbuster fights. Both times (Cotto and Margarito) she ended up in hospital with anxiety attacks. Yet promoter and one-time amateur boxer Frank Maloney's mother Maureen couldn't stay away from ringside. Frank says his mum 'was always confident, watched all of my amateur fights – even when I got knocked out! She liked us doing it. Good discipline, and she's there at every fight I do now.'

Jane Haye, mother of former world heavyweight champion David, is a university librarian and is far from impressed with her son's antics, giving David a slapped wrist when he slates his opponents in the media. Jane would never allow David to have a tattoo, and watches his fights with her hands over her eyes.

My Sky colleague Glenn McCrory had boxing brothers, Gary and Shaun (with Neil in the corner), and a deeply involved mother. Glenn simply says, 'We fought for food and me mam used to spar with us! She could really shadow box too!' Trainer

313

Freddie Roach's mum, New England's first female judge, used to break up her sons' fights with baseball bats.

Tough mamas!

I'll never forget Brazilian knockout king Acelino Freitas, who was named 'Popo' by his mother after the sound babies make drinking their milk. I interviewed Acelino on several occasions, once after his forty-five-second demolition of Daniel Alicea in Sheffield. He couldn't wait to be handed a mobile phone – even with his gloves still on – to talk to 'Mama' back in Brazil. It was all live. Super TV.

Then there's former world heavyweight champion Chris Byrd. His mother Rose had five boys and three girls; six of them were boxers at one time or another. And she has worked the corner for all of them! Chris's dad Jo might have given the instructions, but Rose was his second. Wiping his face, instructions in the ear. Rose ran their gym too. Plus she managed to have quite a successful boxing daughter as well: Tracy was a two-division world champion.

'Super' Zab Judah's mum Katharine Hines was a karate fighter from a very poor area of Brooklyn and is so proud to see her son's name in lights. She feels like she's in the ring with him. 'The Golden Child' Daniel Jacobs had the same affection for his late grandmother, Cordelia, who raised him like a mom and made him into the person he is today. Meanwhile, Ireland's amateur star Kenny Egan has his mum Maura to thank after the marathon drinking sessions he went on when he won Olympic silver. She sorted Kenny out, and she needed to: she didn't want her heart broken.

Maybe the best way for mothers to be involved in boxing is to be protective and helpful but not to become too dependent and live their own lives through their sons, like Julie Brook, Falak Khan, Jackie Calzaghe and Jacqui Barker, who are a huge support from behind the scenes but stay firmly away from the line and heat of battle rather than actually see their sons, their flesh and blood, getting clobbered around the head.

What if Carol Ingle or Margaret Murray or Anne Oliver had been ringside on those terrible nights for their family? What if they had seen, and 'taken', those punches that caused such damage? It may be rare, but it might just scar mothers more than anyone. I was there at all of those nights and it affected me deeply. They are the women who gave birth to these fighters, fed them, housed them, doted on them. Surely it would have been unbearable. Yes, maybe mums should stay away.

In many ways there really is no one quite like Mum when it comes to unconditional, almost unnerving support. Take my mum: anti-boxing all those years ago, round the leisure centres to see me today. But as I said earlier, I would not particularly want my son Oscar to box, and I'm positive my wife Jo would almost certainly crush any request for him to go down to the local boxing club. While Jo appreciates the physical and structural side of training and discipline, she just wouldn't want to see her sweet little boy get hit, let alone hit back. Worse still, what if he got the boxing bug and wanted to take it further? I certainly see our children being guided down the swimming and tennis route.

I have seen, though, many different situations on my boxing journey. What's right for one family isn't necessarily right for the next. I love and respect fighters. I marvel at and admire their mothers, whatever positive influence and role in boxing they play. When their precious sons embark on something so alien to their nurturing, protective instincts, you just have to, don't you? Many mums are as driven, as passionate, as crazy and as downright bonkers as their sons who choose to step into that squared circle. Extraordinary women, they really are.

Epilogue: Fighting Memories and Final Thoughts

At its worst, it's a dirty rotten prostituting game . . . But at its best, it's the most beautiful thing you'll ever see.

Brendan Ingle MBE

I love this sport from the bottom of my heart, and I have loved covering the intricate, complicated and eclectic mix of fighters, their families, and their unique and tantalizing lives, from scores of clans deep-rooted in a generational history of boxing to the loneliest abandoned souls who have to fight just to survive within the shark-infested world of pugilistic politics. Let alone in that foreboding ring.

As we have seen, families are playing an ever-increasing role in shaping the careers of their prizefighting sons, brothers, husbands, nephews and, now, daughters and sisters. Times have most certainly changed since the days of the Don King/ Bob Arum dominance across the pond, or when British fighters found it hard to break into the big time without tight allegiances to the likes of Mickey Duff and Frank Warren.

The promoters are still critical to the fight game of course. Major boxing television networks such as HBO, Showtime and us at Sky choose largely to make deals with the promotional outfits, whether established or new, rather than the fighters themselves.

'Big' Frank and 'Little' Frank, as we tend to describe Messrs Warren and Maloney, are forever telling me that the families cannot possibly – and shouldn't – run everything, that established and experienced experts are needed to develop the product, make the right matches at the right time and guide their boxing babies through the wild waters. Yes, promoters are there to make a fast or a slow buck – that's the nature of the beast. Always has been. But they know the way it works – or at least the way it has worked.

Promoting can be a cruel business. The big guns like King, Arum and Warren have long invested in building up young fighters into star attractions. Then those same fighters can jump ship, feeling they or their families will do a better job. The promoters can find themselves at odds with a family's particular choice of agent or business manager; they often believe views can be misinterpreted if they don't deal directly with the fighter in question. Bitterness can ensue between the two parties, largely of course down to pounds and dollars, percentages and splits. Who gets what from the pot.

Promoters can of course get so close to their fighters that their young protégés almost become family. Sometimes as tight as a father–son relationship. At one stage Frank Warren became particularly fond of Naseem Hamed. Barry Hearn and Chris Eubank were a hysterical double act – an odd couple on the surface, but for so long a boxing match made in heaven. Likewise Jess Harding seemed inseparable from Spencer Oliver, and had the heartache of that Albert Hall nightmare to deal with. The Omen left fighting for his life, the moneymaker knowing that the exciting and profitable journey was over while natural paternal feelings flooded in.

In my role as executive producer for Sky's boxing coverage, I have my own love/hate affair with the promoters. My three phones are constantly ringing and beeping (although they do normally give me Christmas Day off!). The guys are charmingly effective, razor sharp, and as intriguing as the fights they offer us. While the hardest of men go to war and then complete proceedings with a hug and a kiss afterwards, the television executives and promoters enjoy their own version of friendly fire. We have mini-battles, neither giving much ground, albeit mixed with plenty of laughter and respect for the quality and needs of each side.

We certainly know the importance of the gaggle of promoters, on account of their expertise in the field and their relationships with the worldwide television stations and other media outlets. The press craves enticing personalities, desires unusual stories and hopes for exciting fights; the promoters normally know how to provide most of these. They appreciate the importance of building a stable that is attractive to the TV players, who of course shell out the money and demand returns.

Superstars like Floyd Mayweather and Manny Pacquiao understand that importance, with their strong ties to US giants Golden Boy and Top Rank, but the trend has been to look after number one far more than ever before. Don't think anyone other than Mayweather or Pacquiao truly calls the shots. The multi-million-dollar cash cows hold the key after all. With that comes assistance from external sources, like the old idea of 'agents', the new craze of 'business managers', and the constant array of savvy lawyers, precise accountants and financial investors. The richer a fighter is, the grander his army can be.

The next step seems to be launching one's own promotional company. Oscar De La Hoya breathed fire into this new way of developing assets when he split with Top Rank. This assisted the 'Golden Boy' during the Indian summer of his career, but he still needed the intelligent mind of Swiss businessman Richard Schaefer alongside, and look where we are today. The canny pair spearhead one of the major boxing promotional organizations in the world; they may even be out on their own at number one. It all comes back to the fact that 'promoters' in whatever guise, whether led by the old masters or the young, ambitious former fighters, are still very much central to anything boxing-orientated.

Yes, the fortunate few British sportsmen who have transcended the game, like Prince Naseem Hamed, Lennox Lewis and, to an extent, Ricky Hatton and David Haye, tried hard to break away from the traditional promoters in an attempt to cut out the middle man – but look closer, and promoters or promotional companies were still involved. After leaving Frank Warren, Hamed employed Barry Hearn to promote his extravagant UK shows; Lewis had his Lion promotional business; Hatton utilized Dennis Hobson, Golden Boy and Frank Maloney; and Haye, with trainer/manager Adam Booth, launched Hayemaker Promotions, which included young protégés like George Groves, and had a connection with Golden Boy.

Of course for every David Haye there are scores of heavyweights who never get near world-title level, for every Naseem Hamed plenty of lighter-weight fighters who are barely mentioned outside the trade. These prospects, contenders and journeymen are dependent on promoters to get work, often indirectly through their own independent managers or international agents.

Promoters are necessary, but the move to strike out on their own, especially when the stakes get higher, has meant more families becoming entwined in the complicated mesh of boxing. Fathers, mothers, brothers and sisters are now closing ranks around their fighting stock. Fighters have more chance of a faithful relationship with blood ties, as much as that can happen with vast sums of money floating around. The hardness and direction of dads, the bosom and heartfelt bond of their mums, the protection and friendship from their siblings – structure, advice, love and true trust.

Family provides more of these things than anything or any-one else. We all need them in our working lives. I have certain friends and confidants, and within my own family my step-mum Joan provides that. She is an adviser, a listener, taking off any rose-tinted glasses to tell it to me straight, whether I like it or not. It is very useful to be told the truth, not to be protected by sugar-coated responses.

Guidance is essential, and as I always say, boxing is about timing and levels. Professional, external experts must ideally mix with the support and comfort of the fighter's inner circle to make it work. What the family provides is a nest, any amount of time, experience and understanding, and a love no other source can supply. All vital components of the boxer's make-up.

Fighting families are as a result absolutely fascinating. How unique boxing is, often involving the whole family, compared to other sports, especially individual ones. When do you ever hear about an extended clan being deeply involved in, say, golf, motor racing, darts or athletics? The fighter's dedication to training can be wrapped around the package. So many chess moves happen both in and out of the ring. Help is at hand.

What characters they all are too, steering their ship, spying on their loved ones, incorporating their particular talents in so many different ways – often as crucial and as influential as the all-important boxing stars.

Most fighters, you see, are heroes. Win, lose or draw, these gutsy, courageous folk have my utmost respect. All of them. Just to get into the ring. Thanks to Adrian Dodson, I know that whether one's record is 25–0 or 22–78, every single boxer deserves enormous credit. Particularly when they also have the pressure on their shoulders of wading through the quagmire – what Lennox Lewis used to call 'politricks'.

I have had so many special days with these amazing people already in my twenty years working in boxing. Some I've introduced to you in these pages, but others stand out too. So here are a few final fighting memories, and some last thoughts on the sport I adore.

My very favourite ringside moment was sitting next to Mr Racing himself, John McCririck, at a jammed Madison Square Garden in December 1997 when Naseem Hamed and Kevin Kelley dished up a seven-knockdown thriller in four unforgettable rounds. On the undercard was another absolute belter. Junior Jones and Kennedy McKinney went to war, and it was a mini version of the main event that swung one way then the other. McKinney had to haul himself back from the very brink to shock the spidery New Yorker and take an incredible victory.

That week also provided some of my favourite boxing quotes. Hamed was teasing Kelley by saying, 'When I knock you out, I'll give you a nice job – putting up my posters. I want them nice and neat. No creases now, Kevin.' But the best came from McKinney, who looked straight over at Jones at the pre-fight presser and said, 'Your arse is grass, and I'm your lawnmower, baby.'

Sensational.

In terms of a celebrity crowd, it has to be the MGM Grand in Las Vegas when Floyd Mayweather tackled Sugar Shane Mosley. It was A-list all around. Fighters, movie and pop stars. You name it. Leonard. Hearns. Duran. Tyson. Ali. To my left were Angelina Jolie and Brad Pitt, Meg Ryan and P. Diddy; to my right Leonardo Di Caprio, Jack Nicholson, Bruce Willis. Just in front: Arnold Schwarzenegger. An unimaginable cast of the rich and famous.

Talking of ringside celebs, my most memorable interview must surely be with Russell Crowe, who was in Manchester to support Kostya Tszyu for his mega-match with Ricky Hatton. I was rather star-struck but was amazed at how much he knew about boxing. I really engaged with him, and told my family what a smashing bloke Crowe was. So nice that the very day after the fight Crowe flew to New York, arrived at a hotel and had an altercation with a security guard. He was charged with second-degree assault and possession of a weapon.

It's not all just about the glamour of movie stars and the Vegas strip. At Sky, we can live rather antisocial hours and sometimes put up with endless travel. Take a recent escapade to Poland for the Vitali Klitschko–Tomasz Adamek fight in September 2011. My alarm in London went off at 4:30 am; a cab, train and two flights later, I arrived (via Frankfurt) in Wroclaw. My case never made it. My Euros were then not accepted. I should have taken Zloty of course! Having eventually sorted out a suit and tie for the show, I ventured out on the city tram to the Olympic Stadium, but when I got there, I found myself at an athletics track some twenty-five miles from the correct venue! Huge traffic issues held me back further, and I eventually arrived at ringside when the show was already deep into the undercard, sixteen hours after my day had begun and, by this time, much lighter in both clothes and money. It was worth the trek though to see 50,000 screaming Polish fans decked out in red. Even if their man was dismantled from start to finish, Adamek was still a hero in their eyes.

There are many fighters who are close to my heart. Tommy Hearns and Barry McGuigan are my boxing heroes (David Gower and Sammy Lee are my other sporting idols). But there is no doubt which modern gladiator holds a place in my heart.

I shed genuine tears for Diego Corrales, who lost his life at the age of just twenty-nine, at daredevil speed on the Nevada highways. I remember when my team texted me to tell me he'd died. I really loved Diego. The tattoo-laden wildman did a lot of bad things in his short life, but he did a lot of good things too. A magical and enchanting guy who was very clever out of the ring and a fearless warrior in it who fought with his heart on his sleeve.

A bizarre partnership we might have looked, but Diego and I just clicked, on and off camera, during and after shoots. On one occasion, Cainey and I were driving through the desert to the City of Sin. We called Diego and asked where we should head to. His reply: 'Where do you want me to come and meet you?' Such an absence of ego is rare in boxing; he was just a thoroughly lovely human being. When we arrived at Mandalay Bay, Diego and his wife were waiting in reception. They helped us with our bags, took us around Vegas and looked after us like we were their own family.

It was so tragic what happened to him. Marvellous man. Miss him to pieces.

In this sport where life and death can cross in mysterious ways, there was more heartache when we lost Ireland's excellent hope Darren Sutherland. The Olympic bronze medallist had turned pro with a fanfare, was tipped for great things, but despite being unbeaten and with the boxing world at his feet was found hanged in his flat by his own promoter, Frank Maloney. Such a sad ending for the brightest of pugilistic prospects. I had spoken to Darren less than forty-eight hours before his untimely death.

Maloney collapsed on finding his starlet's body, and doctors discovered that he had already had a heart attack on the Friday Fight Night. He was hospitalized, and fortunately the doctors sorted Frank, to the extent that he couldn't understand why he was prevented from using his mobile phone on the operating table. Such is his passion for the business. Maloney had invested so much time in Darren, and they were very close.

There have of course been many intriguing meetings with fighters along the way too. I have a big soft spot for Paul 'Trussy' Truscott. Few may know the spindly lad from the hard South Bank area of Middlesbrough, but what a story, and what a guy. He's infectious to be around. In the past, most of the kids from his estate have wasted their lives. Trussy was sorely tempted to go the same way, but boxing fortunately gave him the vision and hope he needed. He showed me some of the street corners where many of the teenagers hang out with cider bottles, drugs and weapons. Some sensible ones have listened to this little guy with his high-pitched Teesside accent, who uses his post-fight interviews to preach to the tearaways: 'Don't do drugs. Go to boxing, go to bal-let. It doesn't matter what you do, but don't do drugs and streets.'

The younger boys look up to Paul like some sort of Rocky figure. It's amazing to see. A fighter making a real difference. The once talented amateur has only ever won a Commonwealth title, but those who draw up the honours lists should take note of these local idols. The great thing about Trussy is that he still lives on the estate, in a different house to the original one, which the council bulldozed. He's not a wealthy guy, he's been down on his luck, but he's salt of the earth. A real trier. I love those types.

Another many may not remember, but I found him to be one of the most amiable guys along the road, was Yorkshire's useful switch-hitter James Hare. He was modest, talented, and a joy to interview. His dad was a builder, and the family had constructed this dream home near Roberttown. We did a feature with James one day at the huge mansion, and filmed him peering over the countryside. My voiceover reported that he was a 'Lord of the Manor'. James was a little embarrassed by this – he was so far away from some wealthy landowner – but the name caught on. MC John McDonald proudly announced him as 'Lord of the

Manor' at his next title fight, and James managed a wry smile and a gentle shake of the head in the ring. Then one of our leading trade magazines, *Boxing Monthly*, ran an article entitled 'Lord of the Manor'. James Hare's new rather aristocratic title just ran and ran.

I saw him not long ago at a Kell Brook fight in Sheffield. 'Hello, my lord,' I said to him. Top chap. Or is that top bloke?

Another of the nice guys is Julius Francis. A more approachable heavyweight you couldn't meet. For a while he was a bit of a cult figure in British boxing, especially during the build-up to that surreal fight with Mike Tyson.

My close friend Hodges once accompanied me to a London Fed Boxing dinner and I sat him next to Julius, who was a guest on our table. Now, Hodges is remarkably posh. And opinionated. Not everyone's cup of tea. But he also has a heart of gold. Hodges' opening gambit to Julius was, 'My dear chap, goodness gracious, look at the size of you! Are you a bouncer or a boxer?'

'I'm the British and Commonwealth heavyweight champion,' came the reply from Mr Francis.

'You must be fairly decent then. Jolly good.'

Not in a million years would I have expected my City mate to bond with a south Londoner who helped educate the street kids in his area. But they did. At the end of the evening, Hodges swapped numbers with Francis.

The next time I saw Hodges, he was dressed in a blazer, red chinos and loafers with a suited and booted chum from the broking world and was cheering Julius on loudly at the York Hall, Bethnal Green. Hodges received some very strange looks. His friend Holmes said, 'Sit down and keep your mouth shut for the rest of the evening!' After Francis's latest win, Hodges was embracing him backstage. Extraordinary. The power and raw appeal of the fighter. In all my time of knowing Hodges, I've never thought I'd see anything like that.

There have been many other amusing incidents. One summer's afternoon a few years back I was sitting in my flat relaxing and my phone rang.

'Adam, this is Christopher Livingstone Eubank.'

'Hello Chris, how the devil are you?' I said.

'Can you come to Portugal tomorrow please? Meet me by the Café El Zig Zig next to the seventh sand dune [imagine the lisp!]. You fly to Faro.'

The line went dead. Mmm, I thought. Mad, but tempting, because it is Mr Eubank, and he was in training for a major rematch with Carl Thompson set for Sky Sports. I was on holiday, but I thought, let's do it. So I met a cameraman, Damien Saber, at Heathrow and we flew out on this rather blind last-minute mission.

When we landed in Faro, my mobile rang. 'Adam, this is the Sky operator. I have a Christopher on the phone. He's rather well spoken.'

'Adam, I can't meet you,' came this distant voice. 'I have to return to London to have tea with the Queen.'

'What? Rubbish,' I said.

'It is true. She wants to take tea with me.'

'We have just flown all the way out here to meet you, Chris, and you have to return home today? Ridiculous.'

There was a silence.

'OK. I shall delay my return to England until tonight. Meet me by Café El Zig Zig at Quinta do Lago in two hours. Oh, and you need a four-by-four.'

Again the line went dead.

We thought it would be wise to hire a jeep, and we hurried to collect the camera equipment. It was a race against time or it would be a totally wasted trip, which was already costing a great deal of money.

I knew that Quinta do Lago was an exclusive golf resort near

Vale do Lobo, and we headed straight there. On arrival, we asked at a few of the hotels where this café was. One or two blank faces were followed by 'It's by the sea, across the estuary.'

An estuary. Ahh . . . the 4×4. So we set off towards the beach in our open-top jeep, and by this time the sun was burning hot. As usual I was in my pinstriped suit. Hardly ideal. We went down this verge, and saw the water. Estuary? More like the bloody Danube! I looked over at my cameraman Damien and we instantaneously thought, let's do it! It was all a bit Thelma and Louise. Damien floored it, and we literally flew through this so-called estuary (it turned out later it was conservation marshland) to get to the other side. Brilliant.

Well, temporarily. By the time we got to the middle of this wide stretch of river, we started shipping water. Too deep. Stuck.

Desperate to meet our mad interviewee, we ditched the car and waded towards an island. Damien, sensibly wearing shorts, carried the camera above the waterline, and I had the problem of dragging the tripod through, while my suit was fast becoming completely ruined. It was a bizarre situation.

The sun continued to beat down as we made it slowly to the other side and the beach. We then had to find this damn Café El Zig Zig, lumping the very heavy equipment with us, and it was now dreadfully late. We were bloody annoyed, especially when there was no sign of Mr Eubank anywhere. Surprise surprise. What a nightmare.

We asked in the café where he was, and they told us Chris had long gone. So after a couple of cool drinks and some time out, we decided to get a few GVs of the stunning area (thankfully the camera still worked) before attempting a return to the mainland.

Then, as Damien was filming and the sun was starting to set, this silhouette caught my eye. There, running up and down over the gorgeous sand dunes, was our man. At last. Damien swung the camera round and we got one of those unforgettable shots as Eubank dipped over each dune. It was like a magical mirage.

As Chris approached us he shouted, 'You passed the test, Mr Smith. Few do. Told you a four-by-four was necessary.'

When he came to a halt, I told him about the adventure. The abandoned jeep. Those minutes of mayhem. He laughed. For a long time. Then Eubank proceeded to give us magnificent access: we took superb shots of one of our great modern fighters shadow-boxing in the fading Portuguese sun, and we were given some wonderful lines during an in-depth interview beside the crashing Atlantic waves.

Then Damien and I departed, helped back to 'the other side', and enjoyed a fabulous night out before returning the next day with Eubank treasure. Some twenty-four hours. To this day I still don't know if Chris Eubank has ever had tea with the Queen. Or whether the jeep, which was fished out of the estuary, ever quite recovered from a couple of British TV men acting out some pseudo-James Bond moment.

A Eubank postscript. Despite moving from light-heavyweight right up to cruiserweight to meet Carl Thompson in 1998, 'Simply the Best' actually came in over weight on the scales. When he returned an hour later, and successfully made the limit, I asked Chris how he had done it.

'It was easy, my dear man,' Eubank replied. 'I lay in a herbal bath, reading verses of Oscar Wilde, and the weight simply dropped off.'

Splendid. One in a million. And such fine taste. Oscar Wilde was a genius, after all. In promotional terms, Chris Eubank was one too.

Christopher Eubank Jnr, of course, is one of a host of new blood making excellent early progress in the ring. There is considerable pressure on the youngster's shoulders with his famous daddy driving him on, but there's so much to look forward to with boxing today.

Britain doesn't boast quite as many champions as in recent years, but the good news is that we are getting our chances against the best in the world, pushing them close in proper, hard fights. Matches are as competitive as I can remember in my time at Sky. In 2011 we saw Haye–Klitschko; Sturm v. Macklin and Murray; Alvarez v. Hatton and Rhodes; Martinez v. Barker; Cleverly–Bellew; Burns–Katsidis; Rios v. Murray; Froch v. Johnson and Ward; Khan v. McCloskey, Judah and Peterson. Fiery stuff.

Amir Khan and Carl Froch should become world champions all over again in 2012. Ricky Burns and Nathan Cleverly are going great guns. Kevin Mitchell and Kell Brook may well graduate with top honours, and there's a plethora of talent behind them. George Groves, Tyson Fury, David Price, Scott Quigg, Carl Frampton, Billy Joe Saunders and one of my personal favourites, Liverpool's heavy-hitting Joe Selkirk. Can Frankie Gavin also start to show some of that sparkling form and knuckle down as a serious pro?

As for the amateurs, what a setting for the GB men's and women's team at the Olympic Games. There's no place like home, and super-heavyweight Anthony Joshua leads a host of medal possibilities including Thomas Stalker, Andrew Selby, Fred Evans and Luke Campbell. Watch out for the likes of Natasha Jonas, Savannah Marshall and Nicola Adams as the girls go for gold for the first time. Boxing always goes in cycles; this summer could kick-start another surge for British boxing.

On the international stage, is there anyone to break the formidable and supreme Klitschko brothers' dominance? Time and again they turn back their challenges in front of massive, delighted audiences who relish the chance of being present at a Klitschko event.

Yet where is the real competition? The next big, bright thing? Is there a hunt on for a young Tysonesque American who can breathe much-needed fire into the once so glamorous marquee division? If not, there really should be.

How many chapters remain in the Floyd Mayweather boxing story? Summer jail time awaits. Will he ever share a ring with rival pound-for-pound king Manny Pacquiao, and how much has the Pac-Man got left in the locker after his fortunate trilogy victory over Juan Manuel Marquez?

Andre Ward could lead the new breed. Ironically, the super super-middleweight comes from a strange family upbringing himself. Andre was raised by his father, a single parent. Frank Ward had two jobs to support the family but also fought, once compiling a 15–0 amateur record. Andre was inspired to follow in his dad's footsteps and began boxing at eight. Frank never missed his son's fights, despite his other work.

Unfortunately, Frank died suddenly of heart failure in 2002, at just forty-six. Andre was distraught, but rather like Oscar De La Hoya and his late mum Cecilia, he used his dad's untimely passing to motivate his career. Andre went on to strike Olympic gold in Athens, and is now the leading twelve-stone fighter on earth.

Fortunately he had another mentor: Virgil Hunter has been there for Andre's entire boxing journey. Virgil is the only trainer Andre has ever had, and is also his godfather. The way his story has panned out, it makes one think. However awful the loss of his father was, at least there was another supporting figure. If Frank Ward had undertaken that role of trainer, it's possible his death would have had even more of a detrimental effect on Andre's professional life. As it is, Andre Ward has done brilliantly, and strives to perform for the next generation. His wife Tiffiney and children Andre Jnr, Malachi and Amira are always in the front row at ringside cheering him on.

Will the classy Californian become the next real superstar for the States? Or could Mexico's extremely popular Saul 'Canelo' Alvarez – he with the many boxing brothers – actually turn into the global face of boxing? Victor Ortiz, James Kirkland, Guillermo Rigondeaux, Yuriorkis Gamboa and Adrien Broner, the fighter I believe could be the pick, add to the evidence that there is plenty to look forward to.

Boxing may not be quite the universally known sport it once was. But times have moved on. The introduction of satellite and cable channels, as well as a lack of loyalty or financial muscle from terrestrial networks, has meant the sport is not as widely viewed. Yet Sky Sports continues to produce plenty of live fights along with our weekly *Ringside* magazine show which brings guests from Sugar Ray Leonard all the way down to the grassroots of the sport. On the flip side, the mass market found on the internet means that news and video are more accessible to the public, and I really do believe that boxing still has the power and attractive qualities to be right up there – number three or even number two to football when there is a mega-fight. Sometimes I feel boxing is smouldering in the ashes, like a sleeping giant waiting to be woken. When it is, everyone will know about it again.

There has certainly been a shift in world domination towards the Eastern Europeans – intelligent, brilliant athletes with text-book skills but who sometimes lack the spark, magnetism and engaging personalities of those found elsewhere. The problem in America is that teenagers are choosing easier paths out of desperate situations than, say, twenty-five years ago. The big bucks on offer in basketball, American football and, to a lesser extent, baseball and ice hockey are tempting sportsmen into safer, more profitable fields and away from boxing. Maybe the potential heavyweights we so crave are getting lost this way.

The press must relight the fighting flame and get behind us

too. We have a great bunch of dedicated boxing writers led by the *Sun*'s Colin Hart, the *Daily Mail*'s Jeff Powell, the *Guardian*'s Kevin Mitchell and *The Times*' Ron Lewis. But we need more paper space. We need boxing back on the back pages.

We must be wary of the threat of UFC and other mixed martial arts, which are really beginning to tempt the youth of today. They are incomparable to the classic Marquess of Queensberry's fight game, but we need to be on our guard, and look to make our sport more appealing than ever before. There must be room for innovation as we move forward. Think of Twenty20 cricket, which has angered the purists, or faster snooker, or the injection of 'razzmatazz' in darts. Sport has been forced to become more in tune with a modern crowd's demands.

Prizefighter is an interesting start, with quick fights, lively crowds and a bag of booty at the end of one entertaining night. Yet even Prizefighter needs to freshen up with new ideas or it will become stale. The Super Six Super-Middleweight tournament had its difficulties with fighters pulling out, postponements and, to the casual fan, a complex system, but we had high-class matches, a plethora of world title fights and some cracking action. There was a similar competition at bantamweight, which slipped a little under our radar, and there's been talk of another in the red-hot light-welterweight division.

There have been proposals for tri-nation tournaments, international duels, and Frank Maloney recently put forward the concept of a 'Heavyweight Factor' to find the best novice around. The new wave of promoters like vibrant Eddie Hearn and popular Ricky Hatton must surely help attract more fans, and indeed more fighters, into our sport. With Floyd Mayweather and Oscar De La Hoya both promoting in the States, Juan Manuel Marquez in Mexico, and the Klitschkos in Germany, there is certainly more glamour associated with becoming involved. Maybe we could see more reunification bouts, but the belts aren't what really matters – we just want good fights and then good rematches, which been absent for so long.

What would be useful is if there could be some added appeal for the amateurs. The World Series of Boxing is one new idea to have been introduced. Almost unique in this most individual of sports, it is a team competition, and pits the best against the best. No vests or head guards are worn, and there is no computer scoring. As with professional boxing, there's a ten-point must system, but the athletes are still eligible for the Olympics.

For years the critics have questioned the gap between the two levels of the sport. Many have long felt that the amateur game is more like fencing and working for the 'computer'; maybe the World Series will help smooth the transition and make top amateurs better pros. In its inaugural year, seventy-six WSB matches and 390 bouts were televised worldwide in eighty countries, reaching a potential audience of fifty million!

There are other positive figures to move forward with. An enormous resurgence has taken place around Britain. Regular boxing classes are now taking place each week in tens of thousands of schools and gyms. Already 5 per cent of primary and 26 per cent of secondary schools have a formal link to an accredited boxing club. Registered amateur club members have tripled since 2005. Rebecca Gibson, Head of Development for the ABA in England, says there has been 'a major increase in funding'. Hopefully a few shiny medals at London 2012 will help Charlotte Leslie and her All Party Parliamentary Group move forward with vigour.

Meanwhile, white-collar boxing has become so much more widespread. Donning the gloves in carefully monitored situations gives City slickers and office workers a way of working off stress, channelling aggression, achieving a goal, and most importantly taking better care of their physical health. The flamboyant

London promoter Spencer Fearon is a partner and trainer at The Real Fight Club by Liverpool Street station, a state-of-the-art facility that is always heaving. Another popular London boxing figure, Isola Akay MBE, established The All Stars Boxing Club on Harrow Road in 1974. Back then, the area around the gym was known as 'the front line' because many youths were in and out of trouble. Akay invited the police to train at the gym alongside the boxers, which saw a reduction in street violence. All Stars still takes in around three hundred people each week, and queues of boys and girls are regularly seen outside.

Simon Marcus runs the London Boxing Academy Community project. He was approached by the Youth Offending Service and the police for help with teenagers who had been excluded from school. They needed to be occupied during the day, so Simon and trainer Chris Hall began an alternative school to provide help for some very violent young men. Their timetable is based around sport, mainly boxing, and the school helps transfer those skills into academic educational work.

In May 2008, I hosted a charity gala dinner in Kensington to raise funds for the LBA, at which Simon Marcus told politicians, fighters and people from all walks of life, 'There has been a six-fold increase in gang culture, with children as young as five joining local gangs. We use boxing and other sports to capture the imagination of excluded students, and reintroduce them to education and mainstream society. Through sport, we teach our students to understand the values of teamwork, discipline and responsibility, which help them achieve academic qualifications and walk away from drugs, crime and poverty.' The LBA and others are trying to persuade kids that being in a group inside a gym will provide that togetherness and sense of belonging that gangs are seen to attract. The low achievers in education need to be educated in this.

It is working. Attendance levels are excellent, GCSEs are

being achieved, and talented athletes have been unearthed and developed.

The LBA are based in Tottenham, which was of course a focal area for the riots in the summer of 2011. Simon also sits on the 'Riot Panel', set up to help re-educate the youth, and to try to make sure those awful scenes of looting are not repeated.

These days there is definitely more pressure on parents to encourage their children to find goals, and quickly. In an age of computers, technology and a troublesome knife culture, we need to get our kids up and running and into sport. Push their boundless energy into something positive for their lives and we'll all enjoy a safer and better future in Britain.

In January 2012, Johnny and I attended a wonderful event at Wembley Stadium, the Sky Sports Living for Sport programme awards. We were delighted to see young boxer Nick Ward become the eventual winner, having turned his life around after a meeting with Johnny's old stablemate Dermot Gascoyne.

As we approach the grand showcase of the London Olympics, boxing has become a hot topic. It is time to strike, now, with family and future generations right at the epicentre. Thousands of people all over the UK are obviously more than happy to see a boom in boxing helping to keep their young children healthy, fit, focused and, most importantly, happy and as safe as possible.

In a fractured society, boxing can be the most inclusive of sports. People come to it from all walks of life. Plenty of good stock comes from a travelling background. British champions like P. J. Gallagher and Martin Power have provided us with a decent sprinkling of television moments. PJ was a particular favourite. The 'family' on his north London caravan site was more reminiscent of Noah's Ark: all kinds of animals would come out of hiding on a shoot with PJ!

Jimmy Vincent, the eccentric journeyman who ground it out

to become a domestic champion, used to live on a sprawling site under the flight path next to Birmingham airport, while welter-weight John O'Donnell is billed out of Shepherd's Bush in west London, a stone's throw from my house. When I asked John which road he lived on, he told me his family home was under-neath a road. Quite a large one – the A40 Westway that takes one into the heart of the capital. 'Thousands of people drive over us every day!' he laughed.

Currently we have hot middleweight hope Billy Joe Saunders, living on a travellers' site in Hatfield, and that entertaining big heavyweight Tyson Fury, whose genes are deeply rooted in boxing, mainly of the bare-knuckle variety. Tyson's dad 'Gypsy John' was feared all over the country and graduated into a tough pro too. Unfortunately his hard fights outside the ring landed him an eleven-year jail sentence for gouging a rival's eye out. The feud had lasted twelve years and was initially over just a bottle of beer. Not really the sort of family you want to poke fun at.

With his fiercely protective, overbearing father 'inside', Tyson has seemed a little lost at times, both mentally and certainly physically. During his rise, Tyson's been trained on and off by his Uncle Hughie, but that relationship hasn't run smoothly. The tools, talent and star appeal may all be there for this good-looking, marketable heavyweight, but has he had the right sort of family love around him? Tyson certainly hasn't had the ideal direction.

This culture of boxing is of course different from the main-stream. These large travelling tribes have contributed much to the world of pugilism, but often don't possess the structure or stability required for success. They are constantly moving around sites. The kids love fighting, though, and will box forty or fifty times a day.

Take the Buckland brothers: all-action British super-featherweight champion Gary and novice southpaw pro Mitchell. Disagreements on their traveller site in south Wales are sometimes sorted out in trainer Tony Borg's gym – much to his dissatisfaction! Gary and Mitchell just get down and fight. No head guards. No gum shields. No wraps. No rounds. Just 'Last man standing'. They go at each other for forty, forty-five minutes, while Tony explains, 'There's no need for a ring – it might as well be a phone box!'

One such fighter was Tony Doherty, who won thirteen consecutive Welsh amateur titles and was unbeaten in his first twenty-one pro fights. He was a real talent, but then he lost a couple of bouts and drifted away. A Romany boy who speaks travellers' Gaelic and whose ancestors read palms, he sold bundles of tickets, but perhaps a lack of dedication and discipline with weight was his downfall.

Simon Doherty, 'The Blacksmith', taught Doherty how to fight: bare-knuckle fighting, that is. No biting, kicking or nutting. No weight limits, no rounds, no count-outs. These men can fight for three hours; they just don't want to surrender.

Tony is the youngest of seventeen. All his family boxed apart from one, who has cystic fibrosis. Another brother is Paddy, from *My Big Fat Gypsy Wedding*. One of Danny Dyer's deadliest men, he won *Celebrity Big Brother* in 2011, rides a horse everywhere, and has fifteen grandchildren. There is also a Frankie Doherty who is seven and fights all day, even when injured. They are reared to be fighters. Frankie's dad is Hughie, the son of Frankie 'The Punk' Doherty – a legendary bare-knuckle fighter. Hughie is also training his eighteen-month-old son Charlie on the pads. There is no childhood innocence there.

Traveller families are a tough breed of fighters because they have been victimized and marginalized. They are hard, hard men. Few, though, make it to the pinnacle of pro boxing.

In recent decades we've also seen an influx of immigrant families to Britain, and some of them have made a real crack at the pro boxing business, possibly on account of previous family hardships and the fact that they possessed the drive to try something new and and be successful. The Hameds from Yemen, the Khans from Pakistan, even Enzo Calzaghe firing up the Welsh dragon, having arrived by boat from Sardinia.

At a lower level, we've enjoyed that exciting livewire Takaloo. Born Mehrdad Takalobigashi, his family fled Tehran in the late 1970s after the Shah was overthrown and carved out a very successful life on the Kent coast. Takaloo boxes for his family.

Mongolians Choi and Shinny Bayaar left a huge heritage to support their families by moving to Lancashire. Shinny was so determined to win a British title that he undertook strict exams on our history of kings, queens and other royalty to gain citizenship. Meanwhile Choi has an enormous cult following down south – a new version of the boxing family.

Families see this precarious but most rewarding sport as a passport to economic mobility and security, to providing their loved ones with spoils. Some work for this family business and some never have to work again. There can be friction, even damaging jealousy, but better the blood you know than the devil you don't.

Other fighters have chosen to adopt a family around them. At the start of this book I mentioned Vernon Forrest, the tall, talented former world welterweight champion who was one of the most wonderful human beings you could hope to stumble across in the boxing world. Vernon set up an amazing company called Destiny's Child which was a project to shelter, house and protect disadvantaged folk from quite horrific situations. Moreover, Vernon ensured that many of them found full-time jobs, or worked in the local community in Atlanta, Georgia.

A few years back our Sky cameras picked up on this heartwarming tale and we spent quality time with the smashing group of characters that Vernon brought to his fights. No entourage, few relatives, just this extraordinary extended family. Vernon drew his ring powers from their stories, and the turnaround in their lives. There was real affection between them. Vernon had this mansion due to his ring riches, and every one of his group had their own front door key to come and go as they pleased. And there were about thirty of them!

Vernon dedicated his life to his Destiny's Child family and was one of those genuine good guys. How tragic that the waster who shot him dead after a botched car robbery and ensuing chase was actually murdering an entire group who depended on Vernon. Criminal. Pure evil.

More good comes from pound-for-pound greats Manny Pacquiao and Oscar De La Hoya, who also see their supporters as a family extension. Oscar has enormous time for his fans. The dazzling ex-fighter with the matinee-idol looks pumps money back into the schools and hospitals of the poor East Los Angeles neighbourhood where he came from. He personally hands out turkeys every Thanksgiving to the hungry, and enjoys helping his people.

Pacquiao's fellow Filipinos worship him; he has God-like status among them. Millions watch Manny fight; crime halts all over the Philippines every time the Pac-Man appears in the ring. He gives huge lumps of money to the victims of natural disasters and in return thousands of his family of fans turn out to support him, whether at ringside, as he steps off a plane, or even at press conferences. When Pacquiao came to Britain before tackling Ricky Hatton in Las Vegas, we knew Manchester's Trafford Centre would be hosting scores of Hatton fans, but we couldn't believe the numbers of English-based Filipinos there. They made more noise at the final leg of the press tour than even the most passionate boxing fan club we've probably ever known in the history of the British game.

Back home, boxers turned managers Paddy and Tommy Lynch were recent recipients of the Henry Cooper Award for Services to Boxing by the British board. These dynamic brothers kept Birmingham kids off the streets and took no fewer than nine fighters to British titles after more than fifty years in the sport. Entitled to 25 per cent of a boxer's earnings, it is rumoured that they hardly took a penny from them – another extended boxing family.

There are more tales like these in this astounding sport of boxing, but I shall leave some of the final words to one of my heroes, Barry McGuigan. 'Family is crucial, critical,' he told me one day in the make-up room at Sky as we were preparing for the latest show. 'I had family all around me. Some fighters have no one to counsel them, no one to talk to. We all need help. Boxers may have the reputation of being as hard as nails, but we are sensitive souls. We don't show fear, but it's there inside. Who better to help than your family?'

I sincerely hope you've enjoyed this peek inside boxing from a slightly different angle, and that it will make you think about all the complications that can be involved, in terms of support and love and correct career progression. There is no definitive guide. There is no right or wrong. We all make mistakes, but then we need someone there to pick up the pieces. We think we know it all, but there are daily twists. Actually, everyone is different. The more intelligent and single-minded may need fewer family members around them; the insecure, nervous and deeply affected may crave more. It's far from easy to arrive at a winning formula. The boxers themselves need talent and dedication, but they also need luck. One's family may be the only true trustees, the best option of all.

Well, it's back to my family now, until the weird, wonderful and compelling world of boxing tempts me away yet again . . . and that will be just around the corner.

Beautiful Brutality. There really is nothing quite like it.

Acknowledgements

Thanks to everyone who played a part in bringing *Beautiful Brutality* to book, including: Giles Elliott and all at Transworld Publishers; Daniel Balado-Lopez for his copy editing; my Sky colleague Bob Mee for his invaluable advice; Jonny McWilliams and Melissa Chappell at WMG; Susannah Toman Baker and Alice Rose for their feedback on the early drafts.

And thanks to all the fighters and their families, particularly Ricky Hatton for the foreword, and Margaret Murray – James's mum – for making me truly believe in boxing.

INDEX

ABOUT THE AUTHOR

Adam Smith is Head of Boxing at Sky Sports and has been one of the main commentators, presenters and reporters of their coverage for nearly twenty years. He lives in London with his wife and three young children. This is his first book.